INSIDE THE LEGAL PROFESSION

Professor Longan's new book, Inside the Legal Profession: Conversations with Leaders of the Georgia Bench and Bar, is a welcome addition to the legal landscape. Its well-chosen guests all have fascinating stories. Topics range from how to survive the law school experience to many of the premier problems of our day, including Guantanamo Bay, mandatory minimums, partisan gerrymandering, and gender discrimination in employment. Historical moments and recollections, along with questions from Professor Longan's law students, add depth to the interviews. Regardless of whether the reader has Georgia connections, Professor Longan's collection presents an engaging pathway to and through the practice of law. I highly recommend it.

—Mark R. Brown, Newton D. Baker/Baker and Hostetler Chair of Law, Capital University Law School

Professor Longan has compiled a library of interviews with an eclectic group of lawyers. Each interview is interesting in its own right; but as a composite, they provide an excellent introduction to the many facets of law practice. The varying life experiences presented give starting law students an unvarnished look at what practice can be. Law practice has stress, long hours, hard work, high points, low points, great satisfaction, and a few disappointments and failures. What a special vehicle this book provides to introduce students to exactly what the journey they are embarking on can be.

—A. James Elliott, Professor of Practice, Emory University School of Law

I was a teacher of drama for many years, and I know good drama when I see it. Few professions create as much natural drama as the law, and this book takes you into the rooms where the drama happens. In these interviews, prominent lawyers and judges detail their experiences in the profession and explore the knowledge, skills, and personal character necessary to succeed. It's always good to learn important lessons, but these stories also make for great reading. They have the characters, plots, conflicts, and suspense that make for great drama. For its combination of life lessons for law students and lawyers and its excellent storytelling, I give this book one of my few A+'s.

—Mary R. Wilder, Professor Emeritus of English, Mercer University College of Liberal Arts

MERCER UNIVERSITY PRESS

Endowed by

TOM WATSON BROWN

and

THE WATSON-BROWN FOUNDATION, INC.

Inside the Legal Profession

Conversations with Leaders of the Georgia Bench and Bar

Patrick E. Longan, Editor

MERCER UNIVERSITY PRESS
Macon, Georgia

MUP/ P688

Published by Mercer University Press
1501 Mercer University Drive
Macon, Georgia 31207

27 26 25 24 23   5 4 3 2 1

Books published by Mercer University Press are printed on acid-free paper that meets the requirements of the American National Standard for Information Sciences—Permanence of Paper for Printed Library Materials.

Printed and bound **in the United States.**

This book is set in Adobe Garamond Pro and Georgia (display).

Cover/jacket design by Burt&Burt.

ISBN 978-0-88146-887-8 (print)
ISBN 978-0-88146-888-5

Cataloging-in-Publication Data is available from the Library of Congress

LCCN 2023931616

This book is dedicated to all the lawyers and judges who are good stewards of the best traditions of the legal profession and who strive to help the next generation of lawyers learn and live up to those traditions.

Contents

PREFACE

by Patrick E. Longan[1]

All first-year students at Mercer University School of Law take a course on professionalism and professional identity. I teach that course along with my colleagues Daisy and Tim Floyd. The students learn that to find success and meaning in the law they need to cultivate a certain kind of professional identity, one that is infused with the traditional values of the profession. The course teaches that lawyers must be competent, faithful to clients, faithful to the law, public-spirited, and civil.

It is important, but not enough, for the students to know about the importance of these virtues. Cultivating them is hard work, and there are many obstacles to their implementation in practice. We discovered early in the evolution of the course that we needed to focus not just on the transmission of knowledge but also on motivation. We had to show the students the rewards of all that striving towards the right kind of professional identity. To do that, we needed to introduce them to lawyers and judges who are exemplars of the type of professional we are urging the students to become.

That need led to the creation of the "Inside the Legal Profession" component of our course. On Monday and Friday mornings over the course of the semester, I interview judges and lawyers with the entire first year class as the audience. I follow the format of the famous "Inside the Actor's Studio" interviews that James Lipton conducted for many years. I discuss with our guests their careers, both the joys and the challenges, and I leave time at the end for the students to ask questions. The interviews are routinely recorded, and from those recordings the transcripts that appear in this book were made.[2] More than fifty of the interviews are

[1] William Augustus Bootle Chair in Ethics and Professionalism in the Practice of Law, Mercer University School of Law, Macon, Georgia.

[2] The transcripts have been lightly edited for clarity and length.

posted to YouTube, where collectively they have garnered thousands of views.

Over the years, I have had the privilege of interviewing judges from the federal trial and appellate courts, the Georgia Supreme Court, the Georgia Court of Appeals, various Superior Courts, State Court judges; a Juvenile Court judge; and a Magistrate Court judge. Lawyers from every part of the profession have participated: prosecutors; defense lawyers; big firm litigators and transactional specialists; solo practitioners; family law attorneys; government lawyers; law professors and administrators; in-house counsel; plaintiffs' lawyers; insurance defense lawyers; and bar counsel. Our students have heard from members of the profession at every stage of a career, including brand-new graduates who talk about those first months of practice, young lawyers navigating the partnership track in law firms or struggling to make successes of their own firms, and senior partners and distinguished judges with the perspectives of decades in the profession. The roster of guests has been diverse by gender, race, sexual preference, and ethnicity. At Mercer, we have been honored by the generosity of all of the busy and important people who have volunteered their time to help introduce our new students to the many lives in the law from which the students might choose.

It was difficult to choose just a handful of the interviews to include in this book, but the lawyers and judges who appear represent an excellent cross-section of our guests. Five are graduates of Mercer Law School. United States District Judge W. Louis Sands describes his journey from the time when he was a child and told his mother that he wanted to attend Mercer University—this at a time when no African American could do so—through his Mercer education, service as a prosecutor, private practitioner, and Superior Court Judge, to his nomination, confirmation, and service on the federal bench. Angela M. ("Angie") Coggins talks about what it is like to serve as a public defender, the career choice she made as an intern in Mercer Law School and that she followed for more than thirty years. Tomieka R. Daniel, who has participated in the series every year since its inception, gives the students a look inside the challenges and rewards of representing clients who cannot afford lawyers for civil matters and thus turn to her as a legal services attorney. Justice Hardy Gregory, Jr. describes his service as a plaintiffs' lawyer, a superior court judge, and a Georgia Supreme Court justice. Along the way, he dispenses wise advice based upon his more than fifty years at the bar. Richard A. ("Doc") Schneider tells of his serendipitous choice to attend Mercer Law School and how that led to a remarkable career at King & Spalding in Atlanta, including working for two other famous Mercer lawyers, former judge and attorney general Griffin Bell and legendary trial lawyer Frank Jones. He also shares the origins and rewards of his avocation as a singer-songwriter. Lamar W. Sizemore, Jr., who along with Judge Sands is a member of the famous Mercer Law Class of 1974, talks about his three careers: as a highly successful plaintiffs' lawyer, as a Superior Court judge, and as a mediator. Along the way, he imparts memorable lessons for lawyers, such as how to deal with an adversary who mistreats you, and for judges, including his admonitions to err on the side of mercy and to "just rule."

Others who appear in this volume have connections to the Mercer Law faculty. Professor James P. Fleissner has taught at Mercer since 1994, and the graduating classes have selected him to receive the annual teaching award seventeen times. He talks about his earlier career as a federal prosecutor and about how to take advantage of the opportunities that law school affords. Dean Daisy Hurst Floyd, now University Professor of Law and Ethical Formation at Mercer, describes her career trajectory from being an associate at a big law firm through her appointment and service as Dean of the Mercer Law School. Along the way, she had occasion to be a client, and in her interview she candidly describes the circumstances that led her to need a lawyer and the lessons she learned about lawyering from being a client. Justice (then Judge) Verda M. Colvin is an adjunct professor at Mercer; she shares the insight and wisdom of someone who has succeeded in private practice, as a state prosecutor, as a federal prosecutor, and as a judge. Her dedication to excellence and her courage to be herself as a judge rather than mimic what other judges do have inspired our students every time she has visited our class.

Two of the interviews in this volume are of lawyers who have no direct connection to Mercer but who nevertheless made the effort to come to Macon and speak with our students. Emmet J. Bondurant talks about his varied and highly successful career: as a Supreme Court advocate, as the founder and leader of a highly successful commercial firm, as an attorney for two detainees at Guantanamo Naval Base, and as the pro bono lawyer for a man wrongfully convicted of murder and sentenced to death. He memorably describes his motivation for some of his most high-profile pro bono work: "I hate bullies." Former Georgia Chief Justice Harold D. Melton (now a partner at Troutman Pepper in Atlanta) shares his experiences as the first African American president of the student body at Auburn University; as a law student at the University of Georgia who placed at "the top of the bottom half of the class;" as a lawyer in the Georgia Attorney General's office; as counsel to Georgia Governor Sonny Perdue; as a Justice on the Supreme Court of Georgia; and finally as Chief Justice of that Court.

Students need to see and hear from lawyers and judges who have found success and meaning in their professional lives. They need to have exemplars, people whose stories inspire them and whose paths they may want to follow. With the help of those whose interviews appear in this volume, and the help of the dozens of others who have participated in the "Inside the Legal Profession" project, we have been able to provide such exemplars for our students. It is my hope that all who read this book will find similar inspiration in the stories it contains.

A Conversation with Emmet J. Bondurant

Introduction by Jason J. Carter[*]

When people set out to be lawyers, most of them imagine themselves as a champion for something. Maybe you imagine winning trials on behalf of big companies who pay handsomely, or striking blows for underdog plaintiffs whom no one else believes in. Maybe you imagine yourself representing an innocent person who was wrongly convicted. Or you might dream of striking a blow for justice in a case that changes the contours of our political system or our legal profession. Maybe you imagine yourself as an advocate transforming the justice system itself.

Any one of those things can make a career. And Emmet Bondurant has done them all. As you can see from the interview that follows, he has also done them with toughness, determination, courage and with a laugh and a twinkle in his eye.

Just the resume facts tell a champion's story: in 1963, when he was 26, Emmet argued *Wesberry v. Sanders* in the US Supreme Court. That case applied the one-person-one-vote rule to congressional districts, which not only made them more fair, but began to end the rural stranglehold on Southern politics and pave the way for our modern political system. In 1983, he argued one of the most important sex discrimination cases in US history, *Hishon v. King and Spalding*. There, he took on the biggest law firm in Georgia and established that Title VII forbids gender discrimination by partnerships.

In 1991, after a yearslong battle, Emmet secured the release of Gary X. Nelson, a man wrongly convicted and sentenced to death.

Emmet also advocated for reform of Georgia's indigent defense system, culminating in 2003 with the passage of the Indigent Defense Act, which created for the first time a uniform state-wide indigent defense

---

[*] Partner, Bondurant, Mixson & Elmore, Atlanta, Georgia.

system under the supervision of the Georgia Public Defender Standards Council. Emmet was elected and served as the Council's first chairman from 2003-2007.

In 2019, Emmet argued *Rucho v. Common Cause* in the US Supreme Court, seeking to end partisan gerrymandering. This argument, which occurred fifty-five years and four months after his first argument, marks what I believe is the longest Supreme Court career in history.

Throughout this career in public service, Emmet has also been without peer in representing clients. He has handled innumerable trials in every conceivable forum. He is a Fellow of the American College of Trial Lawyers and of the American Academy of Appellate Lawyers—a rare double in these legal Halls of Fame. The *National Law Journal* recognized him as one of the Top 10 trial lawyers in the United States; *Best Lawyers in America* named him as the 2010 Lawyer of the Year for Antitrust and Bet-the-Company Litigation and the 2012 Lawyer of the Year for Arbitration and First Amendment Litigation. *Chambers USA* has constantly listed him as a Leading Antitrust Lawyer, and *Atlanta Magazine*'s poll of Georgia Super Lawyers showed him as the top vote getter for many years.

In my view, Emmet has achieved as much as one can achieve as a lawyer. I have been lucky to have placed my office next to his for my entire legal career, and I can say that he has achieved all of this with an open door, an open mind, and a mentor's heart. I have never seen Emmet turn someone away when they were looking for help.

EMMET J. BONDURANT, 2019

PROFESSOR PATRICK LONGAN: Emmet, thank you very much for joining us.

MR. EMMET BONDURANT: I'm honored to be here. Thank you.

PROFESSOR LONGAN: We've got a lot to talk about because you've had a long and quite varied career. But I want to start by asking you, why law? All those years ago, why did you choose law over all the things you could have done?

MR. BONDURANT: Haha. (Laughter.)

PROFESSOR LONGAN: That was not a joke. (Laughter.)

MR. BONDURANT: You will see the point. I was an undergraduate of Georgia. I couldn't figure out what to major in. I changed majors eight times, and one of my fraternity brothers said, "why don't you try law school?" Georgia had a combined degree program, and I could use the first year of law school as the last year of undergraduate school, and so I went to law school with no intention of being a lawyer but with an idea that it was a good background for something else, whatever that "else" was. I was also—it was the end of the Korean War, pre-Vietnam War, and I was in an Air ROTC program, and soon I was going to get drafted into the Air Force, so I went to law school with no intention of being a lawyer and completing a degree. It turned out that I liked law school. I found the first year, as I'm sure you did, a bit of a culture shock because it was so utterly different from undergraduate school. But I stayed, so forget all the stuff about long-range planning, it worked out, and I'm glad I ended up with that career choice, but it certainly was not a grand plan designed from childhood to be a lawyer.

PROFESSOR LONGAN: Was there some event or something that happened that caused you to think, "I really think I want to try this lawyer business"?

MR. BONDURANT: Well, I found the subject matter interesting. I found it was an entirely different way of thinking from taking an undergraduate course, in which you were learning dates and collected data, and you were having to learn critical thinking in a very challenging way. I liked it. As you got into it you found that some of the subject matters were interesting. Particularly constitutional law was interesting; criminal law was very interesting. I have to confess real property law didn't exactly excite me.

PROFESSOR LONGAN: They're taking property right now.

MR. BONDURANT: Yeah, the Rule in Shelley's Case or the Rule in Wild's Case have escaped me over the years, or I have escaped them, so...(Laughter.)

PROFESSOR LONGAN: Well, you've done a lot of different things over your career, and I want to have a chance to talk about all of them. I know you founded your own firm. You've been highly successful. You've done pro bono work. You've worked on policy questions. But I think where I want to begin is with your work regarding voting rights. Here's why I want to start there: in a sense it can create some bookends for us at the beginning of your career and the present. Early in your career you were involved in—I want to make sure I get this case right—*Wesberry v. Sanders*[*] before the Supreme Court of the United States involving congressional districts in Georgia, and you argued that case at age twenty-six. What was that like?

MR. BONDURANT: It was fun. You have to understand, and all of you are too young to have known this, but Georgia operated under the equivalent of the Electoral College under which the representation of the General Assembly was terribly malapportioned, and it carried over to the governor's race. The six largest counties in Georgia each had three members of the state house, and double that in terms of what we call county unit votes: the equivalent of the Electoral College. The next

---

[*] 376 U.S. 1 (1964).

thirty had four, and the remaining counties had two. So that Echols County, for example, on the Georgia-Florida line, in 1960 had a population of 1876 people. It had two county unit votes in the election of governor, the equivalent of Idaho or Wyoming's contribution to the Electoral College. Fulton County, which obviously was Atlanta, had many more people. It had six county unit votes, which meant the governors were always elected by the rural forces in Georgia which, as you can imagine at that time, was the reactionary force to everything going on from school desegregation to economic development to education and everything else.

So, I got interested in the topic. I had an opportunity, after a clerkship, to spend a year at Harvard in the master's program in which my master's thesis was going to be a cutting-edge paper as to how one might challenge the county unit system in federal courts. At that point in time the federal courts were operating under a 1944 dictum written by Felix Frankfurter that said that all issues involving elections were political questions, that the federal judiciary was too pristine and couldn't get their robes dirty by going into the political thicket where they might be scratched by briars. That whole area was out of bounds. Well, just as I was finishing what I thought was this great cutting-edge paper as to how that might be challenged, the Supreme Court decided something called *Baker v. Carr,** which was a 1962 decision from Tennessee, in which the court ruled six-three that, in fact, federal courts could take jurisdiction. My paper overnight became a rear-guard action, being subsumed by the *Baker* decision.

When I returned to Atlanta, there were three cases pending in the wake of *Baker.* There was one challenge of the state legislature; there was one challenge of the county unit system; and the third case was *Wesberry v. Sanders,* in which two young lawyers in Atlanta who were Jaycees brought a suit to challenge congressional districts. They lost in the district court two-one in an opinion written by a Mercer alumnus, Griffin

---

* 369 U.S. 186 (1962).

Bell, who was then on the Fifth Circuit. Because I'd done all this work, I got introduced as a very young lawyer to these people working on these cases, and candidly took over *Wesberry*, which they had lost. It was sent to the Supreme Court, and the Supreme Court took it.

I argued it in November 1963, four days before the Kennedy assassination, which is a date we all remember. It was probably not the best judgment for me to argue the case, being as young and inexperienced as I was, but angels tread where fools fear to tread or vice versa, and I did, and it turned out okay. In February of 1964 the Court came out with a six-three opinion, written by Justice Hugo Black, which held that under Article I, Section 2 of the Constitution, members of Congress within a state had to be apportioned based on population. One person, one vote rule came out of that case. Five months later in legislative cases, *Reynolds v. Sims*[*] and three others, the Court applied the same principles to state legislative districts. So as a result, the Georgia General Assembly in both houses had to be reapportioned. That is why you have equal representation on a population basis in both state legislatures and congressional districts.

PROFESSOR LONGAN: Talk for a minute, if you would, about the argument itself, and how you felt as a young lawyer standing in front of those justices.

MR. BONDURANT: Well, the Supreme Court is an awesome place in many respects. This was the Warren court, the same court that had ruled in *Brown v. Board of Education*,[†] and was particularly, in comparison to courts in the last thirty years, a progressive court that believed that the law was an instrument for reform and not protection of property interests per se. They did not believe in a calcified Constitution frozen in time, and whatever James Madison thought in 1787 when the federal convention was held, and thus the Court dealt with a number of issues that had long been neglected by the federal courts. In

---

[*] 377 U.S. 533 (1964).

[†] 347 U.S. 483 (1954).

that period of time, you had the one person, one vote rule, which revolutionized both state and congressional elections, which were terribly malapportioned. In Georgia, for example, Georgia's congressional districts had not been reapportioned since 1930. And this was in 1960. In Alabama and Tennessee, their state legislative districts hadn't been reapportioned, even though their state constitutions required it. So that was a major reform of the whole electoral process. The Georgia county unit system failed, so you had a popularly elected governor and not one elected by this county unit system that skewed all the votes to the rural areas.

I don't remember being particularly intimidated by the court. I had argued some cases in the court of appeals, the federal courts of appeals before that, and I would offer those as an object lesson for all of you. We talk about pro bono work. A lot of that is great training for you as a young lawyer that you will not get in the ordinary course of a practice at a significant law firm, because a client who is a paying client isn't going to pay a rookie to go to the federal courts of appeals on a case of importance. It just ain't going to happen. So, the first year that I was practicing I was then at Kilpatrick, Cody, Rogers, McClatchey & Regenstein in Atlanta, which was then a mere twenty-lawyer firm. I got appointed in three cases to represent inmates at the Atlanta federal pen on federal habeas corpus actions, technically §2255 cases,* challenging some part of their convictions or incarcerations. As a result, I got to argue three cases in the Fourth Circuit Court of Appeals that I wrote the brief in. I went up and argued the case. No partner told me how to write the brief, that he'd do the argument for me or anything else. It turned out I won all three of them, which will get you a lot of prison mail. (Laughter.) But it also gave me experience in a federal appellate court with serious matters vastly years ahead of where I would have gotten it in the ordinary course of practice at Kilpatrick Cody. I had

* 28 U.S.C. §2255 sets forth the procedures under which a person in federal custody may seek to have his or her sentence vacated, set aside, or corrected.

argued more cases in the federal courts of appeals than most partners in that firm and all the associates in my first year of practice.

So it was serendipitous in the second year when I had the opportunity to go to the Supreme Court. I had been in some form of combat, not at the Supreme Court level, but federal courts of appeals were not particularly user friendly in habeas corpus cases, so it was a great opportunity. And while it was a pro bono service, sacrificial and all that sort of thing related to good works that lawyers ought to do free, it was great training for me, and it was an opportunity that I would not have had had I stuck to the firm's ordinary billable work of representing small loan companies in collecting overdue debts from people who had borrowed a little money from them.

PROFESSOR LONGAN: So you did your first Supreme Court argument in November 1963. Your next Supreme Court argument is next month. Can you talk a little bit about that case so the students get some context?

MR. BONDURANT: Well, the next case is clearly on a par with *Wesberry. Wesberry* changed the face of Congress because Congress went all over the country. They'd been elected from basically rurally dominated districts that had not been reapportioned for years, and so forth. The case we're currently working on is from North Carolina. It is a partisan gerrymandering case, and you have read a great deal recently about partisan gerrymandering. But it essentially involves whichever political party is in power using voting history data, how people vote in the smallest areas in which data is recorded, called Voter Tabulation Districts, and then stacking the political deck by sorting those districts out as to whether they're Democratic or Republican. You can with great precision, with the help of computers and a program called Maptitude, draw districts that are contiguous, compact, that don't look strange or anything else, that are absolutely equal in population that screw one political party or the other and exclude them from power.

In North Carolina the Republicans took control of the legislature in 2010 and set out to gerrymander the congressional districts and convert North Carolina, which was a fifty-fifty state, and still is, which had a seven-six Democratic majority in the delegation, to ten-three by gerrymandering the districts. The districts got held invalid because they used racial quotas for two of the districts, which violated the Equal Protection Clause. So, in 2016 they came back and adopted a new plan, in which they adopted written criteria that said this is going to be a partisan gerrymander, we're going to use political data, meaning voting history data, to preserve the current Republican majority.

We challenged that in the federal district court in 2016 before a three-judge court on four constitutional grounds: one, under the First Amendment because, for those of you who have not yet had Con Law, the First Amendment prohibits viewpoint discrimination, prohibits the government from discriminating against people in any respect based on their political beliefs, their religious beliefs, their viewpoints about issues. We challenged it under the Equal Protection Clause, equal protection of the law, which is obviously favoring Republicans over Democrats, but also under Article I, Section 2, which was the basis of *Wesberry v. Sanders*, and Article I, Section 4, which is the provision that says a state's legislatures shall determine the time, places, and manner of election of members of the House of Representatives. Well, the Supreme Court, in two cases that have been overlooked by everybody but us, said this is only a delegation of power to the states to adopt procedural rules. This is not a delegation of the power to dictate electoral outcomes or favor or disfavor a class of candidates. But what is a partisan gerrymander but an attempt by the legislature to dictate in what are called crack districts?

In North Carolina, Republicans will win those specific ten districts, and then Democrats will win the other three districts, which have been packed with super majorities of Democrats, or if you want to look at it on the other part of the sentence, favoring or disfavoring a class of candidates. If you're running in the first congressional district in North Carolina, which has been packed with a seventy percent Democratic majority, you know who's going to win that election. The Democratic incumbent is going to win. The Republican has no chance. Republican voters are worth nothing in that district, and the general election is a formality. Conversely, if you're in one of the ten districts that have been ethnically cleansed of Democratic voters, you know a Republican is going to win those districts. And guess what, in a wave election, the gerrymander held. Ten Republicans, three Democrats, even though the split in the vote was basically fifty-one to forty-nine, although there is one district, as you know, in which there are questions of absentee ballot fraud and which may be changed.

Well, the Supreme Court for the last thirty years has said, "this is a very complicated problem. We agree this is antithetical to the Democratic process, but nobody has proposed a manageable constitutional standard by which to rule on these issues." Well, we have, we did, and the three-judge court in our case unanimously ruled that the districts in North Carolina had been unconstitutionally apportioned. In an opinion that was a mere 214 pages long, the Supreme Court remanded it for reconsideration in light of the case from Wisconsin, and the court entered a new opinion that is now 321 pages long. So, it is up in the Supreme Court along with a case from Maryland, which we also worked on, which is, guess what, a Democratic gerrymander of a single Republican congressional district. So that issue is probably, from a pure democracy representative government point of view, the most important case in the Supreme Court this term of court and will determine in the future whether or not either political party, when they gain power, can essentially entrench itself in political power and exclude the other from gaining power by gerrymandering the districts.

It can be done very effectively. The Republican majority in Congress since 2012 is solely responsible to the gerrymandering in districts in five states: North Carolina, Michigan, Ohio, Pennsylvania, and Wisconsin. That accounts for the entire margin. If you had apportioned members of the House in those states based on some proportional representation, how the popular vote broke down in those states, the Republicans would never have had a majority in the House of Representatives for the last decade.

PROFESSOR LONGAN: We're going to look forward to seeing how that case is decided, and when it is decided I'll make sure the students all have a chance to see the opinion. I want us to switch gears for a minute and ask you about another case that you handled. You represented one of the Guantanamo detainees. If I pronounce this right, Muhammad Abdullah Al-Anzi.

MR. BONDURANT: Actually, I represented two of them.

PROFESSOR LONGAN: Two of them, all right. One of the things the students are learning here is that part of being a professional is keeping your eye on public service. Part of that is representing people who are unpopular. It's safe to say that Guantanamo detainees were not popular people in the United States, and yet a number of lawyers came out to defend them. Could you talk a little bit about that, what that experience was like, and why you did it?

MR. BONDURANT: Well, you'll get more of this in Con Law in law school. You've got to believe that the justice system at core is, just as the word implies, justice. That there are procedures, that there's some element of fairness in all of this, that you have impartial courts applying impartial rules to get a fair result. Guantanamo is, along with the Japanese exclusion cases, probably the greatest departure from the constitutional system that we all believe in that you have ever seen. You've not had Con Law, but during World War II the United States declared all people of Japanese descent on the West Coast to be security risks, rounded them up, put them in concentration camps in the High Desert in Nevada and in California, and kept them for the duration of the war, without trial, without anything, solely based on their Japanese ancestry. Those cases went to the Supreme Court, and the Supreme Court chickened out, deferred to the military authorities, refused to rule that these people, who were American citizens, in America, had any due process rights to challenge their detention. The Court has subsequently recognized that is probably, along with Dred Scott and a few other cases, the biggest blight on judicial jurisprudence in the United States and everything the legal system is supposed to stand for.

Well, the Guantanamo cases are another example. We all know about the war in Afghanistan, and so forth. What you don't know is that it was a cottage industry in Pakistan to sell people who were non-Afghanis, who ended up in Afghanistan for various reasons, to the CIA as supposed Al-Qaeda agents, and the US took them into custody, held them in places like Abu Ghraib, in many instances tortured them, and took them to Guantanamo. Guantanamo was selected by the Bush Administration because it was thought to be a judicial black hole, that is, that the federal courts in the United States could not exercise jurisdiction, the Constitution didn't apply, we could ignore the Geneva Conventions, we could ignore the rules of war, and we could hold them for however long we wanted to, and we could do any goddamned thing to them we wanted to, and we did.

Al-Anzi was a Yemeni who went to Pakistan, according to him, to teach the Quran to children. I'm candidly skeptical of the explanation, but whether he was or was not involved in that activity, when he was taken by the Pakistanis he was in Pakistan, turned over to the US, theoretically considered one of the worst of the worst, and taken to Guantanamo. Among other things that happened to him was he was waterboarded, except their method of waterboarding was to take him outside in mid-winter in Afghanistan and put him down on a stone table and hold his head under water in a barrel at the end of the table until he was faced with drowning. He had no fingernails; he had no toenails. I personally examined those. They used electric shock treatment, an electric generator which they hooked up to various body parts, which I won't name, to try to extract a confession, and the result was that if you confessed, that proved you were in Al-Qaeda. If you didn't confess, that also proved you were in Al-Qaeda because you had been trained to resist interrogation.

I've seen all the super-duper secret documents which they had on him, and they had nothing. They held him there for eleven years before he was released. We filed habeas corpus on his behalf. Notwithstanding that the Supreme Court had ruled that these petitioners had a right to challenge their detention under habeas corpus, the Court of Appeals of the District of Columbia reversed every case the petitioners won and affirmed every case the petitioners lost. Essentially, the Court said, if there is a piece of paper in which some government person said they had grounds to hold him, that was presumed to be true, and since the petitioner couldn't depose anybody, he couldn't disapprove it. So those cases, to say I'm bitter about those cases is an understatement. We lawyers tried as hard as we could, and dozens of lawyers all over the country did, with big firms and small firms, and ran into a stone wall, not at the District Court level in DC, but at the Court of Appeals level, of ideologues, two of whom are on the Supreme Court, including John Roberts, who essentially abdicated all judicial responsibility in those cases. The Supreme Court, after ruling in four cases in favor of the petitioners, refused to review any of those cases, and the whole episode is a travesty for the legal system that holds itself up as an example to the world of how a legal system is supposed to work, is a total abdication of the process.

Al-Anzi was released recently. We represented earlier a guy named Ahmed Errachidi, who was a Moroccan cook who was, again, sold by the Pakistanis to the CIA and held for seven or eight years. The government in those cases takes the position this is all highly classified. They wouldn't even tell you whether or not they were holding the guy there. As you got into the case, you normally in discovery in cases get documents from the other side. Well, any documents we got from the government, you had to go to a super-duper secret room in Washington. After you'd gotten a security clearance, you could only look at the documents there and could not make notes that you could take out of the super-duper secret room. If you had a hearing, the documents were brought in a plain brown envelope like pornography to the court by a security officer, opened in a sealed courtroom so you could try to use them. You really thought you had walked through a looking glass in terms of that process.

The government in my view lied and got away with lying in those cases. The government took the position—and all of you have watched enough TV to realize how silly this is, these are people that were being held as security risks supposedly for their intelligence value, they were interrogated thousands of times—the government claimed that they did not make one tape recording, one video, one verbatim transcript of any of those interrogations. They only had what the translator told an American what he thought the guy had said. What was produced to us was a single summary sentence of thousands of interrogations, hundreds of hours, and so forth, that supposedly supported the government's position. If you were arrested on a drunk driving offense in Hahira,* you would probably be interrogated on video by the local sheriff. If you took a deposition in any civil case with more than a hundred dollars involved, you're going to have a court reporter and a verbatim transcript so that you can record what the adversary said, cross-examine him, and so forth. The US Government holding people for, supposedly as the worst of the worst, to gain intelligence to help us fight the war on terror, claims not to have done any of that, when there are government documents that show the opposite is true, and the courts would not go into it. So that's a terrible episode.

The lawyers who stood up in those cases did absolutely the right thing, and hundreds of law firms spent millions of dollars and hours of pro bono time trying to make the justice system work as the Constitution intended it to work. And we failed. The courts failed us. It was not the bar that failed. It was the federal judiciary that failed.

PROFESSOR LONGAN: I want to give the students a chance to get a feel for the broader range of your career, and you haven't spent your entire career just doing these kinds of high-profile, largely pro bono matters. You started in what was then a big firm. Now it's laughable to think twenty lawyers is a big firm. But when you were forty years old, you founded your own firm, and the firm has been extremely successful doing commercial litigation, antitrust litigation, the business side of litigation work. Can you talk a little bit about that side of your career

* Hahira is small town in far south Georgia.

and what you found rewarding about founding and running your own firm these many years?

MR. BONDURANT: Well, the pro bono work I refer to as my playtime. I tell people that other people play golf. I sue people. (Laughter.) But the reality is if you're going to be in private practice and you're going to support a family, it's hard. You have to balance conflicting demands, and you can't spend all your time on your playtime.

Our firm does nothing but complex commercial litigation of various kinds, both trial and appellate litigation. That is really interesting; it's really challenging. You're playing in a fast-pitch league, doing some very demanding cases that take a vast amount of time and effort on the part of a lot of people. The nice thing about a litigation practice is that no two cases are alike, and you're learning the nuts and bolts or the details of how an industry would operate or how a particular transaction occurs or some medical procedure. I defended a patent case involving, I'll give it to you literally, transrectal biopsies of the male prostate with long needles and things like that, and I learned more about prostate cancer than I care to know, but subsequently was diagnosed with it. So there is a balance.

But there are opportunities to do high-quality legal work, to be extraordinarily well paid for it, depending on whether you win or lose sometimes, and do these other things, as well. One of the things that I have thought important, and let me give the old Kilpatrick firm credit, I was allowed as a very young associate to get involved in some very controversial cases on a pro bono basis that a lot of corporate clients, if they had been asked, would not have approved of, but I never got a peep of disapproval from the firm. They didn't cut my workload in order to do it. That was night/weekend work, as it is with us, but we do not let clients tell us the kinds of cases we can handle. You may remember when the Guantanamo cases first came up, one of the people in the Bush administration urged corporate clients to boycott the law firms that were representing Guantanamo detainees, and there was immediately some pushback on that. But if you're going to do those cases you've just got to face the fact that there are going to be people who disagree with you, and who don't think that people like the Guantanamo inmates should have a day in court or don't think somebody like Gary Nelson who was convicted of murder should be released. But your job in the legal system is to be an advocate, to make the system work, to make sure that the person is properly, if they're in jail, properly convicted, or if you're defending a civil case or you're prosecuting a civil case, to make sure that your client has the best day in court they can have, and a fair decision that you have put heart and soul into to achieve.

This is not one of these things you can do casually. You've got somebody's life in your hand if you're doing criminal work. You've got their financial welfare in your hand whether you're representing them as a plaintiff in a personal injury case, in which they've been horribly damaged, or whether you're representing a defendant in a business case whose very survival may depend on whether you win or lose. And so you're taking on a real responsibility. But it is both challenging and it is rewarding. It is painful. You will remember the wins, but you'll remember the losses much more because the losses hurt a lot. The lows of losing are much lower than the highs of winning. But it is something that's very demanding.

I tried a case in Tampa more than ten years ago now that lasted for five months before a jury. It was a corporate dispute involving four or five hundred millions of dollars, in which the other side was an eight billion dollar company trying to squash a competitor who we represented, and we fortunately won, but that's the kind of thing to be a lawyer you really relish the opportunity in those cases. But if you're going to let other people tell you the kinds of cases you can take, or you can't take a case for somebody who can't pay you who deserves a day in court because of their political views or they want to force their views on you, you're not really the sort of professional, independent lawyer that at least I would want you to be, and I think you, in your own quiet moments, would want to be yourself.

There are clearly costs to those things. I have brought cases that I can tell you with absolute certainty cost my law firm tens of millions of dollars either in referrals or direct client representation. It has that price, but it is a price, in my view, that is well worth paying, and we have survived, maybe not because of it, maybe in spite of it, but we are the kinds of lawyers we want to be. If you want to be the kind of lawyer that is timid and lets clients tell you what you can do and what you can't do for other people, you're probably in the wrong profession.

PROFESSOR LONGAN: Emmet, I've got a long list of questions that I made up, but I'm going to stop. I'd like to turn it to the students and see what questions they have for you in the time remaining. So, what questions do you-all have for Mr. Bondurant? Yes, sir?

LAW STUDENT: So, naturally, your career has come with some stress. How have you dealt with that over the years?

MR. BONDURANT: You just gut it out. (Laughter.) Clearly, it is a stressful career, there's no question about it, and you know there are a lot of lawyer alcoholics, there are a lot of lawyer suicides, but at the same time you just—it's like any other competition: you basically have to rely on both yourself and your colleagues to do the best you can, and as long as you're giving it your best you're going to lose some cases. I've lost cases that I should not have lost. The courts were wrong. I was right. I'm still right. (Laughter.) I make no apology for that. But it does require work. This is not a casual occupation. This is not a nine-to-five job. You take it home with you, and you wake up in the middle of the night wondering, damn, have I missed a filing deadline? That's the nightmare that we all have. But with concentrated work you can be an enormous success at this.

But it is—I kid you not, if you want to do something casually, go sell insurance or go in the advertising business or something like that. This is not that kind of a job, because it is demanding. I found as a young lawyer—I did reasonably well in law school—when I got to Kilpatrick as a young associate, I thought I was pretty damn smart until anything I drafted came back, they marked it with a red pen, and it looked like it had been dipped in blood. (Laughter.) You realize that you really had to up your game, but that was great training, and I am indebted for it. Would I do the same thing to a young associate? I don't apologize for it. It's just a matter of learning that you're playing in a fast-pitch league, and you've got to up your game and you've got to come playing your A game every day.

LAW STUDENT: What are some of the obligations or aspects of lawyering that you dealt with early in your career that you have to deal with less or that changes when you develop in the game?

MR. BONDURANT: Well, early in my career I was a young associate at Kilpatrick, which was a great law firm. It had really fine lawyers with damn high standards. You did not have your own office. We were in what was called the mole hole, which was an office in which were four or five young associates with no windows next to the library, and you did a lot of writing, and so on, as well as handling a lot of small cases. Were those intellectually challenging cases? For that level of my experience and career they were intellectually challenging. The first time you go to State Court of Fulton County in a little civil suit that you've never tried a case before, it is about as stressful as going to the Supreme Court of the US, but that is part of the learning experience.

What's the advantage of being an older lawyer? The advantage is that I can pick and choose. There are a lot of things that I would just basically say I don't want to be involved with. I don't want to waste my time on those cases. Sometimes they're paying cases. Sometimes there are clients that you meet that even when they want to pay you very well, you may be able to figure out in advance that they're somebody you can never please no matter what you do, at which point you refer them to the person in the bar you like least. (Laughter.) But as you progress in the profession, you do less of the things that you don't want to do and delegate that, but our view, and our firm is a little different from a lot of others. When we have major litigation, we probably have only one partner and one associate on it, and they would be working more or less at an equal level, not in a purely vertical level, in which the partners on Mount Everest are getting distant reports of what's going on in the field. I think you need to be involved in the day-to-day work in preparation of the case and working with young lawyers to do the same thing so that you- all know all about the case instead of you're reporting to me what you find, and I've never even seen the witnesses.

LAW STUDENT: I have a two-part question. What were the outcomes of your Gitmo cases, and then if you were to advise the attorney general and the president going forward, from a constitutional perspective, what would be your proposed alternative to Gitmo?

MR. BONDURANT: I would—let me take the second first. If I had been the attorney general, I would never have had a Gitmo. If you wanted to try these people as war criminals, I would bring them to the US courts, and I'd try them under the Federal Rules of Criminal Procedure as we have done with many espionage cases, many terrorist cases in federal courts throughout the country.

The outcome of all the Gitmo cases was that despite all the efforts we made we did not accomplish anything for the prisoners. No prisoner was released as a result of a favorable legal ruling. Every favorable legal ruling was reversed. Every unfavorable legal ruling was affirmed. I'll give you the example of Errachidi. He was the cook who was a Moroccan who was sold by the Pakistanis to the CIA, spent six or seven years in Gitmo. We brought habeas corpus on his behalf. The federal court simply stayed our ruling in our case pending outcomes in cases in the Supreme Court, which simply meant it was put in the refrigerator and frozen, and then one day in 2007 or 2008 I got an email from the government. "The government has made a determination to release INS 127." That was his number at Gitmo. "This is not to suggest he's not a threat to the security of the United States or that he's not a terrorist. We're going to release him anyway."

So we then said, "Well, how can we facilitate this?" He was Moroccan. It turned out that Jason Carter, who you may or may not know, who is Jimmy Carter's grandson and was an associate, his office was next to mine, and we were speculating, "how do we get in touch with the government of Morocco?" Jason said, "Well, I know the king of Morocco." (Laughter.) Through the Carter Center, they communicated with the Moroccan government, and within two days they told the state department they'd take Errachidi back. He was brought home and released by them and has since written a book about his experience.

One of the funny side stories of that was when you first get one of these cases—mine came from the Center for Constitutional Rights in New York—they didn't even know whether he was being held. His family in Morocco had heard from somebody that there was somebody named Ahmed, the cook, being held at Guantanamo. So, you call the government and say, "we've been asked by the family to represent this guy. Can you tell me whether he's being held at Guantanamo?" "No, that's classified." "Well, how can I file habeas corpus if I don't have the facts and know whether you're even holding him? It's kind of silly for me to file it if you're not holding him." "We can't tell you; it's classified."

So, you have to get a security clearance, file a lawsuit alleging he's being held, without knowing he's there, and then, of course, they admit he's there. Well, he was supposed to be the worst of the worst. He was known as the colonel within Guantanamo, and that was supposed to mean he was some kind of leader, and this was all top secret, classified and so on. Well, about three or four years into his detention, an article appeared in the New York Times Sunday supplement, the magazine section of the Times, in which they were interviewing the commandant at Guantanamo. He was describing his efforts to negotiate with the prisoners to get more cooperation in return for more privilege. Guess who he was negotiating with? The colonel whom he named was Ahmed Errachidi, this top secret, worst of the worst. They produced no evidence that he was anything other than a nobody, and ultimately released him as a nobody, and he's gone back to Morocco as a nobody. He spent seven or eight years of his life in solitary confinement at Gitmo, which is not a place for a beach vacation, I can assure you.

LAW STUDENT: Could you speak about what has motivated you over the years to do these things that seemingly you go against the public by—or representing Gitmo detainees or causing trouble in North Carolina—

(Laughter.) Can you talk about what has motivated you to even pursue those type of cases?

MR. BONDURANT: It's hard to psychoanalyze yourself. Let me try. I believe deeply in the justice system. I hate bullies, and I hate for the system to be unjust.

I represented Gary Nelson, who was convicted of rape, murder, sodomy of a six-year-old child in Savannah in 1978. We spent twelve years on that case. He was wrongly convicted. He was inadequately represented, but worse than that, the prosecution in Savannah violated every known constitutional right you've ever heard of, including suppressing evidence, knowing use of perjured testimony to get a conviction. Fighting for somebody like that, who can't possibly afford lawyers, particularly lawyers who charge the outrageous sums that we charge our civil clients, is important, and if the justice system is to work, if it's to mean anything, if it's to live up to the word "justice," people like you and I and all of you have got to say, "that's my job, to correct those injustices and to take those cases."

The Nelson case, he was on death row for twelve years. Virtually every young lawyer in my office worked on that case at one time or another doing something. He became a human being to them. The secretarial staff would send him yarn because he learned to crochet while he was in prison so he could earn cigarette and candy money. He would knit baby blankets and baby sweaters for shower gifts for the secretarial staff. He was a real person. I was convinced if we had lost that, a number of our young lawyers would have left the firm and said to hell with practicing law because there is no justice in this system. Others would have needed psychiatric help just because of their attachment to him. We fortunately were able to win. Habeas was granted.

I argued that in the Georgia Supreme Court the day after I ran the Boston Marathon, which is another story. I didn't win, no. (Laughter.) But I did finish in about four hours. But Gary was released in 1991. We relocated him in Athens with the help of social workers from Savannah because my theory was, if a cap went missing in Savannah he would be the number one suspect. He has lived a blameless life since then, and that was really worth the effort and worth the investment by the firm of firm time, and everybody who worked on it thought that this is why I really wanted to be a lawyer. It was not just the paying cases. The paying cases are important. Winning those are really important, feels good and you get a check every month, but it also feels good to do something for somebody that nobody else is going to help.

LAW STUDENT: I was just interested in how the social unrest of the 1960s kind of helped mold you as a person or a lawyer. Can you speak to anything specific in that era?

MR. BONDURANT: One of the things that candidly I regret was that there were practically no Georgia lawyers, no white Georgia lawyers with the large firms, involved in the civil rights movement in the early sixties, when others were going to Mississippi as part of Freedom Summer and things like that. But that was a period of great change. It was a period in which the courts were a leader in reform, not an obstacle to reform. That is a major change in the way that the federal courts have performed since then. You can tell which side of that equation—I'm not a strict constructionist who believes that the law ought to be ossified in the state that it was in 1789, in which there were a lot of things that went on that would not be acceptable today.

PROFESSOR LONGAN: Emmet, thank you for being with us today.

A Conversation with Angela M. ("Angie") Coggins

Introduction by Franklin J. and Laura D. Hogue[*]

No one knows how many cases Angie Coggins tried to jury verdict in her thirty-one years as a public defender. Well over a hundred, no doubt. No one knows how many clients she represented during those three decades. Several thousand, easily. But what we can know with certainty is that every one of those clients would remember "Ms. Coggins." To them, she was the lawyer whose effusive personality and warmth left no doubt that she cared for them, worried about them, and that she would bring her prodigious skills as a criminal defense lawyer to their aid. She saw behind their worst moments, their bad decisions, and yes, often, their heinous crimes to the human being of worth, the person whom she believed could be salvaged, remade, and, so she hoped, able to return to society a better person.

To know a client, Angie would tell you, you must know their roots and their community. Family, friends, teachers, pastors, coaches, doctors, and neighbors. She paid attention. She listened. She worked tirelessly. Well-known at the Houston County jail as "the best lawyer that money *can't* buy," she practiced law the way she lives her life: with passion and integrity, her heart always open to her clients. Whenever a potential client would call us seeking representation and let us know that the Houston County Public Defender represented them, we would ask, "which lawyer?" If they answered, "Angie Coggins," we would always tell the person, "you already have the best lawyer you can get; save your money and keep her."

Angie entered the practice of law in the late 1980s, when women graduating from law school made up just over twenty-five percent of the class. She was only twenty-four years old. Even at that young age, she

---

[*] Partners, Hogue & Hogue, Macon, Georgia.

knew who she wanted to be, knew that her talents would best fit the needs of poor people accused of crimes. Angie was born to be a public defender. It was her calling. And she threw herself into it completely.

Angie's dedication to her profession and her desire to see young lawyers practice to their full potential led her to become an effective teacher and role model, teaching criminal defense to hundreds of lawyers in the Bill Daniel Trial Advocacy program, sponsored by the Georgia Association of Criminal Defense Lawyers, of which she served as president in 2017, as well as at the National Criminal Defense College's annual Trial Practice Institute. She even taught trial practice halfway around the world in the small Republic of Georgia, where she and six colleagues started a training program for a nation hoping to emulate the best practices of American criminal defense. After seven trips to that country, several hundred Georgian lawyers now know a unique personality, sometimes sporting pink hair, sometimes blue, and always in the trendiest, funkiest shoes, so many shoes, who helped them elevate their lawyering to a whole new level. She made an unforgettable impression as an ambassador for the best of American trial practice.

No one can know the full reach of Angie's influence in the lives of those thousands of clients, the thousands of young lawyers she taught, and even the prosecutors and judges who saw her practice. But what we can know is that she has left an indelible legacy on the practice of law and a shining example of the best that criminal defense lawyering can offer.

ANGIE COGGINS, 2015

PROFESSOR PATRICK LONGAN: Angie, tell the students a little bit about what led you to law school and, in particular, what led you to do what you do.

MS. COGGINS: It will be very corny and very cheesy, but it is the truth. When I was in the eighth grade—back in my day we called that junior high school. I know most of you probably refer to it as middle school—we had a class called Youth in Law, and it was all about the juvenile justice system, and so we had all kinds of great projects and cool things to do, building little juvenile detention centers out of popsicle sticks and things along those lines.

PROFESSOR LONGAN: Really?

MS. COGGINS: Really. My dad helped me craft it. It was great, and I would have the shower and the cafeteria and the yard. It was very fun. But it wouldn't have been fun to be there. The other thing that was fun was we had a mock trial. And in the mock trial one of our classmates was accused of going down to the creek with another classmate and stabbing her, and I got to be the defense attorney in that case. I don't know why I wanted to do it. I just wanted to do it, but once I had participated in that, my fate was sealed. I knew from that moment, eighth grade, I knew I wanted to be a defense lawyer. Now, I didn't know then what was a public defender. I don't think I had any sense of public defender, but I knew I wanted to represent the underdog. I knew I wanted to represent the person that needed good, quality, effective assistance without having to pay tons of money for it.

PROFESSOR LONGAN: A lot of us never recovered from eighth grade.

MS. COGGINS: (Laughing).

PROFESSOR LONGAN: At least you turned it into something positive.

MS. COGGINS: I did; I did. I got it in my mind. I went straight through undergrad, straight to law school, started at the public defender's office in my third year of law school, and I've been there ever since.

PROFESSOR LONGAN: Well, talk to us a little bit about what that means. Describe your job to us and tell us about your clients, how they end up being your clients, and the kinds of things that they're accused of doing.

MS. COGGINS: We represent people from one end of the spectrum to the other, from shoplifting to murder. Now, we no longer handle death penalty cases because Georgia established the capital defender system, and I'm thankful for that. Death penalty cases take a lot of time; they take a lot out of you. I was involved with a couple before the capital defender system came into existence, and it's excruciatingly painful and difficult, as is any case, but that's the ultimate punishment, and it can be very trying if you think you have a person who's going to lose their life at the hands of a jury. Fortunately, none of our clients ever did. I was involved with three death penalty cases, and each of them ended up with life sentences, so I was very grateful for that. When you ask, "what kind of people do we represent?" we represent people like you or your sister or your dad or your aunt. It's just people who find themselves in situations where they are facing prosecution by the state, and they need somebody to stand in the gap.

PROFESSOR LONGAN: The latest statistics I've seen in Georgia, about eighty percent of the criminal defendants are indigent and need somebody like you.

MS. COGGINS: I would think that's right. We actually do not keep up with the statistics. We have an indigent defense coordinator who is responsible for determining whether somebody qualifies for the public defender's office. It's very simple. It's based on the federal poverty guidelines, so if one person makes "X" number of dollars, they qualify. If they make over "X" number of dollars, they do not qualify, and you deduct for each dependent the person has and whether they have child support payments and things along those lines.

PROFESSOR LONGAN: You're a very experienced defense lawyer, and you told me just before we started that you have 180 cases open at one time?

MS. COGGINS: On average. We have eight attorneys in the felony division and three attorneys in our misdemeanor division, and on average we carry between 180 to 200 cases at any given time. State court carries far more than that because they have a (snapping fingers) greater turnaround.

PROFESSOR LONGAN: I didn't warn you I was going to ask this, but I've got to ask this: with 180 files, can you do it the way you want to?

MS. COGGINS: Oh, yes, I do it exactly the way I want to do it. (Laughter.) I do it exactly. When I first started in the public defender's office back in 1989, we had three attorneys, and we each carried a caseload of about three hundred. So, you learn how to manage time. You learn how to prioritize. The truth of the matter is all those cases are not going to come up at once. I've been doing this since 1989. I was telling Pat earlier, our backlog in Houston County has actually decreased here lately, and I think that's due in large part to our judges finally taking control of the trial calendar and finally prioritizing cases by age as opposed to nature of offense. A lot of times, oh, yeah, a person charged with armed robbery, they need to be up first versus the case that's three years old. So, they've switched it around, and so now our backlog has increased. But back to your question—you learn how to manage, and like I say, not all those cases are going to come up at once.

I have had situations where I have been overwhelmed and felt like I wasn't going to be able to effectively represent my client, and the one time I can remember specifically going to a judge about it, I had twenty-two cases set for motions. Now, I file motions, and I argue motions. I had twenty-two cases on one motions calendar, and I went to Judge Lukemire and I said, "look, there's just—I'm good but I'm not that good. There is just no way I can handle twenty-two." He was very gracious, and we sat down and went through the calendar, and we went through those cases that were older, and so he selected the older cases to force the DA's office into making some decision: let's fish or cut bait here. I think I ended up with maybe fourteen on the motions calendar instead of twenty-two, but I handled that just fine.

PROFESSOR LONGAN: Your clients didn't pick you. You're appointed to represent them. Do you find it difficult to build trust with your clients?

MS. COGGINS: It depends on circumstance. One great thing about our office, and I wish more public defenders' offices would do this, and I'm not sure, I don't know how others operate completely, but we have consistency in representation. I've been representing some of the same clients since 1989. I've grown up with them; they've grown up with me.

PROFESSOR LONGAN: Repeat customers?

MS. COGGINS: Yes, it's like getting married, once you're assigned to a public defender, till death do you part, at least in our office. We like the continuity of representation. So, if, for example, you come in charged with shoplifting this week, you get assigned to me, I'm your attorney throughout that. You come back two years from now or six months from now charged with violating your probation, I'm your lawyer. That really helps in building a level of trust. I just treat people the way I would want to be treated. I want your respect, so I'm going to give you respect. The media gives us a bad rap; books give us a bad rap; movies give us a bad rap, but the truth of the matter is we're the ones in the trenches, and we're the ones who know what we're doing, and we fight really hard for our clients.

PROFESSOR LONGAN: I would think that the first time you get a client they would look at you and think, "who's paying her? The same people that are paying the one that's prosecuting me. Whose side is she on?"

MS. COGGINS: That is a common misconception.

PROFESSOR LONGAN: Good. (Laughter.)

MS. COGGINS: It is a common misconception, and you will have clients who will say, "you're getting your check out of the same window. You know, you go to the same window to pick up your paycheck." It's not true. The state pays for the district attorneys. We are county funded. I'm very proud of Houston County because Houston County was far ahead of the curve here in Georgia. We've had a public defender's office in Houston County since 1974, and our county commissioners are very supportive of our office. They understand what a difference we make, how much money we save the county every year, so they've always been very financially supportive and just supportive in general. You just have to work through that with the client. You just have to prove to them—and it's no greater effort. It's not as if you come back every day and say, "I didn't get paid by the state today." You just show them in your actions, in your demeanor and how you treat them and how you are prepared for court. I mean, there's no better way to prove to a client that you mean what you say than to be prepared and ready when you go to court.

PROFESSOR LONGAN: I'm not sure the students would appreciate the historical context here for the Houston County Public Defender's Office because the public defender system statewide went into effect what, about ten years ago?

MS. COGGINS: Yes. Actually, about twelve years ago now. I don't know if you guys read the newspapers or pay attention, but just a week ago there was a bill that got tacked onto part of Governor Deal's criminal justice reform bill, and it was about to undo all that was done twelve years ago to give consistent representation throughout the state of Georgia. Way back in the day Georgia did not have a statewide public defender system. We had just a hodgepodge of indigent defense. You had some counties that did contracts. You had some counties that did panels. You had some counties that had public defenders' offices, and so people were getting very disjointed sense of representation. There was no way to really have standards and to have guidance for people who were representing the poorest people who needed the best representation. There was no way to keep an eye on that. And so

Norman Fletcher, Chief Justice Norman Fletcher, commissioned a blue ribbon panel to study indigent defense throughout Georgia and to come up with a plan for what we needed to do to make it better, and ultimately the decision was made to create a statewide public defender's office, statewide public defender system, so that in every circuit in which there was a DA's office there was a public defender's office because fair is fair and equal is equal. We are an opt-out county from the statewide system.

PROFESSOR LONGAN: Right, because you were already—you were there.

MS. COGGINS: Our office was actually the model office. We were the office on which the panel was based because my mentor, Terry Everett, who was the public defender from, let's see, I guess '89 until 2007, did an amazing job. We had a great public defender's office, always dedicated, always efficient, but she really, really brought us up to the level where we are now, and Nick White has just continued to maintain that level.

PROFESSOR LONGAN: Well, help the students understand what it's like to be you.

MS. COGGINS: It's awesome. (Laughter.)

PROFESSOR LONGAN: That's good. Is there a typical week, a typical day, a typical month that you can describe?

MS. COGGINS: Yes. One thing about Houston County is we are a one-county circuit. Many public defenders' offices have several counties within their circuit, and so they have to travel and what we call ride circuit. They have to go from one place to the next. Cordele has been in the news a lot because their public defender's office has been sued by the Southern Center for Human Rights because they still are underfunded, they still are understaffed, and people are not getting the representation they deserve and to which they're guaranteed under our Constitution.

But in Houston County we get our year-long calendar about midway—for example, we'll get 2016's calendar in about the middle of the summer of 2015. So, a typical week in Houston County, on Monday I get a jail list. It tells me everyone who is in the Houston County Jail from A to Z. It lets us know the nature of the person's charges. It lets us know whether they have bond. It lets us know the date of the arrest. We go over that jail list every Monday. As I say, our indigent defense coordinator creates a list of who's been arrested over the weekend, and that's a daily thing. We get a jail list every day. Now, we don't get the big jail list every day. We get that on Monday. But Tuesday through Friday we get another jail list. Prints out, tells us who's been arrested since the night before.

Our indigent defense coordinator determines who's been arrested, goes over to the jail, sees them, qualifies. If they qualify, they're immediately seen by our paralegal, interviewed, file comes back to the office, file gets opened. We have bond hearings every Thursday morning. We have pleas in association with that. We have probation revocation hearings every other Wednesday and every Thursday afternoon. We have two trial weeks every month, and thus we have motion hearings once every month. We have arraignments once every month. It's very organized. That is a huge benefit to Houston County, because it is very organized, very efficient. The judges are involved. We stay on top of things.

PROFESSOR LONGAN: When I envision you at work, I envision you at a very dramatic jury trial. That's what public defenders do in my mind, but you've told me that's not right. How many cases do you try?

MS. COGGINS: I don't keep stats. It's just not my thing. I was telling Pat earlier I went, one time, eighteen months without trying a case. It's just—and that's hard to believe in a public defender's office. That doesn't mean my co-workers weren't trying cases, but I personally have gone up to eighteen months without trying a case. Sometimes I just can't get a case to try. I filed two demands the last trial term, two trial demands, I was ready (snapping fingers) let's go, and the DAs offered misdemeanors on both of the cases. Felony burglary down to misdemeanor criminal trespass, felony fleeing down to misdemeanor fleeing or speeding, I can't remember. It was a misdemeanor with time served, so everybody was happy.

PROFESSOR LONGAN: Except you, you wanted to go to trial.

MS. COGGINS: I love trying cases. I absolutely love trying cases, but there's always a risk involved, and at the end of the day if the client is found guilty, he or she may be the one going to prison, not me, so if it can be resolved and the client is happy with the resolution, then, hey, I'm happy to go eighteen months without trying a case. I get plenty of courtroom experience, though, because, as I mentioned earlier, probation revocations are little, mini trials, and those, I can't even count how many probation revocation hearings I've had.

PROFESSOR LONGAN: You love going to trial. Tell us more about what it is you love about your job.

MS. COGGINS: I love my clients. I just—

PROFESSOR LONGAN: Are they loveable?

MS. COGGINS: After they meet me they are. I just have an affinity for this kind of work. It's all I've ever wanted to do. I've never thought about doing anything else, and I know people probably think that's hard to believe after as many years that I've done it, but I just, I love it. I love what I do. I love taking care of somebody. I love guiding them. I love standing in the gap. I believe in the Constitution. I believe in the rights, the guarantees. Where's my flag? I believe—I just—I can't put it into words. I just love what I do.

PROFESSOR LONGAN: How do you not burn out living like that?

MS. COGGINS: You do. You do burn out, and you take a week's vacation, and you go to the beach, or—one big thing that I have is the Georgia Association of Criminal Defense Lawyers. I am the executive vice president right now, in line to be president, but I've been a member of that organization since I started practicing law. It is an amazing group of people. It's people who do what I do. It's people who experience what I experience every day. We are the largest member-run organization in the country. I think we have anywhere from 1600 to 2000 active members, so that's people who are doing criminal defense who want to be a part of a group that helps support you, helps train you, helps teach you and comfort you and give you solace, laugh with you when things are funny and cry with you when you've had a bad day. I can reach out to any one of those people.

Then on top of that, my office is made up of an amazing group of people. We just—we're like family. We have the benefit of being a smaller office. We're all in one office, and you don't have a whole lot of turnover because we have such a good group and people are really committed to what they do. I've been there twenty-six years. Cindy, our office manager, has been there twenty-four. Claudia Minor has been there twelve or thirteen years. Nick has been there since 2007. We just mesh really well, and we take care of each other.

PROFESSOR LONGAN: What's the hardest thing about your job?

MS. COGGINS: Well, when a client goes to prison, even if that's where they're supposed to be—it hurts. It's just devastating. You've got to think of all the other consequences. It's not just somebody going to prison. It's their child being without a mother or their husband being without their wife, they lose their job, they lose their home, they lose connection to the community. It's just sad, and it happens, and it rightfully happens, but it still is very painful.

PROFESSOR LONGAN: It's hard for me to imagine how it feels, because you're standing there, they're convicted and they're led away, I mean, right then.

MS. COGGINS: I cry a lot. Even if the State proves the case, you still hurt. I go to trial on some cases where I believe my clients are going to be convicted but they want to go to trial. Or there's no offer. Or the offer is horrible. Whatever the case may be. But I had a gentleman who was convicted of aggravated child molestation, and he got twenty-five without parole. No prior felony convictions, some forty-odd years old. The alleged victim was fifteen. And he's serving without parole. It breaks my heart. That's not right. It's not fair. It's not just. Those types of sentences are draconian, and they have no place in our system. So when he crosses my mind, I think about what all I've lived in the last five years. What have I done in my life in the last five years? He's lived his life in prison, and he's got more to go.

PROFESSOR LONGAN: How do you get past that?

MS. COGGINS: You don't. I think it's pretty obvious that I'm not past it because I'm about to cry right in front of you guys. You just have to—you just have to take a deep breath and take your next step and just hope that they're doing okay.

PROFESSOR LONGAN: Obviously you've represented people accused of child molestation; you've represented people accused of murder, kidnapping, burglary, aggravated assault, and I could go on down the list.

MS. COGGINS: I will tell you this: A repeat shoplifter is the most hated client in the world. (Laughter.) I hate a repeat shoplifter.

PROFESSOR LONGAN: Alright, I'll bite. Why?

MS. COGGINS: Because they're whiny. (Laughter.) They're whiny as clients. And in Georgia if you're a repeat shoplifter, on your fourth, you have to get a year in prison, right? A year in prison. You're supposed to get a year in prison for shoplifting a hair brush, but that's what the law says, after three your next one's a felony, no matter the amount of the property, no matter what it is, it's a felony, and the statute says you get ten years to serve one. So, try explaining to somebody who's stolen a hair brush that they have to get a year in prison when you've got somebody who's charged with stabbing someone five times, and they may get probation?

PROFESSOR LONGAN: I would whine, too. (Laughter.) Well, here's my question. You've represented—and I assume you've represented a number of people who actually did do things that they were accused of.

MS. COGGINS: Sure.

PROFESSOR LONGAN: Do you ever get the question, how can you represent such people?

MS. COGGINS: All the time. I'm sure several people in here wanted to ask that very question. It's not the nature of—you're not defending the crime. You're not saying it's okay to go out and murder someone. You're saying to the government, to the State of Georgia—if you think my client did something, then you better be able to prove it. Bring it, don't sing it. That's why it's easy.

PROFESSOR LONGAN: But you're very good at what you do, and so I assume that you have obtained acquittals or gotten evidence suppressed that allowed people who had done terrible things to walk free.

MS. COGGINS: I haven't had a murder case dismissed yet because of a motion to suppress, but I've had several drug cases. Again, this is not moral court, people. It's legal court. If you believe in any kind of greater judgment, that's going to happen some other day. This is legal court. I had an assistant DA, who is now a state court judge, who would just on a regular basis say to me, "your client knows he did it." I don't care. I know he did it, too. Prove it. I would have to say to him, "this is not church. This is not moral court. This is a legal courtroom. You bear the burden of proof. Come on, let's go."

PROFESSOR LONGAN: Have you ever had somebody for whom you obtained a dismissal or an acquittal and who went out and re-offended?

MS. COGGINS: Every day. (Laughter.) We have a lot of repeat business. This is one thing that is very—you talk about burnout, this is one of the things that's very tough because in my line of work, if a client successfully completes his or her probation, I never see them again. So, the success stories are kind of out of sight, out of mind. What I deal with unfortunately is the about fifteen to twenty percent of clients who, for whatever reason, just can't make it. They fail to report; they get a new offense; they're addicted to drugs, so they're going to be repeat offenders. That becomes a little discouraging because you obviously focus on what you see as opposed to what you don't see. But the statistics are there.

The majority of people who are placed on probation complete their sentence successfully, and they never get in another day's trouble, and I never hear from them or see them again. Occasionally clients will come back and let me know how they're doing and that they have successfully completed their time and things are going well for them. I remember one young man in particular, he was charged with trafficking drugs, we ended up working it out with possession with intent, but he did have to go to prison. But he went away, under the first offender statute, because he'd never been in any trouble before. He successfully completed his prison time. He successfully completed his probation, started his own business, became a pastor, and he came back to let me know that he had accomplished all those things. I still have his card. Those are few and far between because I think most people when they get past it don't want to revisit it, so it's not as if they want to come back to my office and tell me all about how well they've done. They get through it, and it's in the past, and it's done.

PROFESSOR LONGAN: But you say those are few and far between.

MS. COGGINS: The success stories are many.

PROFESSOR LONGAN: Right.

MS. COGGINS: My knowledge of the success stories is few and far between.

PROFESSOR LONGAN: Well, tell me generally as a defense lawyer, how do you define success? That can't mean just dramatic acquittals in jury trials. I mean, what does success mean for you?

MS. COGGINS: Doing my best for the client. You truly—there's been times when I felt like I dropped the ball somewhere, and you don't feel like a success in those moments. You don't feel like a success when you have sets of motions to be heard, and you fear that client number seven is going to suffer over client number ten. That's hard to handle. But, like I say, the more you practice, the more you do, the more successful you become at prioritizing and being able to give client seven and client ten everything they deserve. Creating that trust with the client, standing up to judges and DAs and just giving it your all.

PROFESSOR LONGAN: In past years, I have asked the students, in a forum that's private so nobody sees it but me, if there's any kind of client they could not represent. Almost uniformly the answer I get is somebody accused of child molestation. You've represented a lot of people accused of child molestation. Is there any kind of person you wouldn't be able to represent?

MS. COGGINS: No, because, again, you're not defending the allegation. You're not saying it's okay to molest a child. You're saying if you as the State of Georgia think this happened you better be able to prove it. I've had a number of child molestation cases where my client was innocent.

PROFESSOR LONGAN: But you've had a number where they were guilty, too.

MS. COGGINS: Of course. And if the state can prove it, then the system works the way it should. If the state can't prove it, the system works the way it should.

PROFESSOR LONGAN: Are there particular cases you can think back on in your career that taught you particular lessons, that really stand out in your mind? There have been so many.

MS. COGGINS: Yeah. In combination with advice from a friend there was one case that helped me to realize that I need to just let my client be my client. We all teach our children: don't judge somebody based on the way they look, right? Judge them based on the content of their character, get to know them. How they dress, the way they wear their hair, all that really shouldn't matter to you. You should get to know them as a person. Well, when you're a defense attorney or I guess any attorney, you talk to your client about presentation: we're going to court. You might need to cover up that tattoo; we're going to court, you might need to take the braids out of your hair.

I had a particular young man, Maurice Collier was his name, he's deceased now, but I remember him, this is way back when we were in the old courthouse, this is probably early 1990's. He was an African American man, had dreads, little tiny dreads, and he was charged with stealing his own car from the police impound lot. (Laughter.) Which was hilarious. He said, "I didn't do it. Angie, I didn't do it." I said, "I'm good, Maurice, let's go." So, we're prepping for trial, and I'm telling him, "you may want to think about cutting your hair. You may want to think about it. You know, people, they shouldn't do it, Maurice, but people judge based on how you look, judge based on how you dress, your hair is a little different." He said, "I'm not cutting my hair." I said, "I'm fine. If you don't want to do it, don't do it, but just understand what I'm trying to tell you." So we go to trial on this theft of his own car, we have an all-white jury, and within the hour they were back with an acquittal.

That moment in combination with, like I say, what a good friend taught me, was to let your client have the dignity of being themselves. Right? If the jury is going to convict somebody because they have dreadlocks, then that's on them. But don't try to change them or make them be something they're not. Let them have the dignity of being themselves.

PROFESSOR LONGAN: And yet you gave him the advice, and he could accept it or reject it.

MS. COGGINS: Of course.

PROFESSOR LONGAN: You gave him the advice, and his appearance could have affected the outcome.

MS. COGGINS: It could have. But I don't give that advice anymore. No, because that moment representing Maurice—and the friend of mine is Cynthia Roseberry. You know Cynthia.

PROFESSOR LONGAN: Sure.

MS. COGGINS: She was the federal public defender here in Macon, and now she's working with the federal clemency project. She was appointed by, I guess appointed by Barack Obama to be the director of the federal clemency project, and she talks a lot about -isms and schisms and problems that we have in the system with just that, judging somebody based on how they look as opposed to the evidence the state brings.

PROFESSOR LONGAN: You see people once they're in the system, but by getting to know them I'm sure you learn about why they're in the system. What is it in the community that you serve that causes people to end up in the criminal justice system?

MS. COGGINS: Well, drugs, and some people are just thieves. (Laughter.) I'm just being honest. Some people just have a compulsion, and they just can't seem to help themselves. Circumstances, it just—there's—I don't have an explanation for that.

PROFESSOR LONGAN: Poverty.

MS. COGGINS: Other than the general explanation: poverty, drug addiction. You get in a fight with your best friend, and you punch them in the face, and then all of a sudden you're charged with a crime and you're coming to jail.

PROFESSOR LONGAN: For years I invited you, when I was in charge of the counseling course, to come and demonstrate to the class how you counsel a client about a plea bargain. How do you handle that? If you get an offer that you think is good, do you tell your client what they should do?

MS. COGGINS: No.

PROFESSOR LONGAN: They're going to ask you, "What should I do?" How do you handle it?

MS. COGGINS: I tell them, "You have to do what you think is best for you. I can't tell you to take this offer. I can tell you that I think it's a good offer. I can tell you that I think it's a terrific offer, but ultimately you have to decide whether it's an offer you want to accept. We can counteroffer. We can try to even get a better deal than what's on the table." I tell clients, "look, a trial is a risk. It's always a risk. It's a roll of the dice, a toss of the coin. Whatever you want to call it, the majority of the time a trial is a risk. You may walk out the victor; you may walk out in chains."

PROFESSOR LONGAN: But surely you get clients that say, "Angie, I'm torn, tell me what to do."

MS. COGGINS: Yes, of course. They say, "Tell me, what would you do; what would you do if it were you?" I say, "I can't speak to that. It's not me." That's really a place where you cannot put yourself in that person's shoes because it's not you. You don't know all that's coming into play. You don't know what all is affecting that decision. It's not me, so I can't tell you what I would do, because that's not fair.

PROFESSOR LONGAN: The other big counseling moment that I see or foresee in your job is the defendant who wants to testify. Now, I imagine you've got a lot of clients who want to testify and probably shouldn't, right?

MS. COGGINS: Yes.

PROFESSOR LONGAN: How do you talk them down?

MS. COGGINS: Just patiently go over all the advantages and disadvantages of testifying. I remember a particular case, a client was charged with armed robbery, and he wanted to take the stand, he wanted to take the stand, and ultimately had he insisted I would have let him take the stand.

PROFESSOR LONGAN: It's his right.

MS. COGGINS: Of course, his absolute right. There's a lot of decisions that the attorney makes that are the attorney's to make: strategy, what witnesses to call, what kind of defense to put forth, what charges you want the judge to give. I try to involve my client in every aspect of the case because it's not my case. It's their case, so I try to involve them in every aspect. You know, "do you want to ask for a lesser included or you want all or nothing?" Even that I discuss with the client. As for testifying in this particular case, I told him, I said, "look, there's no reason for you to take the stand. You've said you're not guilty by going to trial. There's nothing you can add to the testimony that's already been provided. All you can get up there to do is say 'I didn't do it, and we've already told the jury you didn't do it.'" He ultimately decided not to testify. Thankfully he was acquitted. So, there was no fallout from that.

PROFESSOR LONGAN: Ever had one who made the other choice and lived to regret it?

MS. COGGINS: I can't know if they lived to regret it. We had a murder trial one time and prepped, prepped, prepped, prepped, prepped our guy, and he did great. One of the things that we had discussed was, "don't ever call anybody a liar." You just don't. They may be lying, but you don't call them a liar. So in the middle of this axe murder trial with a surviving victim, by the way, who identified our client—

PROFESSOR LONGAN: Strike one.

MS. COGGINS: Yeah. (Laughter.) But it was necessary, it really was necessary in this case for him to testify. Great job, did a great job, did a great job on direct, he's doing a great job through cross. The DA starts asking about why people were saying things in contradiction to what he had said. And we had talked about this. The people to whom the DA was referring were our client's friends and our witnesses. I think they were, like this witness said "X" and this witness said "Y," it wasn't that great of disparity, but it was enough that the DA starts crossing our client about it. I can remember—and the chairs were, like, little swivel chairs in the witness box, and so the DA is questioning about, "well, Mr. Smith, why is it that so-and-so said that and so-and-so said this?" I swear I remember sitting in the courtroom watching him, you know, you get your breath, you're holding your breath, and he kind of leans back in his chair, and I'm thinking, "It's good, he's going to say something." He leans back, and then he rocks forward and he says, "I don't know except that they're lying." (Laughter.) (Making thumbs-down gesture). Actually, the jury was out, this was literally a case where the surviving victim identified our client as the one who had axed her in the head, the jury was out for over eight hours on guilt/innocence and ultimately did convict him, but, yeah, that was a rough moment. "I can't think of any reason except that they're lying."

PROFESSOR LONGAN: Exactly what you told him not to say.

MS. COGGINS: Yeah.

PROFESSOR LONGAN: I'm going to turn this over to the students in just a minute for any questions that they have, but I always give our guests a chance to say anything you think the students need to hear, anything, any advice, maybe something you wish you had heard when you were a first-year law student. What advice do you have for the students?

MS. COGGINS: One piece of advice I would give to you, this is going to sound silly, but please do your best to take the word "like" out of your vocabulary. I don't know what it is about young people, if you will, but the word "like" is so overused. Please take it out of your vocabulary. We're public speakers. Don't say "you know," don't say "I mean," don't start your sentence with "uh" or "um," and please, please restrict the use of the word "like" in your conversations. As far as actual advice about where you're going, just know your heart. Know your heart, know what you want to do with this law degree, commit to that. If you go into defense work, commit to that. Commit to the ideas. Commit to the belief. Commit to what it is you're doing for other people.

PROFESSOR LONGAN: And if they want to do what you do they should come work for you under the third-year practice act.

MS. COGGINS: Indeed. We will put you to work under the third-year practice act. I was telling Pat earlier we've got several third-year students who are working with us now, and they've done everything from probation revocation hearings to motions to suppress, to sitting second chair. Andrew Feagan is a third-year student here, and he recently assisted on a burglary case, and he did the opening statement, he crossed one of the officers, and that case ended in an acquittal. Yeah.

PROFESSOR LONGAN: That's a good thing.

MS. COGGINS: That's a good start.

PROFESSOR LONGAN: All right. Let me turn this over to the students for a few minutes.

MS. COGGINS: Sure.

PROFESSOR LONGAN: What questions do you have for Angie this morning?

LAW STUDENT: You mentioned that you get a lot of repeat business, if you will. How do you handle the clients that weren't exactly happy with your representation of them and now you've got to represent them again?

MS. COGGINS: That's a very good question. I do not say this to toot my own horn, but I've been there so long, I have a very good reputation, and it's a rare occasion that I have somebody that's unhappy with me, because you get to know the person as a person through the repeated representations. But we do have those situations where clients come back after having entered a plea of guilty, they're back on a probation violation, and they will write a letter saying, "I want anybody but Angie Coggins. Anybody but Angie Coggins." Well, that's not the way it works. You don't—you're entitled to appointed representation, but you're not entitled to the appointed attorney of your choice. You get who you get. And with our office, again, it's the continuity. So, if I represent you this week, I'm going to represent you next week. We just have to work through whatever differences we may have at the moment. I see it all the time with clients, because I'm the chief assistant public defender, all the little complaint letters come to me and people send the inmate request form and they say, "I don't want Ms. Hall, anybody but Ms. Hall." I write back, "Ms. Hall's a fine attorney; she'll represent you effectively and zealously. Just because you don't like her doesn't mean she's not going to do a good job for you." Truly, through the continuity of representation, those kind of issues, like I say, they finally resolve themselves because our clients ultimately see that we do have their best interests at heart, and even if you don't like me I'm still going to do my best to kick the DA out of the courtroom.

LAW STUDENT: You said that it's about defending the person and not the crime. For something that's a repulsive crime, especially if it was to be a repeat offender, how do you process that mentally? I don't understand that, if you defended some person that was charged with child molestation, and they were acquitted and they come back as a repeat offender for another child molestation case—I'm trying to figure out where you get that strength to do it.

MS. COGGINS: I don't know. I don't know from where it originates, but it's there. And that's a valid point, and you will, like I said, know your heart. If you believe, "I go into this job, but I can't represent somebody charged with child molestation," then don't represent somebody charged with child molestation. Now, if you're in a public defender's office you're not going to have much choice, but in private practice you pick and choose, and if you don't want to represent somebody who's charged with child molestation, tell them to go see Hogue & Hogue. Just send them to the next person. But it's—it sounds so trite but it's the truth: The Constitution says you are entitled to effective representation of counsel. It doesn't say you're entitled to effective representation unless you're charged with child molestation or unless you're charged with murder or unless you're charged with repeat shoplifting. People make fun of the phrase "true believer." I don't know why. We should all be true believers whether you're prosecution-minded or defense-minded, we should all be true believers in what our Constitution guarantees. It's that simple.

LAW STUDENT: I'm sure you see new attorneys very often. What are some of the common mistakes that they make when they're trying cases besides saying "like"? (Laughter.)

MS. COGGINS: Being unprepared. You have to know your case. You have to know your case better than anybody in the courtroom. Everybody has their own style, obviously everybody has their own way. I'm a very client-centered person, I'm very touchy-feely, very emotional because the person sitting next to me is just that, a person. It's not a number; it's not a charge; it's a person. So, I want to do my best for that person, and a surefire way to guarantee that is to be prepared: know your case.

LAW STUDENT: As a public defender, maybe when you were first starting out, did you ever feel at a disadvantage being the public defender because of the stigma that's always attached to individuals who don't have enough resources to get representation?

MS. COGGINS: I have felt that on occasion. When you have judges that were former prosecutors, and that's all they ever did, was prosecute, you tend to feel like there's a little bit of a bent, that they're going to be pro-prosecution as opposed pro-defense or pro-objective. I should say, the majority of the time, in my circuit at least, I feel like our judges treat us very fairly. Occasionally I feel like they're helping the prosecution with their job, telling them what questions to ask or what they need to do to get this piece of evidence into evidence, but overall, no, I've never felt that way with judges, DAs, or jurors for that matter.

I will tell you this: in all the years that I've tried and all the cases I've tried, I've only been truly disappointed in one jury's verdict. Conviction/acquittal, when a jury renders their verdict, in most cases I feel like they've done exactly what they were sworn to do. There's no—I shouldn't say there's no better feeling, but it's a great feeling when you've tried a case and the jury has acquitted, and then you speak to the jurors and they say, "You know, we thought your guy was guilty, but the state didn't prove it," because that's the burden. The jurors have listened. They've paid attention to what the judge told them; they've paid attention to the law. I've found that, that when jurors come in, just like you guys sitting here, and they have preconceived ideas and they look at you in the red shirt and you're sitting next to me at defense table, "I know that guy must have done something wrong or else he wouldn't be here." But once they get in that box, once they get in the box and they take that oath, they really do a good job.

In all the cases I've tried, in all the verdicts that have been reached, in only one was I disappointed, and it's because we spoke to the jurors afterwards. It was an alibi defense, and one of the jurors said, "well, we didn't really think the state proved his guilt, but you didn't prove his innocence, either." Well, that to me is a wash. He should have been found not guilty, but they found him guilty because we didn't prove his innocence, so that was a little upsetting, but overall I've been very pleased and satisfied with juries' verdicts.

LAW STUDENT: How do you deal with a client that maybe doesn't understand coming in that your having a good relationship with the state, as well as with the judge, can really be a benefit to them rather than what we see on TV, which is that they don't get along, prosecution and defense?

MS. COGGINS: Just a matter of discussing it with them. If they bring it up, if that ever becomes a topic you say, "look, a good relationship with the DA can sometimes work to your advantage, because if they like me, then in turn they may like you, and we may be able to work out what's charged as a burglary down to a criminal trespass, and you may have only committed a criminal trespass." So it's easier for me to talk to the ADA and say, 'Hey, look, you really don't have the evidence on this case. Cut my person a break, do whatever.'" You just have to walk them through that.

LAW STUDENT: I'm wondering, this is with my limited knowledge, but I think there are maybe more prosecutors who then become defense attorneys, rather than vice versa, defense attorneys who then become prosecutors. I'm wondering if you have any opinion about why that happens or if you know of any colleagues who've done that and why they chose to switch sides?

MS. COGGINS: I know of a number of people who have been in the public defender's office who went to the prosecution, but I can't tell you why. I don't know if it's because they didn't like the work or whether they had a little bit of a pay grade increase when they go to the DA's office. I really don't know, but it kind of equals out. There's plenty of prosecutors who ultimately go into private practice, and they do defense work because they've learned it from the inside out, and that's a distinct advantage I would imagine.

LAW STUDENT: You are a woman, and you're pretty petite, and as you say you have a heart for the people, so you're kind of touchy-feely. What are some of the challenges that you face when you're dealing with male offenders or male clients just person-to-person, going in and out of the jails? What are some of the challenges and how do you deal with them?

MS. COGGINS: Again, just, when you meet the person for the first time, just treat them with respect, just like you would anybody. You meet somebody in an elevator and you say hello, and you strike up a conversation, or you sit next to your classmate and you start talking. It's just a matter of trying to establish the same kind of rapport or relationship that you would with anybody. They're no different than you. They're no different than me. Circumstances have placed them somewhere different, circumstances that may have been beyond their control, or circumstances that were well within their control, but it's just another person who needs to just be treated like you would want to be treated. I don't know how to explain it.

LAW STUDENT (FOLLOW-UP): Just to carry on a little bit, I guess what I'm really getting at is, have you dealt with anyone who took your friendliness a little too far as far as maybe have, you know, asked you out on a date or asked for your phone number? (Laughter.)

MS. COGGINS: It's funny you say that. I do have one particular client who adores me, and he writes me letters all the time and tells me that he loves me, and I'm the best thing that's ever happened to him, and he's right, I am the best thing that's happened. (Laughter.) Just take it all in. (Laughter.)

We go to the jail on a daily basis, and back in the day we had to drive over to the jail and we meet, I'm this close to my client when I meet with them, we're not through a glass wall or any partition, I'm right there with you. I've only had one occasion, literally one occasion in twenty-six years that, it could have been a woman, it could have been a man, but in this particular case—it was a man who was very angry and jumped up and leaned over the table, and you just say, "I'm done." And you walk out. You let them calm down and go back at a later time. You don't have to be disrespected, and you don't have to take any kind of abuse. Just get up and walk out.

PROFESSOR LONGAN: Time for one more.

LAW STUDENT: Sometimes we hear that you have to take your emotions out of it. Do you agree with that?

MS. COGGINS: Yes and no, John Cole (pointing finger upwards). (Laughter.)*

PROFESSOR LONGAN: It was yes and not yes.

MS. COGGINS: Oh, did he change it to yes and not yes?

LAW STUDENTS: He did.

MS. COGGINS: When you say take your emotions out of it, I don't know how I could do this job if I weren't emotionally invested in it, because while I say I'm not defending the crime, I'm defending the—there's a person, there's someone's life and liberty and freedom and career and hopes and dreams, so I can't help but be emotionally invested. When you're prepping the case, you know, obviously you can't

---

* Professor John O. Cole taught at Mercer University School of Law for forty-five years and was famous among generations of students for using the phrase, "yes and not yes," when he was explaining a particular point about legal reasoning and argument.

let yourself be clouded. You can't let your judgment be clouded by your emotional attachment to the client or to their problem or their case. So, you learn to separate that, sure, to be able to see the forest for the trees and those kind of things.

I wanted to tell one more story. We do preliminary hearings every other Tuesday in Houston County and I had a guy who was charged with robbery by sudden snatching. He had supposedly driven through the parking lot of Kroger and snatched this lady's purse. We're having a preliminary hearing. I'm handling the preliminary hearing for the guy. The lady comes in. We've subpoenaed her. We've had the victim come in. She takes the stand, and when she takes the stand, she has a purse that clearly has fingerprint dust all over it, and so I'm crossing her about the purse and about the snatching, and the client leans over and says, "that is not the purse I snatched. The purse I snatched was white." (Laughter.) I said, "shush." (Laughter.)

PROFESSOR LONGAN: Please join me in thanking Angie Coggins.

A Conversation with Justice Verda M. Colvin

*Introduction by Gracie K. Paulson**

Verda M. Colvin is a Justice of the Supreme Court of Georgia. She would tell you she is just an ordinary person like anyone else, but I, and so many others who have the pleasure of knowing her, will tell you she is extraordinary. Not because of her position and accolades, but because Justice Colvin exemplifies the themes in the conversation between her and Professor Patrick Longan that you are about to read—striving for greatness, never settling for mediocrity, and a commitment to service. She genuinely cares about every individual she encounters, engages each person before her as if she has an unlimited amount of time, and continually sees the best in humanity. Justice Colvin pours herself into her work, her personal relationships, and her faith in equal measure with an excellence that is inspiring to encounter.

I was fortunate enough to experience her contagious optimism firsthand while serving as her staff attorney when she took the bench in the Macon Judicial Circuit in 2014 as the first African American female superior court judge for that circuit. In fact, we started our first official day on the job together. I was a month away from graduating from law school, and she was coming off a highly successful career as an Assistant United States Attorney in the Middle District of Georgia. I will never forget how surprised I was when she came to my law school graduation ceremony. We'd only just met about a month prior, and here she was committing valuable time on a Saturday morning to watch me walk across that stage. Looking back, I now see that I should not have been one bit surprised to see her there that morning. She believes in the importance of investing in people's lives, and that day, she was investing in me.

Justice Colvin entered the superior court system with a zeal and

---

* Associate, Roberts & Stevens, Asheville, North Carolina.

energy that was perhaps unexpected by many but quickly recognized as an asset to the bench. Her enthusiasm for fostering change was palpable. Although I had not practiced as an attorney in the Macon Judicial Circuit prior to Justice Colvin's judicial appointment, I could sense a change in the attorneys I saw come before her from one appearance to the next. Her expectations propelled cases to move forward expeditiously. Her days were packed with hearings, speaking engagements, trips to the jail, presiding over various matters from bond hearings to temporary restraining orders, committee meetings, and soccer games. I remember wondering how she got it all done and still had anything left. My conclusion was and still is that she is a woman of incredible inner strength, integrity of character, and mental resilience to doubt and discouragement.

While the awards and recognitions she has received over the years are many, Justice Colvin remains humble and grounded. Community service has always been her passion. True to her servant's heart, Justice Colvin began her legal career in private practice where she thrived on representing clients without resources for legal counsel. Her judicial career reflects the same commitment to serving the less fortunate. I watched as participants who entered her mental health court as people without hope graduated from the program with GEDs, jobs, restored family relationships, and a brighter future ahead of them. I watched as she brought the courtroom to tears with her stern but compassionate speeches of warning and motivation to the youth in her Consider the Consequences program.

It has been six years since I last sat next to Justice Colvin on the bench. In those six years, she has moved from the bench of the Superior Court to the bench of the Georgia Court of Appeals, and now to the bench of the Supreme Court of Georgia. She has invested in countless lives, encouraged the downtrodden, given purpose and a plan to those without direction, and been a guiding light to many a lost soul. As her reassuring words echo in my mind when I face the challenges of life, her investment in me endures. Her voice guides me to strive for greatness, see past peoples' current circumstances, be passionate at whatever I set out to do, and speak it into existence. At the end of the day, I think she would agree that is the purpose of her service throughout the court system of Georgia, her career as an attorney, and her life—to impact lives for good.

JUSTICE VERDA COLVIN, 2015

PROFESSOR PATRICK LONGAN: Thank you for coming.

JUDGE VERDA COLVIN:[*] Thank you for having me.

PROFESSOR LONGAN: I really appreciate you being here. I like our guests to go back initially to the beginning and describe how and when they decided that they were going to spend their lives as lawyers.

JUDGE COLVIN: I have this age-old story that everybody has. It starts off when we're young. I was in first grade, went to—my mom put me in private religious school, and so I was very indoctrinated, and I wanted to do something to help save the world, so I wanted to be a missionary. It was either a missionary, a doctor, or lawyer, but I really wanted to be a missionary, and she was, like, you can't be a missionary; they don't make any money. (Laughter.) So I let go of that ideal and that dream, because that's really what I wanted to do, and so I thought, okay, I'll be a lawyer, because my thought was, I don't know if I really want to see all that blood and gore I would see as a doctor. As I got older my mom said, "you need to be a lawyer because you love to talk," and so I just kind of kept that career path going, but I knew I wanted to be in the service arena somehow. I wanted to make the world better. That's the reason why a lot of you-all are here. So I kind of kept that path. I'm very structured, very disciplined, and once I set a goal nothing else comes in my way, but at some point in seventh grade I remember we were going across the stage talking about our careers, and, like many young women do, for some reason you stop giving yourself the ability to think big, and I went across the stage as a legal secretary. I think now, what was I thinking? I don't know what happened. But I

[*] At the time of this interview, Justice Colvin was a Superior Court Judge for the Macon Judicial Circuit. For clarity, we have left her title as Judge in the transcript.

got back on track, decided I wanted to definitely be a lawyer and continue to pursue that.

PROFESSOR LONGAN: Tell us about your career before you became a judge and give us an overview of the arc of your professional life.

JUDGE COLVIN: Okay. Well, I just explained to you who—my philosophical approach toward practicing law, so when I first started out, I wanted to work for—I thought I'd work for a firm, but I wanted to work for a firm that was kind of different, New Age, and I found that firm in Charlotte, North Carolina. So, I graduated from Georgia, interviewed like all of you-all will do when you get to your third year, and this firm in Charlotte asked me to come up, and so I went up there, and they were very different than anything I had ever seen. It was truly a conglomeration of what you would expect America to look like in every phase. They had a firm, and it's so hard when I say this, people look at me so weird because I've never seen anything like it, and there are none like this now, but they truly put themselves out and were a firm that was truly multiracial. So, for instance, if they'd just hired a white attorney, the next attorney they hired would have to be African American, Jewish, or Asian, so they made sure they kept—and so it was truly half and half. They didn't do as well with the female end of it, but they had more females than most firms had, so when I went to interview with them, I already knew this, and I thought, what a novel place. They're trying to really live out the creed that America espouses to be, and so, it really gelled, and I was going to work for the first-name partner.

I practiced there for three years. It was considered a civil rights firm, and so that's one reason why they looked the way they looked. They did the Charlotte-Mecklenburg bus desegregation case, and that's how they got their fame. Because they did that case, and because of that case and what it meant for that particular community, they made a pledge to make sure their firm was racially diverse, and so I was just mesmerized, thought I was very fortunate to get that job, and I was. I worked there for three years, but I left after three years because, as I told you, I was very idealistic, and I became disillusioned because while they let me represent the people who couldn't afford attorneys many times, and I was able to do what I wanted to do, at the end of the day it was a business.

They had a novel concept: associates sat in with partners. I'm telling you-all this to say to you— find what fits you, and this fit me. They were so cool that associates would sit in with partners and actually had a vote on things we did with the money. I mean, it was just phenomenal. When they won big cases, we received a bonus even if you didn't work on the case, just totally different than anything I had ever seen. And so as we sat in a meeting one day—it's funny that I would say this because many of them are now in other places, but I'm very candid and that's who I was there—but as we sat there we had won a big medical malpractice case, and they were discussing what to do with the money. Since I was one of those people who wanted to represent those who didn't have money, I said, can we do this, can we put one percent of all of the verdicts we get in a pool for money to fund this litigation that we think is important but that clients don't have money and we can't just pull from our resources? I just remember them looking at me as if I had said the most outlandish thing in the world, and my feelings got so hurt, tears just welled up in my eyes, but I couldn't let them see it. That was just such a disillusionment to me because I thought, I came here for all the principles you stand for, and we can't take one percent to put in a fund?

At that point, that and some other things prompted me to think, okay, I need to do something different. Ken Mauldin, who was the solicitor at the time in Athens-Clarke County and is now the DA, had been asking me to work for him for many years. He would call me in Charlotte and say, "are you ready to come home?" I called him and I said, "okay, I think I'm ready." Well, I could never imagine myself being a prosecutor because I was all about the underdog, but I thought, I can work at the solicitor's office. That's just misdemeanors. Nobody can go to jail more than a year, twelve months, and a fine no more than a thousand dollars. I can do this. So I went to Athens. I worked with him for two years. Then I got married and was pregnant, and I was driving back and forth from Decatur, Lithonia specifically, to Athens every day, and I knew that was too much, so I said, "Mr. Mauldin, thank you for the experience, but I think I need to leave."

So I left, and I started working as assistant general counsel for Clark Atlanta University, which was very different than anything I had done. It was even a different kind of practice than, say, a firm practice because basically I was doing all of the things that universities do. But after nine months, I knew I needed to leave. I was philosophically at odds with things that I felt like I was being asked to do.

So I left and went to work for Bob Keller at the Clayton County DA's office. Best gig I ever had in my whole life. He was the greatest boss ever. He just retired recently from working for the governor. He was head of the board of pardon and parole, and so I worked with him for three years, really cool place, tried cases. Every kind of case you can think of that's a felony I tried. Very rewarding experience, but after three years there, I knew it was time for me to grow. I had kind of done everything we could do.

I was one of the top prosecutors, and so I interviewed for the US Attorney's Office, interviewed in Atlanta, and they were going to hire me for their next slot, but I would have to wait. The US Attorney at the time here in Macon called Atlanta to say, "If you were hiring who would you hire next?" They gave her my name, and that's how I came to be in Macon, because I figured I'll just go ahead and take an Assistant US Attorney's spot. I don't want to give one up waiting for another one. I had one in Alabama that was offered, but I decided I'd stay in Georgia. And so I came here, and I worked in that office for fifteen years. Did everything. I've done some litigation there that we had never done. You-all, I don't know how many of you-all are from Macon, but I was a part of the prosecution that shut down Sedona Tanning Spa & Salon, which was basically a sex shop, and so I headed that prosecution. That was something our office had never done. I did some housing cases that our office had never done, did big drug conspiracy cases, so—and I was also assigned to asset forfeiture.

After working there for fifteen years, and I know this is a question you might ask me, people came to me when Judge Brown was considering retiring, and the first person came to me, Sharon Ratley, and said, "I think you really—he's going to retire," this is before it became public, "I think you need to put your name in the hat." I thought, she's just being nice. I've worked really hard; that's an at-a-girl for being a good hard worker, and I just chalked it up as that. Then the second person came to me, unrelated to the first person and without any knowledge that the first person had already kind of told me that this was going to come up, because nobody knew he was going to retire, and I thought, why did they come to me? So, when the third person came to me—it was my boss, Michael Moore, who's the US attorney now—and I thought, well, maybe I need to think about this.

The ironic thing was two or three years prior to my putting my name in the hat, I had been thinking, I need to do more. I'm very active in the community. Any case that came in our office that nobody wanted to touch I'd do it. I spent many nights up at the office at two o'clock in the morning getting ready for trial because I don't like help, so I tried all my cases myself, even multi-defendant cases. I thought, I've been saying I want to do more, maybe this is it. Well, I will tell you the scary part about signing on is that it's not a permanent gig like being an AUSA. Being an AUSA I had job security. I knew I was going to be there. The only thing I had to worry about was hitting the top of the pay scale and not getting any more raises, but I had security. With this gig you have to run for office every four years.

Well, I tend to be very spiritual, and I thought, you can't say you want to do more, you want to serve more, and not be willing to put yourself out there. I'm a huge proponent of if you say something, then mean it and be willing to do what it takes to make it happen. It was kind of like a dare to myself: if you say you want to serve, then show me you want to serve, and so I thought, I'm doing this. I've got two kids. I'm a divorced mom raising my two kids. My son is in college, and my daughter goes to private school, and I thought, wow, this is an act of faith, but I tell my Sunday School kids all the time, if you believe in something, live up to it. You can't preach what you don't practice, and so I put my name in the hat and went through the process, and the governor called me one Friday afternoon, and I just answered the phone, "Verda Colvin, US Attorney's Office." He said, "this is Governor Nathan Deal." (Laughter.) He called my cell, and I didn't answer, so then he called back on the main line. I was appointed on April 16 of 2014, and I started the next day on April 17.

PROFESSOR LONGAN: Wow. (Laughing). I almost want to ask you if there's anything you haven't done.

JUDGE COLVIN: I know.

PROFESSOR LONGAN: What a range.

JUDGE COLVIN: Yeah, it's been wonderful. I thought the other day, I'm the only prosecutor I know who's done everything from misdemeanors all the way up to federal offenses, and it's kind of been a nice progression.

PROFESSOR LONGAN: Before we turn to your experience as a judge, I want to ask you just a couple of things about your life as a lawyer. One of them is whether, at any point, you felt like you were treated differently because you were a woman and because you're African American.

JUDGE COLVIN: Good question. I've thought about this often. I will tell you-all from what I've told you, you can probably imagine I'm very idealistic. I hope for any African American students you don't think this is Pollyanna, but I don't walk around thinking every day that I'm black and I'm an African American female. I mean, I know that; I mean, that is intrinsically who I am. I don't think about that. There are times when things will happen that I am keenly made aware of it or reminded of it, but for me, having the strength of always being excellent has transcended all of that, I think, and I will tell you how.

When I first started practicing at the firm I told you I worked at, we had a female attorney who was pregnant at the time, she was a partner, and she was supposed to go in and represent this stockbroker before a stockbroker licensing board. I'll just be candid. He had allegedly stolen a lot of money from a very rich couple. Middle-age white guy and had all the signs of all the success of a stockbroker. You know, the stomach, the— (Laughter.) The $1500 suit, he was just so put together. She was going out, she had some problems with her pregnancy, and so they were, like, Verda, we need you to handle this. Well, I didn't know anything about stockbrokers or the law, but I studied up, so when they brought him to meet me and Ms. Ellington, and he looked at me like what—now, I'm just out of law school, so I'm almost—I'm almost fifty now. People tell me I look young. So you can imagine how young I looked at twenty-five. I wore my hair back to make me look a little bit more classy and older, but it didn't work well. He looked, he said, "wait a minute, I'm paying good money, and this is who you-all are giving me to represent me?" So I was, like, what?

At that point I knew it was because I didn't look like him, I wasn't him, and I wasn't in the age bracket that he thought I would be experienced. So, at that point, that was a challenge.

So, I did all the research I needed to do. We went to the board of stockbrokers in North Carolina to see if they would let him keep his license. The older couple was there and were very, very rich, and so I'm going in thinking, this is a lot, his license is on the line. I go in and I do my thing, and I represent him. This beautiful gentleman, white gentleman about sixty years of age, very tall, slender, complete white hair, just looked like he walked out of Business Weekly or something. (Laughter.) He was beautiful. He comes out, and he has one hand in the pocket, and he extends it. He said, "Ms. Andrews," that's my maiden name, Ms. Andrews, "I want to tell you, you are a credit to your gender and your race because before you walked in that room this man was going to have all his credentials stripped. As a result of you walking in that room and representing him, he will be able to keep his stockbroker license, but he will have to pay back all of this money regardless. But you are a credit to your race and your gender." I was like, I can't believe he said that.

I went back to the firm, and I told them. The partners got in the room, black, white, Jewish. I said, "Can y'all believe it? That's racist. I can't believe it." And they laughed, and they said, "Verda, you don't realize, that's huge. You showed him something he had never seen before, and you have made a mark for our firm about what we're about and excellence in which we strive." From that day forward I never allowed my race or my gender to have any effect on who I was as an attorney. What I learned is having a standard of excellence transcends all of that, because once he saw that, imagine how that changed his view and all the other people on that board's view about thinking differently just because I don't come in looking like what they think I should look like. My thought is, when I explain my Pollyanna view, is that I don't think about race or my sex because I think of, if I'm excellent, then when I walk in and present who I am, that just catapults me above the best white guy in the room, because they don't expect that.

I really haven't had that as an issue much. In court sometimes people walk in and they're like, what? Because I'm an anomaly in Macon being the first African American female to be on the superior court bench. Many times they'll say, "yes, sir," and "oh, I'm sorry." I'm, like, that's okay, that's what you primarily see, so that's fine, and so I don't wear a chip on my shoulder. I think that helps everybody, so that's my sense on being who I am.

PROFESSOR LONGAN: Well, you said you got the call from the governor and then the next day you started. What surprised you the most when you became a judge?

JUDGE COLVIN: I think I thought, because I'd worked so hard at the US Attorney's Office, I thought, man, when I become a judge, once I start this, I'll be able to chill a little. I won't have to work so hard. I can just kind of—I've kind of made it. But because of my work ethic, probably, because people tell me you're not doing it right, I work harder. Every night I take work home. Every day I'm always working. I schedule my—my day is scheduled boom, boom, boom, but that's a part of who I am, and I now recognize it doesn't have to be that way, but that's my work ethic, and that's what I expect of others, and that's the part that's surprising to me as I become a judge, because I recognize everybody doesn't have my work ethic.

PROFESSOR LONGAN: Well, you say you structure your day boom, boom, boom. Is there a typical day for you?

JUDGE COLVIN: Not really. Let me tell you what I do. I cover a lot of arenas. I do all the narcotics cases. I do the family violence court, which is a diversion court more or less of people who've been charged with committing some domestic crime with their partner or whoever they live with in their household, and it's a way to give them an alternative versus straight prosecution. I preside over that court, which is bi-weekly. I handle the mental health court, which I have a passion for, and those are people who have usually a dual diagnosis: mental health problems coupled with substance abuse issues. We become like a family because every two weeks I'm seeing them for a total of twenty-four months until they can graduate from the program. In addition to that I do any domestic cases, which are divorce cases, that Judge Raymond is conflicted out of because he practiced in that area for twenty-six years. In addition to that, there's one other thing, and I always forget, it's five different things I do, but I do all of those, and every five weeks I preside, so presiding means you do adoptions, child support calendar, bond hearings, TPOs, temporary restraining orders, so I do a hodgepodge of things, so I don't really have a typical day.

PROFESSOR LONGAN: Well, that makes it fun.

JUDGE COLVIN: Yeah, it does, and I like that. Even in the US Attorney's Office I didn't like being pigeon-holed in an area, so I did cases all over the gamut at the same time, because, to me, that keeps it interesting.

PROFESSOR LONGAN: Would you mind talking just a little bit more about the mental health court? The reason I want you to do that—of course, obviously you have a passion for it—but I'm not sure if the students would be aware that these kinds of programs are out there. Most of them were judicially created.

JUDGE COLVIN: Exactly.

PROFESSOR LONGAN: To try to get to the root of what's causing these people to be in the system instead of just processing them, trying to get to the root and maybe help them.

JUDGE COLVIN: Yes. Our governor, Nathan Deal, implemented a criminal reform act, and basically, he changed some things. It's an effort to not continue to house people when you can do something other than that, so I applaud him in that effort. That's something that was exciting about having my interview with him, to let him know that I think those reforms make a difference. But the accountability courts, mental health is one of those courts—these are people who've committed crimes, but they have a mental health issue that's been documented, and typically that mental health issue coupled with a substance abuse issue caused them to commit the crime. So, you've got somebody who's bipolar. They're not taking their meds. They use drugs to kind of regulate their mental stability. Then they go rob a house because they need the money to get the drugs, because typically they're not working a job, so they don't have the money to support their habits. Rather than possibly put them in jail they can agree to come to my mental health court program.

It's tough. We have five phases through the program, and they have to work each phase. If you mess up you get sanctions, and some of those sanctions include community service, writing essays, and jail time. They can get up to seventy-two hours in jail when they commit so many infractions. Basically, it's an effort on my part, and any judge who does the accountability court, to help teach them the need and the actual positive effects of staying on their meds and not being on drugs.

I run my court kind of different than any other judge I've seen. I become personally invested in these people. For instance—and this is true even in my other duties: child support, narcotics cases—I write people, because what I see in what I do is people lack inspiration. Just in general they have lost hope. They seem to settle for mediocrity, and I just believe everybody is meant for greatness. Greatness for each person is defined differently, but each person was created for a specific purpose, so my lot in life, as I sit on this bench, is to try to show people that you're special, and regardless of what you've done previously you can decide to live a different life. And so in doing that with people in mental health court, I try to inspire them to do something other than what they've done. Like one of my participants, I'm trying to help him start back in college. Some of them I write every week just to inspire them: you can do this, you can do this, and you have come to my court for a specific reason, because you're able to do this.

It's a novel way of handling people who would have normally been in jail, and so we have a three-and-a-half page waiting list since I've become the judge of mental health court. People hear about our program, and they want to be in it. I think a lot of that is because they've never heard anybody say, you can do this; this does not have to be your life. And I try to tell every defendant that comes before me, why do you want to be in an orange jumpsuit with people telling you when to get up, when to go to sleep, what to do? You were meant to—you were meant to be more than that. Don't allow this to be your destiny.

I'm novel in that approach. I have people come sit in my court just to see me. I just believe that is the service that I was put here to give, and so long as I'm sitting on the bench, that's what I will do. I'm trying to get us out of this mediocrity, and that's what so many people who come before me have. So, the mental health court, veterans court, which Judge Self does, problem-solving court, which helps our guys who haven't paid child support, owe twenty-something thousand dollars, it helps them get jobs, get education so that they can begin taking care of their children. We have veterans court, problem-solving court, mental health court and family violence, and I'm the only person I know in Georgia that has a family violence court. We're still trying to make that what we think it should be, but it's not one that's legislated, so it's something we're just doing on our own.

PROFESSOR LONGAN: You became a missionary after all.

JUDGE COLVIN: I did, didn't I? My mental health court typically takes me two hours, because I believe each person needs face time, and the proven results have shown that if a judge spends at least three minutes with each participant they will do better, and they will fare better when they leave. I didn't know that statistic, but that's what I do, because I'm going to talk to each person that comes before me. So, my prosecutor, he pulls up a chair to sit down because, he knows I'm going to go through my little spiel, and I'm real big with quotes, and so I said to him one day, I said, I'm sorry, I know sometimes you probably get tired of me going through this. I said, I think I was really meant to be a social worker. He said, no, no, you weren't. You were meant to do this because you're much more effective in this role saying what you say that you could ever be as a social worker. I told him, thank you for that, because I think he's right in some ways because I have that heart but I'm also tough. I don't put people in jail. I just give them what they want. So, if you don't conform you must want to go to jail. You just don't realize you want to go. (Laughter.) So, I'm going to show you that's what you want so maybe you won't want that in the future. That's what I'd tell people when I was a prosecutor. People would say, how could you do that, put people in jail? I said, I don't put anybody in jail. I facilitate their desires. (Laughter.) So, I tell them, I'm just facilitating your desire. You didn't know that was your desire, but that's what you desired. (Laughter.)

PROFESSOR LONGAN: You've been at this almost a year. This is a different approach than a traditional approach for a superior court judge. With almost a year of experience how do you think your approach is working?

JUDGE COLVIN: It's funny that—that's a good question you ask me because there were sometimes that I wondered. I have Judge Raymond, Judge Self, Judge Ennis, and Judge Simms and myself. I thought, okay, number one, I'm different from them in so many ways. I'm a female, I'm African American, my background is different, my experiences are different. As I went through this process this whole year that I've almost been on the bench, many times I have thought, maybe I should change my voice. My voice isn't like the other voices that they're hearing in other courtrooms, and I struggled with that, and then I thought, I can't change my voice. The very reason why I put my neck on the line to say I will do this, despite not having a guaranteed employment, is to have that voice, to reach in a way that other people may not be reaching, and so if I let go of that voice, what was the purpose of me being put on the bench versus anybody else? So if I lose my voice, then I devoid the bench of having the diversity it needs.

And so, over the course of a year I've kind of solidified the fact that I like having the voice that's different. I like being different. When people come in my courtroom, they know it's a whole different ball game. Even the prosecutors know that. I don't have a lot of patience for a lack of excellence, and I don't have a lot of patience for not doing what I feel like we should do. That may be a little bit different because I'm a little bit more stern, I think, in some ways, but I do have a voice of compassion. I will also incarcerate people when I feel like that's the best option. I think my voice is needed, and I will maintain my voice because I think it helps make us a better court.

When somebody stops you when they're about to go to jail because you denied their bond and they say, I need to go back and say something to her, and they come back and say to me, "Thank you for talking to me and addressing me. You're the first judge I've ever appeared in front of who said my name, who took the time to talk with me." That meant more to me than anything. This guy was going off to jail, but that meant something to him. As long as I'm on the bench, I will give people the respect I think they deserve, and I require that they look at me. When I'm talking I say, look at me, look at me in my eyes. I want you to understand what I'm saying. I write them, they write me back, because people are internally dying, and we see it in our society every day. Look at what's going on in our world. People—and I say this sometimes on the bench, we have lost our moral compass as a people, as a nation in many ways, and so, to the extent I can, I try to bring that back.

Even in child support court I tell them, "Sir, you've got six kids, and you don't have a job. What are you thinking? That's asinine. Do what you have to do to stop having these children and take care of what you have. I can't take care of six children; how can you? You've got to get a GED." That's a mantra of mine. You won't go to jail for not paying a fine if you try, but you will go to jail if you don't get this GED. I'm going to assure you have the basics of what you need to get a job. On some things I'm just no nonsense. I say, "You're twenty-two years old and you stopped school in the eighth grade. What is that? I'm the mother you never had." That's what I tell them. "You're going to stay with me." (Laughter.) "You're going to stay with me throughout this period of probation, so, guess what, you're going to jail if you don't get this GED, because I care about you" and so—and they know it. One of the probation officers told me some saying now they have, something about a railroad, you're off the tracks, Judge, everybody you deal with is talking about it because you're no nonsense. And I'm like, it's just I'm not going to let you accept mediocrity. You may end up choosing that, but you're going to choose it while you're sitting in the LEC or in prison, because you're not going to choose it and be just out willy-nilly on the street. No, we're going to do something different.

PROFESSOR LONGAN: Well, again, in just under a year I couldn't begin, and I doubt you could begin, to count the number of people you have encountered. And you'll encounter that many more next year and the year after that and the year after that, and so on. How are you going to keep it fresh?

JUDGE COLVIN: I know. That's what people tell me in my office, "Judge, we worry about you because you do so much and you pour so much into it." I don't have a lot of resources for my mental health court, so when my guys come in and they have their chip, six-month sobriety, day sobriety or whatever, I buy them treats, I buy things. My family violence court, one guy just graduated, and I said, "What kind of cake do you want?" He said a red velvet. I said, man, you would pick something I just can't go in a store and buy. The store-bought red velvet cakes are never good, so I paid somebody to make a cake.

For me, this is a ministry, I will say that, and not like I'm trying to put a religious aspect because it's separate church and state, but for me, and I guess it gets back to what I wanted to do at first, a missionary, so for me it's a ministry. I use my spiritual strength to pour back into myself, because every time I do a speaking engagement, you're right, it pulls, because I'm so invested emotionally, it pulls something from me, but I feel like this is what I was meant to be. I tell people all the time, and I will tell you-all as law students, have a purpose, make sure your purpose is your passion, and then have a plan for achieving that passionate purpose, because if you're not passionate about what you're doing you're wasting your time and your money. I will say that again. If you're not passionate about what you're doing, you're wasting your time and your money. If you get through this process and you figure, I don't know if I want to do this, you can use your law degree in a lot of different ways, but whatever you do, be passionate about it, because you're wasting your time if you're not, and you're not giving your true gift. This is my passion, and I think it's what my calling is. So, when you do that it's never work.

How do I do it? It's not work for me. It's what I feel like I'm supposed to do. I wake up every day and just do what feels right. If you do that, it will never be work. It will just be going to do what you like to do. Now, I don't like having to be there at a certain time, because I'm not a morning person, but because I'm a stickler for time, I'm there on time every day, and I start court on time. I can't stand to be late. Oh, that's my pet peeve, and everybody who practices in front of me knows that, but be passionate about it or else don't do it.

PROFESSOR LONGAN: Is there anything that you don't like about being a judge, anything you find to be particularly frustrating?

JUDGE COLVIN: It's frustrating to be restricted in what I can say, because sometimes I think certain people need to hear the off comment I want to make, but I can't make it because of my restrictions. (Laughter.) So I just—and sometimes I'll say, you really—and I'll just... (Laughter.)

PROFESSOR LONGAN: I'm sorry, Your Honor, but that's too tempting. You're not on the bench at the moment although you are on YouTube. You want to give us an example?

JUDGE COLVIN: Sometimes I want to say to people, just in life because, I do a lot of things in the community with young people, and because I'm so real, I don't try to hide behind titles. To me—I happen to—I'm called a judge, but for me it's helping folks, so I don't get caught up in that. But I tell young men, I can see them in a store, "man, pull up your pants. You wonder why they keep stopping you. It's 'cause you got your pants down and you got this crazy hairdo. Don't do that." But it's nothing different than what I tell my son. He's got this new hairdo that African American guys wear where it's not the twist but they kind of let it be a little kinky, it's getting back to our roots or something. I don't like it. But anyway— (Laughter.) I say, Son, if you're going to do that, keep it—he goes to school in New York, so he's, like, Mom, it's not like the South. I'm, like, I don't care. I said, "Keep it neat and be respectful. Look like you care about who you are and what you represent, and take your hat off when you enter a building."

I want to tell them certain things like that, but certain things I can't say, but my participants in my court, off the cuff they'll write me, and I say, "get that thing out of your hair, let your hair grow back, and just get it cut. Don't put a star in your head." (Laughter.) Sometimes I think it's because they've never had anybody to tell them, and they will laugh like you're laughing, but, they're, like, you're right, Judge Colvin, you're right, you're right. I'm, like, where is your belt? They'll respond, I don't have a belt. How do you not have a belt? You cannot be a man who's responsible in life and not have a belt. (Laughter.) What's your waist size? I'm buying you a belt. So I've bought so many belts, so now people will say, Judge, I got a belt. I'm, like, Okay. (Laughter.)

People laugh. I believe in the gift of laughter. Sometimes things we laugh about help us remember them all the more. Any guys in here who don't wear belts, they're probably going to think about that next time they put on their pants, and they're kind of—and you see their underwear, let me put on a belt. I bet that judge says something crazy. But, I tell them, look like you care. Just—half of the battle is just caring. Now, do you—look down, look down, do you look like you care? Just care. When you come in this court, care, and so, in my courtroom with my participants they know they've got to wear slacks if they can, if you have them. Don't wear jeans.

We've got to look like we have a purpose and a plan, and I try to tell them that because sometimes nobody ever told them they have a purpose and a plan. Believe it or not, guys, there's a lot of people who've never experienced the support that you-all have experienced. Somebody told me once, "nobody ever told me that I can do what I want to do." That hit me. I didn't make that face, but I thought it just hurt my heart because I'm, like, you can and we're going to write each other. One guy wrote me a card, and he looks like many of you, a white young male, very attractive guy, but he's going through some issues, and he wrote me a card. He said, "I have never had any person, any judge to inspire me. Thank you for doing that." I told him, I said, "We are pen pals for life. You write me; I write you back." So, as soon as I got his card, I wrote him back.

It matters not to me who the person is who comes before me. Everybody needs some inspiration, and even you-all need some inspiration sometimes. So inspire each other, because it's really what you give, not what you get. That's the greatest lesson, and that's the key that most people don't know. Success is not about all the trinkets that come with maybe making good money, because that will never ultimately at the end of the day make you happy. It's about what you give of yourself to make the world and other people better. When I leave home every day, I feel good when I come back because I've given a little bit of myself away, and that's really, to me, what it's all about. When you don't do that, you really—you really deplete your own resources.

PROFESSOR LONGAN: We've been talking about your expectations of the parties, the defendants, and so on. I wonder if you could talk a little bit about your expectations of the lawyers. Maybe part of that may be you have a pet peeve or two. Talk about expectations of the lawyers who appear before you.

JUDGE COLVIN: Be on time. You should be in the courtroom before the judge gets there. Be in court at least fifteen minutes before it starts so you can gather your things and gather your thoughts. I cannot stand it when people are late. I mean, that's just—that's unacceptable. I mean, time is valuable. We have limited time in the world, so come to court on time, number one.

Number two, always come prepared. Know your case better than anybody. I shouldn't be able to tell you more about your case than you know. When people walk in my courtroom, and the reason why I work harder now, I have read every single piece of paper in the file. Every single piece of paper, I've read that, because I owe you that, because you've brought this lawsuit or you're representing this client. So, if I give you that much respect, I expect you to respect me enough to come in court prepared, ready to go. It is no greater pleasure I have than presiding over a case where both sides are equally prepared, and I walk out of that courtroom being directed as to where I need to go with the law and what I need to decide, and I don't have to figure it out from point A to Z because I didn't get any guidance. Just have a standard of excellence for yourself. If you do, you will never be without a gig. If you do, you will always be successful. But if your standard is just get by, that's what kind of lawyer you're going to be, a get by lawyer, and you will never have the respect of the judges who you appear before. You want to do that. So, you might not be the smartest person, but you don't have to be. I think in the end the person who does the best in life is the person who works the hardest. I really do.

PROFESSOR LONGAN: Judge, I want to make sure the students have time to ask you whatever they want to ask you. But everybody who does us the honor of coming and being with us, I give them the opportunity, before the students ask questions, to say anything you want to say, anything that you think these students need to hear, maybe something you wish you had heard when you were a first-year law student.

JUDGE COLVIN: Mercer seems to—I graduated from UGA, and UGA probably does the same job now, but I graduated in 1990, so that's like another lifetime, but—and so I don't know how law schools do it generally, but I will say this to you: don't allow yourself to become discouraged by rank. Don't allow yourself to become discouraged by other people having inroads to the profession that you don't have because maybe their father has a firm or something like that. Know your strength. Believe in your strength. Know that you have something to offer. And no matter what or who you interview with, no matter who gives you the opportunity for an interview or who doesn't because they have all these rankings they do, that doesn't define who you are.

I'll give you a story. When I was in law school, I wasn't law review, but I was huge in mock trial and moot court. I was on the star team. In fact, when I was doing moot court, they came to me, the person who was handling my team, which was the Frederick Douglas team, and they said, "Verda, you scored high enough where you could be on any team you want to be on. You can be on the top premiere team, which we haven't had African Americans on before, but I will tell you if you're not on the Frederick Douglas team, we will have no Frederick Douglas team because you're the top candidate who happened to be a minority. So you can choose. Don't feel obligated to choose a team just because. Choose the team you want to." Well, that's huge to hear that if you don't do the Frederick Douglas team we won't have a team, and so I had to think about all of that, and I think—what is that top team that everybody wants to be on, the All-State or what is it called, the one that goes to all the places? Come on, guys, help me. Oh, no, you-all are first-year, so you may not know. (Laughter.) What is it called? The Tri- what? Whatever that top team that everybody wants to get on for moot court or mock trial, that's the one they said that I could do based on my scores, and I thought about it, so I got on the team that was the lowly team that wasn't one of the top teams. I did the Frederick Douglas Competition because I thought it was important to keep that team going, and my thought is, if I've got a skill, that skill is going to be there regardless.

Ultimately, after doing moot court, then I was asked to do mock trial, but I wasn't law review. Mock trial/moot court helped a lot. But the big firms in Atlanta, they still wanted the law review. I went to interview with a respected Atlanta firm, which is still around now. A big firm that you-all will hear about. There was a female partner in that firm, and for some reason she just gravitated toward me. They didn't have many African American associates there, and I guess I experienced more being an African American as I navigated the interview process after finishing law school. This firm didn't have many who looked like me. The partner went to the partners, she went to the hiring board, she pushed for me to be there. She was, like, she needs to be there. Ultimately it was not to be. But I went on with my career.

Well, I was appointed to the bench, and then shortly thereafter—well, this past year, so almost a year thereafter—she was appointed to the superior court bench in Fulton County. I reached out to her, and I wrote her an email, and I said to her in effect, I want to tell you that you might not remember me, and I described who I was without saying my name. I said, you met this young African American female attorney who didn't have—I had some confidence because I was known at the law school because of all of the things I had done with moot court and mock trial, but I wasn't law review, and so I said, you might not remember me. I described who I was. I said, but you gave me the confidence to know that I could do anything and the belief in myself that I didn't have totally. She said, oh my God, I so remember you, and she said, I feel honored that you're on the superior court bench before I am. She said, I can't wait to go back to the partners at the firm and say, I told you so. (Laughter.) She said that, and she actually said she went and told them that.

But I say that to say to you-all don't allow anything about the experience in law school to define who and what you'll be, because you're bigger than that, you're greater than that, and just have that confidence as you move through, because after first year sometimes it will knock you on your fanny. You think, oh my God, I was top of my class in college, and here I am just trying to hold on. That's okay. At the end of the day nobody counts that. You're a lawyer. So just get through, do the work, and get through and don't allow people to define who you are or how good you are. Look at me. So just remember that.

PROFESSOR LONGAN: Thank you, Judge. What questions do you have for Judge Colvin?

LAW STUDENT: You've spoken a lot today about people needing to derive inspiration, and I'm curious, where do you derive inspiration?

JUDGE COLVIN: I hate to have to say this because it puts me on the spot. I will tell you it's my, I guess my spiritual part of my life, that gives me my inspiration. The longer I live the more I am acutely aware that really we're all here to serve each other. That's really what life is about. I just don't see any way around it. Please understand me, I don't think you have to do it the way I do to do service. I think even if I worked for some huge Hollywood star and just did their contracts, I could still serve people in ways. I could be kind. When I see somebody who needs something outside of the service that I render, I give them a word, because I don't care what economic stance you might be in, we all meet people who sometimes are lacking something, right? Sometimes we're lacking things. So you just meet people where they are. But that's what really keeps me going. That's my inspiration. I truly have a love for mankind, I really do. I haven't met a person who I don't find something good in.

So, you know how in law school there's a lot of gunners. I don't know if you-all still call them that, but, you know, the ones who just suck up to the professors, and you're like (making gesture of disgust), if they talk one more time.... But I just never had anybody who I didn't connect with, and so because of that I just have a love of people, and so when you really love humankind you can't not give back. People never cease to amaze me, so—and I'll say that in court, too, sometimes. You can't make this stuff up. It's just too real to be true. So that's my—that's kind of what guides me.

LAW STUDENT: Did you ever find during law school that you—you talked a lot about your faith—that it was sort of not valued or appreciated within school? And how did you deal with that and maintain it, and then as your career progressed do you feel that you've been able to, maybe not intermix the two, but value the two simultaneously?

JUDGE COLVIN: I have. I have found that. When you're young it's easier to keep it under wraps, so that's something I always knew. Like, I don't know about y'all, but before I did anything, I'm like, okay God, you've really got to help me on this test because I get the concept, but apparently I'm not putting it down on paper just like I'd like because I can't get beyond this B; I can't get an A. So, I kept it in my heart, but I didn't wear it on my sleeve because you're just trying to get to class on time. I looked like a crazy woman. I'm like, ugh, my friends were, like, slow down. (Laughter.) Stop tripping out. I was one of those crazy law students. But I wasn't a gunner. I would just sit in the back, like, oh my God, what am

I doing? What—oh my God. Property? Ugh. (Laughing.) I hated it. I hated it, but my—Professor Smith, he was very nice, but, yeah, sometimes I thought, wow, what am I doing here? Yeah, it is hard, but I kept it to myself, and I think when you're younger, for me, it was harder to just kind of let it out.

One of my best friends, she was law review, and so she would get upset because she'd be, like, Verda, this is not fair, I come to you and you explain the concepts, and I make the A, and you struggle to make the B. I was, like, don't worry about it. She couldn't get over the fact that despite the fact that she would make the A, I'd still have study sessions with her. She's, like, why do you help me? I said, 'cause when I help you, I help me, and it's okay, it's all right. She was white, I'm black, because there were very few African American students, so, the bulk of my friends didn't look like me, but I was, like, that's cool. And it's funny because when we'd try to interview, I'd have to help her with interviewing skills because she was so smart, but I'm very personable, and she struggled with that. She was atheist and she'd ask me, how do you stay upbeat? I just tried to share. When she asked, I would try to share my faith with her, but I kept it kind of to myself.

As I've gotten older, I can't help it. It's just such a part of me that even when—I hope you saw when I was here I tried to not mention it, but I couldn't help because it's a part—when you ask who I am, that's a part of who I am, but I don't put it off on other people. I respect other people's views. It's just my driving force that gets me going, and you will get there with your own way of handling it, but be true to who you are, and don't allow that to leave you, because if I had, I don't think I could have made it through. There were many days where I thought, what am I doing? I want to save the world, but I don't know if I'm going to save it like this. So keep it in your heart. You don't have to share it with everybody. Like I tell young people, some dreams you don't share because some people won't support your dream, so you keep it right here, and you figure out as you move along who to share it with. But some things you just have to hold to the vest, and you just live it out, because everybody won't buy into your dream. And that's okay, but you don't need anybody to destroy whatever that dream is, and so that's why you hold it to your vest. I think that's true even for guys, because you know how other guys are. Sometimes people will want to see you do bad, and I just tell my son that: you can't tell everybody everything.

LAW STUDENT: You've talked a lot about how you've worked in so many different arenas and fields, everything like that. Is there something, maybe like on your professional bucket list, that if you had an opportunity to do or to go into some different arena, now that you've done so many things, that might be something you would want to do?

JUDGE COLVIN: What would I like to do? I don't have anything else on my bucket list as far as law is concerned. You know what I would like to do? I'd like to win enough money where I could have these—now, this is something I've always dreamed of, so I'm going to share this dream with you-all. Most people—and I don't share this with everybody, but I'm just going to put it out there because why not—maybe somebody in here will become wealthier than what I can imagine and need to get rid of some money. (Laughter.) And you'll come find me and we'll work this thing together.

PROFESSOR LONGAN: Remember, Your Honor, you're on YouTube.

JUDGE COLVIN: Oh, that's right, so maybe somebody is out there already. (Laughter.) But, if they steal it you'll all know they stole it, right? I would love to do this: I would love to open up one of these historic homes that have, like, twenty rooms in them. I would like to buy one of those and have, in different cities, particularly cities like Macon that struggle economically, to have this unit where I would allow families who are struggling but they want to stay an intact family, to live there, to kind of get it together. They would have to pay a certain amount of money to the house to keep it sustained, and they would stay there. You'd have a limit, like a year or two, that you could stay there to get on your feet. We would help you then get into housing that would help you and your family stabilize, and you have to continue to pay back for a certain amount of time to keep that housing going for other families to come in.

They do have things kind of like that, but it's very hard to find situations where the whole family is included, a holistic approach. Usually, it's a single mom with kids. I think America has got to get back to recognizing the value of keeping that family intact. I think the beauty of that is that it attracts the most conservative political person because they agree in family values. It attracts the most liberal person because they want to give money for social programs, and if we could—if I could do that, if I could have somebody who would help me set that up, the money to start, I would love to do that. I would go to various cities that struggle in that area to do that. I think it would help draw employment because they know you've got a base from which to build. I would love to do something like that. I think that could really change the dynamics of cities. So that would be on my bucket list. I didn't think this would happen, so maybe if I put that out there, it can come into fruition.

LAW STUDENT: You have had such a varied career, so many different experiences. Is there anything you would have done differently?

JUDGE COLVIN: You know what, I would have. I would have believed in myself more. I didn't have a lot of confidence when I first started on this journey, and the funny thing about it, I exude confidence all the time. Like, when I was in court, nobody knew I was scared. I was scared to death, but I would have believed in myself more. So, for instance, and I wouldn't change anything, but I wonder if, you may have this experience now, but when I was in high school applying to college, Yale and Harvard wrote me personally and said, please apply; we want to consider you for admission. Well, neither of my parents had gone to college, so what did I do? I kept it for a while and just looked at it and thought, that is so nice. Wow, I got a letter from Harvard and Yale, and I never applied. That's why I say to you-all, don't underestimate yourself, go for it. Whatever that go-for-it is, go for it. We only come through this place one time, as we know it, so why have regrets? I'm glad I went to Sweet Briar. I mean, I think it helped me develop confidence, all of those things that maybe I wouldn't have gotten at another school. But I didn't go for it. I let it go. I had other experiences like that. Don't do that to yourself. Go for it. No matter what it is, just go for it. What's the worst that could happen? They say no. But if you don't go for it, you'd never know, so—and maybe I would have gotten here sooner if I had done that. (Laughter.)

LAW STUDENT: I was going to ask you, as far as the mental health court goes, one thing. Sometimes when you see that somebody has a mental health issue, and maybe you think to yourself, if they could, they could potentially work through it, how do you face it when it looks like they're basically set up for failure because of the support group around them? How do you approach that? How can you stay so enthusiastic in your moral compass, coming back day after day, when you look at it and after a certain amount of time you just, you can almost tell that it's headed down that path? How do you still give them the benefit of the doubt?

JUDGE COLVIN: What we try to do, we try to get them out of that environment. I'm one of these people, I'm, like, can do. I just have such positive energy. There's no such thing as can't. I tell people in my office, we're not saying that word. We're not saying can't. So what I do with people like that is we try to get them housing so they can get out of that environment with that person and make a new framework for the people who they associate themselves with. Sometimes, particularly in the criminal context, I have to tell them, you can think beyond where you're sitting. You don't have to allow what you're in to be your end-all, and they will tell me, Judge, that's so hard to do. I'll say, you know what, I get it. So come to the courthouse every time you need—come see me. Tell them that you're out there. I'll come see you.

I can't take everybody out of their situation, but what I try to do is help them learn how to take themselves mentally out of the situation. I tell this to people who are incarcerated, you may be physically located some place, but your mind doesn't have to be there. You don't have to have an incarcerated mind, because if you change your mental outlook, you can change your physical situation, but until you change that, you can't change anything else. I can take you physically out of a situation, but if mentally you're locked up, you're going to still be right there, and so I try to make them think that they can be beyond that by thinking mentally, and it's going to take some work on their part, because that's not an easy thing to do.

Many people who are educated like us don't do that very well, but that's the only way you can move beyond a bad situation. You got to think it before you can be it. I just have to keep coming back, I can't give up on them because if I give up on them, they'll give up, so I have to keep coming back, and I have to keep being positive. The other day I was in court,

I went to Kinko's before court, I found this great quote that I told them all to put on their mirror, and I laminated it for them. That's out of my pocket, but people need to be inspired, so I told them, put it on your mirror and every day read it. Remind yourself of what you can be. And let me just be honest: we all need to do that, because sometimes we lose our way, and if you don't have something to remind you of what you can be, you may fall into what is easy to be, which is mediocrity. Don't ever settle for mediocrity.

PROFESSOR LONGAN: Judge, this has been quite an hour. Thank you for coming.

JUDGE COLVIN: Thank you.

A Conversation with Tomieka R. Daniel

Introduction by Amber T. Jones[*]

When I met Attorney Daniel, it was just an ordinary day. I was doing the work I was paid to do, serving a marginalized population that received Medicaid benefits for my company. My job at the time was to provide resources to that population. The community organizations in Peach County had a focus on domestic violence at the time and were planning an event to that end. I committed to finding an unforgettable speaker for the Domestic Violence Rally at Fort Valley City Hall. Everyone I asked for a referral recommended Tomieka Daniel. They said she was the best. So, I found and confirmed her. Little did I know, I would run into a person who would change the trajectory of my professional development.

"They" were right. I had tears in my eyes as she spoke about the women and children that she protected in her role at Georgia Legal Services through protective orders. She spoke with so much compassion and conviction for the work she was doing to protect the same people that I was advocating for in healthcare. Her influence that fall day inspired me to go to law school. Almost one year later, to the date, I was a 1L at Mercer Law. The very first week, in walks Attorney Daniel in her professional glamor. I was impressed by her professionalism, presence, and passion for the practice of law.

In my favorite book, *The Five People You Meet in Heaven*, Mitch Albom wrote, "No story sits by itself, sometimes stories meet at corners and sometimes they cover one another completely, like stones beneath a river."[†] How relevant her story was to mine. We met at corners and were

---

[*] Contract Negotiator, Lockheed Martin Corporation, Marietta, Georgia.

[†] Mitch Albom, *The Five People You Meet in Heaven* (New York: Hachette Books, 2003).

literally completely covering one another. I knew, at that moment, that I could strive to be who she already was.

Attorney Daniel did not stop there. She came to the law school to assist whenever she was needed. The most memorable influence was when she came to present to the Black Law Student Association on how to dress appropriately to secure a summer internship/associate position. However, she did not come empty-handed. She galvanized the local bar to provide gently used professional clothing that was made available to students. She understood the microaggressions that stood between students of color and us reaching our full potential. She decided that attire would not be one of them. Her heart to serve others was clear, infectious, and longstanding. Throughout our time as mentor and mentee, Attorney Daniel has continued to set law students, young lawyers, colleagues, and her clients up for success: professionally, spiritually, and emotionally.

Tomieka Daniel's honors and awards are numerous, but her commitment to people is powerful. The most meaningful thing that I have learned from Attorney Daniel can be summarized in a quote by Maya Angelou: "I've learned that people will forget what you said, people will forget what you did, but people will never forget how you made them feel."

The legal profession is better, more impactful, and more prestigious with Tomieka Daniel in it.

TOMIEKA DANIEL, 2013

PROFESSOR PATRICK LONGAN: Tomieka, thank you for being with us. Let's start by having you tell the students a little bit about yourself and your background, how and where you grew up. That will eventually lead us to how it came to be that you came to the Mercer Law School.

MS. DANIEL: Okay, sure. I'm a military brat. My dad was stationed at Robins Air Force Base. We moved here around the time I was in middle school. I went off to Clark Atlanta for college and came back to Mercer for law school. I knew when I was nine years old that I wanted to be an attorney. I fell in love with the show, The Cosby Show, and I wanted to be the mom—but minus all those kids. (Laughter.) That was my first introduction to law. That was my first time seeing a black female attorney, and I was so intrigued by her, that's what I wanted to do, so I stuck to it. I came back to Mercer, and when I was here at Mercer, I interned with Georgia Legal Services. I think it was my second year and I completely got bit by the bug.

As a first-year, I came in thinking, you know what, I think I want to be a prosecutor. I want to prosecute crimes against children. That's really what I want to do. So, I went down to Houston County, and I interned with another one of our alums and found myself leaving work crying every day. It was probably the most stressful time, outside of my first year of law school, that I had ever experienced. I quickly realized that was not for me. I interned for about a semester. When I come back to the law school, I like to talk to people about trying out different things because you may come in with an idea of what you think you really want to do, but I don't want you to get pigeonholed into that. I want you to understand that there are so many other opportunities available for you. You should really investigate to make sure that that's going to be a good fit before you go out and take that first job and get somewhere and say, oh my gosh, I'm miserable.

So, after doing that, I interned with Georgia Legal Services, and I felt like the lights were just shining, saying this is exactly where you're supposed to be. It was that "aha" moment for me, and I've been there ever since. That's the only job that I've had since I graduated from Mercer Law School.

PROFESSOR LONGAN: You're coming up on your ten-year anniversary. Looking back on those ten years, can you talk a little bit about your time in law school and what it was like for you, maybe a little bit of the ups and downs. I think it's fair to say everybody in this room has had some ups and downs already. It may help them to hear some perspective, ten years out, about what it was like for you when you were where they're sitting now.

MS. DANIEL: Honestly, law school itself, my first year, was not pleasurable for me at all. I would find myself sitting in class some days saying, why did I decide to do this? I see some of the looks on your faces. Some of you have had those questions for yourself. Stick it out. It gets better, I promise you. But seriously, it was a really rough time period for me. It was a struggle, but I fought through it. I realized this was something that I really, really wanted to do, and so if it's what you really, really want to do you have to tough it out. By the time I made it to my second year, my attitude was, you know what, this is not so bad. They are working me to death this year, but I get it now.

I think my problem with the first year was I didn't understand the process. I hadn't done enough research into law school to really realize what I was getting myself into. I just kind of came in blind. I wanted to be the lady on The Cosby Show. How hard is that? I was brilliant as an undergrad, and I did all these great things and made great grades, so it can't be too much different than that. Lo and behold, it was a totally different world when I got here.

But what I found myself doing in the second year and third year was getting more involved in the law school process. I was very active with student government. I was very active with the dean's office. I was active with BLSA on the local and the regional and national levels. Those really helped to turn my experiences around, and I took advantage of a lot of things. I got to know Dean Donovan really well. She got to know me well. The Career Services Office got to know me well. So, if opportunities came about, they knew me so well that they'd say, wow, Tomieka, I heard about something that I think you'd be great for, or, you know, can you go and represent the law school here? Can you go do recruiting for us here? Because they knew what I was passionate about, and they knew my abilities. That really made my experience a lot easier for me, and it's led to some lasting relationships. There are people at the law school that call me to come back—I mean, I'm here every year. You'll get sick of seeing me. I get called to come and speak at the law school probably about five or six times a year, and to go and represent Mercer sometimes, and to just do things because they know who I am and they know that I'm passionate about what I do.

I would advise you as first-year students, don't try to go through this thing as an island. I was never one that did the study group thing or had a study buddy because I didn't need it. My attitude was, I'm brilliant, I don't need to study with anybody. So, I get here, and I'm in a class full of other brilliant people who don't need anybody, and it's intimidating. It was very intimidating for me to look around and see that for half my classmates, their dad was a lawyer and their granddad was a lawyer, their mom, everybody in their family, and I'm, thinking, wow, there's nobody in my family that's in law. You've got to get that out of the way. You've got to get over yourself and recognize that it's okay to ask for help, and it actually is beneficial for you to get with people who don't think like you so that you can figure out how to bounce things off of each other.

I had a hard time trying to see both sides of an issue. I couldn't see the other side of the argument, and so it took me getting in a study group with somebody that I really didn't like. He's turned out to be one of my best friends, but I really didn't like him. We didn't think alike. I just thought he was a jerk. He was really arrogant. He was from New York. You know, I'm a good southern girl. We just didn't click. But he challenged me because he could always see the argument, and he challenged me to reach beyond myself and kind of look at things differently. I would definitely encourage you to find someone like that. He is one of the reasons, I know, that I passed the bar my first time because he was in my study group. We had a very small study group of folks about whom people around the law school probably were thinking, yeah, they're probably going to bring the curve down, I don't think they're going to make it. But everybody in my study group passed because we were completely opposite, and we challenged each other every day. We made a pact that we were not going to let one of us fall down. Had I done that my first semester in my first year, I think things would have turned out a lot differently for me as far as how I felt about that first-year experience. I don't have warm, fuzzy feelings about first year, but as to my law school experience as a whole, I would not have done anything different. I made a great choice coming to this school in this environment and doing the things that I do.

PROFESSOR LONGAN: Was there a particular faculty member who had a special influence on you and your life?

MS. DANIEL: There are actually two, and I'm going to talk briefly about the first one, because I don't want to get emotional.* Professor Kosek terrified me as a first-year student. But I look back now, even when I go into court and I listen to other attorneys when they present their cases, and I hear the way they speak, and I hear Professor Kosek in my head. I say, wow, they obviously didn't have Professor Kosek, because he made sure that you could present yourself like an attorney should present themselves. Everyone that's gone through Kosek will tell you the same thing. You know that you've been taught by the best, and it shows when you're in court and you look at other people and say, no, they didn't go to Mercer because listen how they're presenting their case. They clearly didn't go to Mercer, and they didn't have Professor Kosek. So, I always thank him for that, for pushing us, but he

* At the time of this interview, Professor Reynold J. Kosek had recently died at the age of sixty-four.

terrified us in class. The whole semester you're sitting there like, oh my gosh, I just cannot believe I'm going to have to speak in front of this man, and he's just going to crucify me.

The other faculty member who played a tremendous role in my process was Professor Baldwin. I adopted him as my father. I was scared of him the first year because he was really hard, and he really challenged you. You're sitting on pins and needles, thinking oh my gosh, oh my gosh, what is he going to say next? But I just spoke with him last week. We still have a relationship after ten years. I really depend on him when I have different issues that are coming up or if there's something that I'm not too sure about, a career choice that I want to make or an opportunity that's been given to me. I'll call him and say, what do you think about this, what should I do about this? I've definitely adopted him as a mentor, and that type of relationship can only be formed when you allow yourself to be open. At first, I was too afraid to go to his office. Your professor will say, oh, come talk to me in my office. They're totally different in their offices. That's the secret. They may be horrible in class, but when you go and talk to them, they're real people, too. I promise you would do yourself a world of good to take that opportunity. If something's going on and you just don't quite get it, take the time out before it builds and builds and builds and ends up hurting you in the end.

PROFESSOR LONGAN: Let's turn to what you do now. Is there a typical day for you at Georgia Legal Services?

MS. DANIEL: I love that question. There is no typical day at any legal services program. I always amaze myself. I'll start the week with a things-to-do list of things that I really need to get accomplished this week: I need to work on this answer, I need to do this, this, and this. But the nature of my practice is last minute. Prime example: I would say ninety-five percent of my practice is representing victims of domestic violence. Here in Bibb County, we have court every Friday with temporary protective order cases. So, we know that we're going to have court pretty much every Friday, just in this one county. My office covers twenty-three counties. Five attorneys, twenty-three counties, so you do the math.

I may get a call on Thursday at two o'clock from a client who says, I need help, I've got court in the morning, and I'm like, seriously? Okay, let me see what I can do. She can't come into the office because she's at work, and if she asks to get off work two days in a row she's going to be fired, but she needs this protective order because her ex-boyfriend won't stop calling and harassing her, and they have a child together. He's threatening to take the child and run off with the child. He's been physically abusive to her. He's sent her to the hospital. She needs a protective order. She'll say, I need your help. There's nobody else that can help me do this. So, whatever I had planned for that afternoon, it goes by the wayside because now I have to prepare for court at nine o'clock in the morning. I've got to stop what I'm doing because it's just that critical. This woman's life depends on whether or not I am prepared properly to handle her case that following morning. That means I've got to get witnesses contacted, maybe have a police officer there to testify. I've got three hours to try to do this during business hours while people are still at work and I can actually reach them.

That's a typical day for me: anything can come up. We have clients who walk into our office all the time with different issues. I do a lot of housing eviction work, primarily representing people in public housing, and just this week I was able to keep two people from being evicted from their homes. One was being evicted for failure to pay a maintenance charge of twelve dollars—evicted for twelve dollars! Another was being evicted because it was alleged that she hosted a cookout in the public housing area, and a fight broke out. There were problems, and they were going to kick her out.

So, you hear stuff like this, and you say, well, wow. When I first started, I'm thinking, you can't pay a twelve-dollar maintenance charge? You got to be kidding me. That's me green, coming in from law school thinking I know everything. Then you get into the situation, and you find out that the client says, I was never given a bill for twelve dollars.

Sure, if I paid my $180 rent, I would certainly pay a twelve-dollar maintenance charge, but I never received it. They never gave it to me. So, again, I got to stop what I'm doing. I've got to go and negotiate with the Housing Authority to help this person get their housing saved. You may not know, affordable housing is pretty nonexistent in Bibb County, so if you lose the one place that you have, and you can only afford to pay $180 rent, where in the world else are you going to get a two-bedroom place in Macon for 180 bucks? It's not going to happen, so that person is going to be potentially homeless if I don't take the time to stop what I'm doing and investigate what's going on.

I get the opportunity to come out and speak at the law school. I have developed a Teen Dating Violence project where I go around our twenty-three counties. I go into high schools and middle schools, and I educate parents and teachers and students about the issues of teen dating violence. I train police officers on the issues of domestic violence. I train shelter advocates. What I did in legal services was I found my niche. I knew that domestic violence was something that I loved to talk about, and I'm a good trainer. I have to say that myself. I pat myself on the back. I'm a good trainer. I can come in and teach people stuff in a fun and innovative way that's not putting them to sleep. When they recognized that that was my gift, they just started sending me out, and they let me do what I'm good at. So, I tell you when you get on the job, figure out what it is you're good at, and do it to the best of your ability. Then you can do what you love. I can honestly say I love my job. I love what I do. I love coming to work every day. I have friends that are not in that same position. They dread going in to work. Do what you love and do it well, and you'll never work a day in your life.

PROFESSOR LONGAN: Can you talk a little bit about the office more generally. Five lawyers for twenty-three counties. How do the clients get to you, and how in the world do you serve twenty-three counties with just five lawyers?

MS. DANIEL: Our office is located in downtown Macon, so a lot of our clients walk into our office, but we serve a very rural area, as well, in those other counties. What we do is we go out into the counties, and we do what's called circuit riding. We will post announcements to let folks know when we're going to be there and what types of issues we cover. At legal services we do public benefits work. We do some custody work, some divorce work. Domestic violence, of course. We do elder law. We do Social Security. We do housing. We do consumer law. When you come into legal services, you're going to get a little bit of everything. You're not going to be stuck just doing one particular thing. You're going to have an opportunity to be able to dabble in everything. We do unemployment cases.

Typically, our clients will walk in or call in. They get transferred to us by the clerks' offices in the different counties. Different agencies will refer clients to us. We get a lot of people who come to us when their food stamps have been cut off for whatever reason. Nine times out of ten DFCS was wrong. I hope there are no former DFCS folks in here. If there are, I don't care. (Laughter.) DFCS was wrong, and they should not have been cut off from their benefits. We tell them why they shouldn't have, and we're able to get them restored.

How do we serve people? It's very difficult. That's probably the most frustrating part of my job, the fact that we have so many people who come to us but we have to turn them away, because you physically cannot help everyone. Just one example: on a daily basis I would dare say we get fifty or sixty calls a day from people who want to get a divorce. We simply can't do it. Our funding restricts us from filing affirmative divorces. There are certain instances when we can get involved in divorces. If the person is a victim of domestic violence and if custody is an issue, then we will consider it. But just that category alone—if we did all divorces that come to our office, we wouldn't be able to do anything else for anybody else.

That's why it's really important we reach out to attorneys in the local community and try to get help from them to do the work that we simply cannot do because of funding cuts. We've just gone through another round of cuts, and our program lost a lot of attorneys because our federal funding has been decreased. We don't get state funding, really, so we depend a lot on grants. We have domestic violence grants and elder law grants. Depending on grants limits what we can do, because if you don't have a pot of money to pull from, you're a lot less likely to work on those issues if you don't have the funding to cover it.

PROFESSOR LONGAN: What happens to the people you turn away?

MS. DANIEL: What we do is we have a list of pro bono attorneys who will agree to take cases from us. We have a pro bono list and a reduced fee referral list. You have some lawyers who say, "well, no, I won't do it for free, but if you send them to us I'll do it at a reduced rate, less than what I would charge someone who comes in off the street, because of my relationship with Georgia Legal Services." We have new attorneys, freshly minted, who want to come in and learn some different areas of the law and make a name for themselves. They will be on our listing, and normally we ask them to take two cases a year. It's not a lot. All we're asking is two cases. Oftentimes they take more than two cases, but we say, give us two cases a year and we'll give you some CLE credit. If there are court costs involved, we can help you with the court costs. We just need somebody who can handle this because we don't have the staff to do it. It works very well in the Macon area, but when you get out in the counties and get out in Dublin and Wrightsville and Soperton, where there may be one or two attorneys, and those attorneys are so inundated with cases that they're getting paid for, we find that they don't have time to take pro bono cases. As a result, it becomes really difficult when you have people who live in the more rural counties and need help. There are sometimes we just can't help everybody because we can't find an attorney who's willing to take the case.

PROFESSOR LONGAN: If somebody does not get a lawyer for one of the kinds of problems that you're talking about, what happens to them?

MS. DANIEL: They end up representing themselves, which, as you can imagine, oftentimes becomes a train wreck. Because can you imagine a woman going in unrepresented, and her husband is trying to take her kids? Whether he has good cause or not, she doesn't know the lingo, she doesn't know how to represent herself, she doesn't have money. The first thing that the judge is going to tell her is, "ma'am, you need to get a lawyer." She'll say, "I can't get a lawyer. He was the one who worked. We've been married for fifteen years. He never allowed me to work. I have no skills. I have no money outside of what he has, and he's completely cut me off. How can I afford to pay for a lawyer?" So, she goes in unrepresented. If the lawyer on the other side is an unscrupulous lawyer, he's not really going to care about what her issues are because he's not representing her. His goal is going to be to do whatever his client wants him to do: take the kids, stick it to her, whatever, that's going to be his goal.

And where does she stand? She may have a very good case. She may have been a victim of domestic violence. Maybe he's been abusive but she never called the police, so she has no police reports. She has no background to lay before the court to say this guy doesn't need these kids. He's been abusive towards them, but she hasn't been able to tell anybody because he's always threatened what he would do to her if she did tell. Then she gets in court. She's unrepresented, and she could possibly lose her kids because she doesn't have a voice for her. Those are the cases that pull at me the hardest, because you want to do more. But you recognize with the caseloads that we have already, we can't do anymore.

Sometimes we can't find anybody to help. I find myself begging private attorneys. If I go to a new county, and I see somebody that I've never seen before, I introduce myself and I say, "hey, what kind of law do you practice? You think you'd be interested in helping some of our clients?" Sometimes they're looking at me, thinking, hey, just back off, you know. My plate is full as well, but that's just because I'm passionate about trying to help make sure everybody has representation.

PROFESSOR LONGAN: Is there one client or one case that you look back on in the last ten years and say, that's one that I'm going to keep with me the rest of my life?

MS. DANIEL: There are two that stand out that are not good cases. My very first custody case, I lost, and I'm very competitive. It's the worst feeling ever, and I just took it to heart. I cried when I was leaving court. Don't think I'm a punk because I cry all the time, but I cried. I was really hurt that this woman lost custody of her kids, and long story short, there were some things that came up during the trial that she had not shared with me, things that were very damaging to her case. The judge picked up on them immediately and removed custody of the kids. I took this to heart for about two weeks. I was completely depressed, and I was just so upset. I felt like I had failed her. I wasn't worth my salt. I needed to maybe think about a different career choice.

Then I got a call back from her telling me that her and her husband had gotten back together. I was thinking, I've been killing myself for two weeks worrying, and y'all are back together. But that happens. I see somebody looking at me, thinking, are you serious? That's the nature of what we do. You put your heart and your soul into the case, and you get so emotionally tied into it, and they get back together. So that's one of them.

Another one was pretty tragic. I represented a victim of domestic violence, met with her, talked about safety planning, talked about what we could do to keep her and her kids safe, and she just kept telling me. "I think this is going to get his attention. I don't think he's going to do anything else. I just really wanted him to see that I'm serious and I want the abuse to stop. I just want him to leave me alone." We were able to get the protective order. He was in jail. He got out of jail, and the same day that he got out of jail, he went to her job, and he shot her in the parking lot. He killed her. That always sticks with me because I always look back to see if there was anything else that I could have done differently that could have possibly saved her life. I took that one to heart, and I think about her every day. Not a day goes by, when I represent these victims, that I do not remember her. I think, is there anything else I should tell her? Is there anything else I should say to her to try and help keep her safe? Sometimes you just can't. You do the best that you do, and at the end of the day you have to relax in knowing that you've done the best that you could possibly do for your clients.

PROFESSOR LONGAN: There may be some students with us this morning who think that they might want to do the kind of thing that you do. What would you say to them at this point in their legal education if they have the inkling that maybe legal services is where they'd like to end up? What advice would you have for them?

MS. DANIEL: I'd recommend that you try and volunteer at a legal services office to get a feel for day-to-day activities and what it is we do. I will tell you, it is the most rewarding work that you will ever find. You know, you go to the big firms, and you get rewarded by getting a big paycheck, and that's great, that's fine. It's never anything that I wanted to do, but that's fine if that's what you want to do. I get rewarded in a different way.

I may represent a client and help her get guardianship of her grandchildren, and the next day she brings me a cake that she baked, or I've had another client bring me a plant that she grew in her house, and she's repotted it, and she's brought that to me. People think, a cake, a plant? I still have plants that my clients have given me. Those things mean so much to me, and they make it worthwhile. We represent our clients free of charge, of course. They don't have a lot of money. They don't have the means, but to see the appreciation that they have is gratifying. Think about it, if you've gone through different social services agencies and everywhere you've gone you've been told, no, I can't help you, there's nothing that I can do for you. I'm often the last resort for them, and they know that if I can't help them, what in the world are they going to do?

They're so appreciative of the little things. Thank you for helping me keep my apartment, thank you for helping me get custody of my kids, thank you for that protective order so that now I can actually sleep at night. That makes it all worthwhile. But it's not for everybody. This work is not. I've seen both ends of the spectrum. We have people who come in and they may stay a year or two and realize, wow, this is totally not for me. Or we have people in our program, in my office in particular, who have been there twenty or thirty years. You really need to just kind of go in and volunteer and see if it's something that you could be comfortable doing.

We've had interns come in, and I say, okay, we got to go to the nursing home and get some documents signed, and they're thinking, "what? I don't do old people." (Laughter.) I've had interns tell me this. I'm thinking, "okay, and you want to work at legal services? I don't think this would be a good fit for you." Or I've got into public housing places and I've had interns tell me, "oh gosh, my boyfriend won't let me go on that side of town. I don't think I can go with you to meet with this client." I don't judge them, that's just your reality. That's fine. If you're not comfortable doing that, then you might want to rethink a career in legal services, because this is what I do. I go into public housing places.

I did a manufactured housing project for two years down in South Georgia. I was still with the Macon office, but I had to travel to Valdosta and everywhere, and I would go into these mobile homes. I've seen some things that I don't even want to repeat, things that just completely grossed me out. I was thinking, why do I do this, again? But you have to understand, sometimes you're going to get in situations where you're sitting in a client's house and you see bugs crawling on the wall, and you're just thinking, if I don't get out of here, I'm going to lose it. But you have to recognize, that's their reality. I can't judge her based on that. She still has a legal issue that I have to help her with. Part of the trick is figuring out what you can tolerate. If you know you don't do old people, if you know you don't like domestic violence issues, you might want to think about a different type of public service work that doesn't require you to deal with those type cases.

PROFESSOR LONGAN: In dealing with other lawyers, do you find or perceive that other lawyers treat you differently because you are a legal services lawyer?

MS. DANIEL: Yes. It's gotten better. When I first started, I got the feeling that people felt sorry for me. I had a friend who graduated with me, and he went off to a big law firm, and he really felt sorry for me. He said, I can't believe you do that kind of work. But after about a year he quit because he hated his job. He said, "wow, now I see why you do what you do. You're so happy." I say that to say there are some lawyers who kind of look at you and say, legal services?

But then you have the opposite end of the spectrum, and they come up to you and say, "I really thank you for what you do. I thank you for what you add to the profession." Judges are very, very thankful. I've had judges say, "wow, I love it when I see a legal services attorney on the other side." The first time I heard that I asked, "what, you do?" He said, "yes, because you-all are always prepared. I don't have to wait for you. Your orders are already prepared, they're ready to go, and you have your clients prepared. I appreciate you being on the other side of the case."

It's things like that that help you realize that, although the money's not great—it's doable but it's not great—but you do get a reputation for knowing what it is that you do because you're the expert in the area that you do. The type of stuff that I do, most private attorneys don't really get into. They come to me. I've had private attorneys call me and say, "hey, I got this issue, I'm trying to help a family member with a housing issue, tell me what you know about this." I think, wow, you come to me for help, that's cool. But you will earn the respect if you come in as a professional, you know what you're doing, you're on time, and you're ahead of the curve. You'll get the respect that you deserve.

PROFESSOR LONGAN: I didn't warn you I was going to ask you this, but it occurred to me as I was listening to you. One of the things that's going to come up from time to time in this course is work/life balance. The kind of work you do strikes me as likely to be very emotionally draining, obviously time-consuming, time-pressured, just like the life of many lawyers. How do you keep balance in your life? Can you talk a little bit about that and how you manage to be a happy, well-rounded person at the same time you work in your practice?

MS. DANIEL: I'm still trying to figure that out.

PROFESSOR LONGAN: You and me both.

MS. DANIEL: One of the reasons that I came to legal services was because I said I wanted to have a life. I wanted to have a family. I wanted to leave work at the office and then be able to do all the things that I do. I'm extremely involved in my community. I'm very active with my sorority, with my church. I just do a lot of stuff. And my job affords me the opportunity to do that.

Generally, I work a nine-to-five job. Unless I'm preparing for court, I've got a big trial or something that's not routine, I'm generally a nine-to-five kind of girl. I have a two-year-old daughter. If she's sick and I need to stay at home with her, that's not a problem. You know, I call in and say, listen, I can't make it today. You don't get that type of flexibility everywhere. If something is going on with my family, and I need to be away from the office, I can do that. My grandmother passed away in the summer. I was gone for a week and a half. Nobody batted an eye, nobody was looking at me, thinking, what about your billable hours? It's not an issue. If I wake up and maybe I'm just not feeling it today, and I need to work from home, I'm going to work from home. I have the flexibility to be able to do that.

You just have to go in knowing what it is that's important to you, and letting the folks know that you work with what's important to you, and that you do have a life outside of the office, so that they're not pulling on your time constraints. That's anywhere you go. You want to let people know. You don't want to say it in an ugly way or be rude, but if you have other obligations, you need to make sure that you don't let those fall by the wayside. By all means, you're going to get your job done, but I think that having a life outside of your job will help you be more effective in the job that you do.

PROFESSOR LONGAN: As a class, we're talking about issues of access to legal services. Let me put you in charge. You get to solve this problem. How would you solve it? We've got an enormous population out there that is at least underserved if not completely unserved at all by lawyers. What should we be doing as lawyers as a profession, and as citizens, to deal with that?

MS. DANIEL: I think more law schools need to take the approach that Mercer has taken with regard to public interest and getting you introduced early on to public interest work, showing you what the need is and encouraging you when you leave here to do some pro bono cases. As to whether or not there should be mandatory pro bono work done, there are pros and cons to that. Do I think that every lawyer should do some pro bono services? Absolutely. But the flip side of that is, and I've seen it, if you force an attorney to do something that they're not comfortable doing or they just don't want to do, they may not do a good job, and they may actually do a disservice to the client. They're coming in with a mindset, I don't believe this woman, I don't want to be here, I have other things that I want to do. So, they're not going to do a good job. But, on the other hand, they may start off saying, "this is something that I'm totally not interested in, I don't want to be bothered with this," and then they get that one client that touches them, and they say, "wow, this is nothing like I imagined it would be." That may be the spark that they need to help them understand, you know what, pro bono work is not so bad.

I think when I graduated, attorneys were forced, when you got sworn in, to sign on for the indigent defense list, and as criminal cases came up you were assigned different cases. I've heard pros and cons from people. Some say, "oh my God, I do not want to do that. I don't practice criminal law. I'm not interested, yadda, yadda, yadda." But it was there to fill a need. Sometimes people realize, wow, this is really something that I do enjoy, and they would have never tried had they not been forced to do it.

Because the need is so great, I think you have to mandate at some point. I really do think that you would have to mandate attorneys to take pro bono work, and just hope that because of the oath that we take that they would still do their best job for their clients. But there may be times when we need to kind of check in on people to make sure they're doing what they're supposed to do. I will add that the judges prefer that folks don't come in to court unrepresented, because when you have unrepresented folks, it clogs up the calendar. It takes a lot more time for the judge to have to sort through the issues. When there's an attorney on both sides, the attorneys can help the clients put the emotions to the side and find some type of resolution. Rather than the judge taking three hours with some unrepresented folks to try to work through the issues, it could take some attorneys thirty minutes to get that done. Judges really, really wish that folks had some type of representation to kind of ease their court calendars.

PROFESSOR LONGAN: Well, I want to turn it to the students here momentarily and let them ask you anything they want to ask you, but is there anything that you want to say to them that you wish somebody had said to you when you were in their shoes?

MS. DANIEL: I will say that the practice of law is nothing like your first-year experience, so let's just go ahead and put that out there. If you're not really having a great time right now, I promise you it will get better. If you get in an area that you enjoy, you will have the time of your life, and you will realize what a real difference you can make in people's lives. You-all are going to be so powerful. You are going to have the ability to make decisions for people that will affect the rest of their lives, and I think you need to take that seriously.

The relationships that you are forging right now, they will carry with you. I think about lawyers that I met in my first year who were slackers or goofed off or they were kind of shady, and when I get people calling me saying, "do you have a referral? I'm down in so-and-so area and I need a lawyer." I think back, oh, I remember, my friend so-and-so is down there. But I think, oh, no, he was a slacker, I wouldn't refer you. This is ten years later, so whatever your reputation is that you form here is probably going to carry with you. You want to think about how you treat people, including staff, classmates, and your professors. That will definitely carry you a long way or it can be a hindrance for you. I can think of three people right now that I would never refer anybody to, I and haven't seen them in years. They may be amazing now, but I just have the memories of how they were. Enjoy your law school career, try out new things. Keep your nose clean because you don't want anything hindering you from being able to sit for the bar.

But I guess the biggest thing is just try out different areas of law, even if it means you have to volunteer with a local attorney for six weeks. Do that so that you don't have tunnel vision, thinking, oh, all I want to do is prosecution, this is it, that's all I've ever talked about, that's all I want to do. I would hate for you to get in that first job at the DA's office and then realize, wow, this is totally not what I thought it was going to be. It would be a great time for you to use this opportunity to broaden your horizons, and it leads to jobs. I volunteered with legal services. I did an amazing job, and they hired me. So, during my third year, while everybody else was interviewing and worried about where they were going to work, I was just coasting because by October I knew where I was going to be working. I'd already gotten an offer. So, go in and you make those relationships now. You help people recognize how great you are at what you do, and then you go on and you do it.

PROFESSOR LONGAN: What questions do you-all have for Tomieka?

LAW STUDENT: I've read somewhere that if you go into public service, after a certain amount of time a certain amount of your student loan is abated. Can you speak to that?

MS. DANIEL: That's a great point. I'm really mad about that because they waited too late to start that program. (Laughter). So, I would be sitting pretty had they done that in 2002 when I graduated, so I'm a little miffed by that, but there are lots of repayment programs. I was approved for a repayment program that for three years, if I continued doing what I do, they would pay six thousand dollars a year towards my student loans. That's just for going to work every day and doing what I do. So, when I got the letter saying that I was approved for that, I was ecstatic. That's eighteen thousand dollars that I'm not going to have to pay back. So, there are so many programs. With Georgia Legal Services they have loan repayment. They pay a percent of my monthly loan payment. I pay the first hundred dollars and then they pay seventy-five percent of the remainder while I work there. I signed up day one, and you know, they're paying on my loans. Why not? It's free money. Why wouldn't you take advantage of something like that? When people say, oh, no, public interest lawyers don't make any money, there are so many perks that we get on the back end, like student loan repayment, that make it a definitely more attractive package for you.

LAW STUDENT: Do you-all do any kind of appellate work at all? Do you ever find yourself in a position where maybe someone already went in without an attorney and screwed it up, and so now you're on the appellate end trying to fix it?

MS. DANIEL: We don't do a lot of appellate work, but we have done some. A lot of what we do, I call it triage work. We have been short-staffed since I got with the program. When I interned there were eleven attorneys in the Macon office. Since I've been there, we've not had more than five. To say we're understaffed is an understatement. We really don't get many opportunities to go in and do appellate work. But we have an attorney in our office who loves appellate work. Any time there's an opportunity, we shoot it to her. She developed her niche. That's what she wanted to do, and she let it be known, and guess what, if you love it, go for it.

LAW STUDENT: Is your legal aid office funded by the government or is it a nonprofit private agency?

MS. DANIEL: We are a nonprofit. We do get some federal funding. A major portion of what we had was some IOLTA money that we really depended on heavily, which has subsequently dried up. This has led to funding cuts and us losing attorneys and paralegals. But it was available at one time.

LAW STUDENT: Is there funding from large law firms through donations?

MS. DANIEL: Yes, and the Macon community has been tremendous. The local law firms donate to our office. We are a statewide law firm. We cover all of the counties except for the metro Atlanta counties, which is handled by Atlanta Legal Aid, so we get funding from large law firms, small law firms, and other private donations. We get a little bit of everything from different areas. Primarily what we focus on is grants. We go after grant work or obtain grant funds to support the work that we do.

LAW STUDENT: You say that you wanted to be a prosecutor for a while and changed your mind. Can you be more specific on exactly what it is that kind of ruined your experience there?

MS. DANIEL: It was too stressful for me. I really thought that I would enjoy going out and advocating for kids who had been abused, physically and sexually abused, because that was the niche that I thought I wanted, but it was too emotionally draining on me. I am a huge child advocate. I love kids. I really thought that was going to be for me. I got there and I just realized I could not divorce myself from the emotional side of the work. I wasn't able to leave it at the office. I would come home and think about the pictures that I'd seen of the kids that had been abused and the stories that I heard, and I just couldn't—for me it just didn't work out. So, it wasn't anything about the job. The office was great. There are some amazing prosecutors down in Houston County. But for me personally, with my personality, it wasn't a good fit.

LAW STUDENT: How do you handle—you said that you got a lot of calls that you just can't deal with, how do you handle that personally, saying no to people when you know it's their last chance?

MS. DANIEL: It's frustrating. When I have to make the call, we generally will send out a letter, our "rejection" letter and we give them some advice on how to proceed pro se basically. But I like to call my clients and tell them. I think I'm just a glutton for punishment, because I'll call this mother and tell her I can't help her in a custody matter, and she starts crying on the phone, "well, why can't you help me? There's nobody else that can help me." That's emotionally draining. I guess it gets easier with time because I've been doing it for so long, and I understand that there are limitations and there's only so much that I can do. I definitely don't take it as personally as I did. Does it bother me? Absolutely. That's why whenever I have an opportunity to meet a new attorney, I go and say, "hey, would you consider being on our list? We definitely need your help, and we'll support you." That's one of the good things that I didn't say about legal services. We have so many forms and orders and briefs. We've just got a wealth of knowledge in different areas.

LAW STUDENT: Generally speaking, if you could take one field, which one would you say that the community that you represent needs the most help with: custody, housing, divorce, criminal defense, or something else?

MS. DANIEL: Family law for sure. Custody and divorce cases. That is what we get the requests for the most. The laws have changed and have put a little bit more of a burden on attorneys when they're doing family law cases. We've got child support worksheets that take a little bit more time, and some of the older lawyers think, I just don't want to deal with that or, it's putting more work on me. I'm going to raise my fees because maybe that will kind of turn some folks away or maybe they'll realize it's going to take more work, so I've got to charge you more. But by far, that is the most under-represented area. And that's the toughest one. You've got folks fighting over custody of their kids, that's the hardest one, and that's when clients need representation the most because there are some real issues. When you talk about division of property, that's just stuff. People can get over that. Okay, so I don't get to keep the car, I'll eventually get over that, but if you're telling me I'm going to lose my daughter, that can really, really, really affect me, and that's when I think attorneys need to step up and say, "listen, I'm not going to let this happen; I'm going to step in and see what I can do to help."

LAW STUDENT: With custody cases, how do you balance the interests of your client and the best interests of the child in those situations?

MS. DANIEL: That's a good question. Oftentimes a guardian ad litem will be appointed to the case to make sure that no matter what happens in this process that child's interests are going to be addressed and they're going to be brought before the court. It's a really fine line. You have to tell your client, I work for you and I'm willing to do what's best for you, but I'm a mother, also, so I'm also thinking about this kid. If I have a client who has a drug problem that I know about, I'm really going to try to encourage her to get herself together before she wants to make a big push to get her kid.

I think a lot of who you are personally comes into what you do in the practice of law, and it's a fine balance that you work, and every case is different. You'll just have to look at it and figure out, okay, you know, I know I'm representing you, and I know these are your interests. These are some issues that I think we need to address before we move any further with going down this road that you've planned out. Oftentimes they may come in with one goal, but when you lay it out and you explain to them, okay, these are some of the issues that the court is going to raise, this is going to be a concern with some of the judges, let's talk about these. No one has ever laid it out to them like that before. They'll say, "wow, you know, that does make sense. Maybe I should go into rehab and get myself together and then push to get my kids back, so that by then I'll have a house. Right now I'm living in my car, I don't have a job, and I have a drug problem." I'll say to them, "the likelihood of the judge giving you your kids right now is slim to none, and let's talk about ways that we can help you."

I don't only handle the case. I may be contacting River Edge, and saying, "what programs do you have available for my client? I have a homeless person, she's drug addicted, what can we do?" I may be making calls that most lawyers are not going to make. I like to take a holistic approach to my practice, and I recognize that her only issue is not this custody case. I need to figure out how she's going to eat tonight, I need to figure out where she's going to lay her head, and I need to figure out how she's going to be able to get clean. Then I start down that track of figuring those things out.

When I first started, my mom really had to pull me to the side, she was like, you're going too far. I had a client that came in and she said she hadn't eaten in two days, and I thought, oh my gosh, you haven't had anything to eat? I'm freaking out. This is my first or second year in practice. I put her in my car, and we go to the grocery store, and I'm just, like, "just get what you need." I wanted them to have food. (Laughter.) My boss said, "you did what?" I said, "she was hungry. I went and bought her some groceries." But that's just who I am. That's just what I do. He pulls me to the side and said, "well, you know, there's Loaves & Fishes, they would have given her two boxes of food for free." I said, "really?" (Laughter.) So, you learn as you go on. I don't take folks on shopping trips at the grocery store anymore. (Laughter.)

LAW STUDENT: We hear a lot that law school is nothing like practice.

MS. DANIEL: Thank God. (Laughter.)

LAW STUDENT (FOLLOW-UP): What about law school is most like practice so that we can maybe focus in and work on those elements?

MS. DANIEL: Nothing. (Laughter.)

PROFESSOR LONGAN: It doesn't mean it's unnecessary.

MS. DANIEL: No, it's absolutely necessary. Law school is training you how to think like a lawyer. It's training you to do those critical assessments that you need. It's training you on how to write properly, because as a lawyer you're going to do a lot of legal drafting, and you've got to learn those skills now. You've got to learn time management. You've got to learn how to present yourself. You may think that your professors are being hard when they close the door at the start time for their class and tell you that you can't come in because you're late. Well, guess what, you go to court and the calendar is set for nine o'clock. I've had judges that have seen lawyers walk in at 9:01, and they'll say, "counselor, your case is dismissed; your client's case is dismissed, you're late." So now your client is looking at you thinking, seriously? My case is dismissed because you're late?

You think that what happens in this building is not going to affect you in the practice, but it absolutely does. You need to learn these habits now because you are going to have some judges that are not going to have any sympathy on you. Oh, your car wouldn't start, your this, your that. I don't care. You're not here. You're late. I don't want to hear from you. There are lots of things that you take from here.

I recommend you take the practical courses in your third year. Unfortunately, they don't come until your third year. That's most like the practice. You'll get to learn how to draft documents. You'll get to do trial practice, so that you can actually see it done. But, again, if you want to do some of the things that you'll be doing as a lawyer, as a law student, we have law students in our office who practice under the third-year practice act. We've got one in court this morning handling a temporary protective order case. How attractive does that make you when you go out and you're starting to look for a job that you can tell your future employer, "oh, I've already handled five temporary protective order cases; I've handled six administrative hearings; they were all favorable decisions"? That really makes you ready for the practice.

LAW STUDENT: What does a career in public interest look like? Do you kind of stay in one office or is there mobility?

MS. DANIEL: Within our program, you would have to stay at an office for two years before you have the opportunity to transfer to another office. Generally, folks stay where they start. I've been in the Macon office. I have no desire to move to another office. You just work your way up in the ranks. I started out as a law assistant, and then I was a staff attorney, and then I was the senior staff attorney and now I'm a supervising attorney. I've had the opportunity to do the special project where I worked on the manufactured homes for two years, and I'll be honest with you, the reason that I did that was I was really getting burned out with the domestic violence work that I do. Because people realize that's my niche and I'm good at it, they were really funneling a lot more of those cases to see me. And I really, really started getting burned out, and I was at the point where I was thinking, wow, either I'm going to leave legal services altogether or I have to do something different, because this emotionally is wearing on me. Can't do it anymore. And my program was flexible enough that I was able to go to my boss and say, "listen, what else can I do? I'm really not feeling this right now."

So I did that. I took my two-year hiatus. It really made me appreciate what I do. God knows, I never want to work with mobile homes again. (Laughter.) But it gave me an opportunity to kind of refresh, recharge my batteries, and I came back with more fire than I ever had. Like I said, I've started this Teen Dating Violence project that at first the powers-that-be were not real sure about, and their reaction was, I don't really know, is that really legal? What benefit do we get from that? It's garnered so much attention that I just had the opportunity on Wednesday to participate in my first ever nationwide webinar on Teen Dating Violence because somebody somewhere told the powers-that-be that I was an expert in this area. So again, I'm making myself known for doing something that I absolutely love. It doesn't get any better than that.

You work your way up. When we had funding, we had this great program every year called Legal Services University where we would come together. You'd just basically have a three-day CLE on all the areas of law that we cover, and I learned more in those three days than you could learn in a year practicing at a regular law firm. But we don't have funding to do that anymore, so I've got to go out and create CLE opportunities for myself. But it is a rewarding career. If this is something that you're thinking about, investigate it, see if it fits with your personality, and if you think you could see yourself as a legal services lawyer, I promise you, you will really love what you do, and you will be appreciated for it.

PROFESSOR LONGAN: Tomieka, it's been delightful. Thank you.

A Conversation with Professor James P. Fleissner

Introduction by William V. Hearnburg, Jr.[*]

Professor James P. Fleissner is Professor of Law, Mercer University School of Law. He teaches Criminal Law and Procedure, Constitutional Law, and Evidence. In addition to many other awards and accolades, he is a sixteen-time recipient of the law school's Reynold J. Kosek, Jr. Excellence in Teaching Award.

He is also the best teacher I have ever had. I graduated from Mercer Law School in 1999. Professor Fleissner taught me Criminal Law and Evidence. He also coached and mentored a moot court team of which I was a member. We won a national criminal procedure competition two years in a row under his leadership. It was from Professor Fleissner that I learned criminal law, procedure, ethics, evidence, professionalism, and how to conduct myself in a courtroom.

It is impossible to convey the impact that Professor Fleissner had on my legal career. Although I have been a business litigation attorney for most of my career, Professor Fleissner inspired and guided me into the representation of indigent criminal defendants, in both state and federal cases, including capital cases. Those cases are among the most personally meaningful that I have handled.

In terms of his teaching, what first sets Professor Fleissner apart is his extensive real-world experience. Professor Fleissner has an extraordinary record of serving our country as a federal prosecutor. Among other jobs, he has served an Assistant United States Attorney, Chief of Criminal Appeals, and Chief of General Crimes for the United States Attorney's Office for the Northern District of Illinois. As Deputy Special Counsel, he played an important role in a Special Counsel investigation and prosecution in a case involving the leak of classified information and the reporter's privilege. And he

---

[*] Assistant General Counsel, State Bar of Georgia.

has not only practiced real-world law; he has excelled at it. So, when he steps into a classroom to discuss evidence or criminal procedure, he knows what he is talking about.

Second, Professor Fleissner does not just teach his students in the classroom, he continues to mentor and advise students throughout their legal careers. Just last week (these words are being written in 2021, twenty-two years after I graduated from law school), I called him to discuss an evidence issue in an upcoming hearing. He is unfailingly generous in sharing his time, thoughts, analysis, and advice. And this was not a one-time occurrence, he has provided guidance and help to me throughout my career (and throughout the careers of countless other students). In every discussion with Professor Fleissner, he displays real excitement and pleasure in working through complex legal issues with me.

Finally, in addition to his experience and his dedication to his students, Professor Fleissner also teaches the underlying philosophy of the law in a way that is engaging and exciting. His class on criminal law opened the door to me to the importance of learning the intersections of law, ethics, morality, and culture. He has also published extensively on a wide range of topics, including legal history, constitutional law, evidence, and criminal procedure.

The following is a conversation between Professor Fleissner and Professor Patrick Longan, a nationally recognized expert on legal ethics, about the legal profession. In it, Professor Fleissner describes litigation thusly: "as I said before, it's combat, but it's done respectfully and as civilly as it can be done." In other words, represent your client zealously, but within the bounds of ethics and civility. As a lawyer who represents the State Bar of Georgia with respect to the enforcement of the Georgia Rules of Professional Conduct, I can tell you that every lawyer needs to be mindful of these words each and every day.

There is much wisdom regarding the legal profession in the following discussion. There is wisdom for young lawyers, old lawyers, and lawyers who are in between. There is wisdom for law students, experienced lawyers, prosecutors, defense attorneys, and all lawyers who engage in litigation. Read the following words and apply them to your own learning of the law and practicing of law. You will be a better lawyer for it.

PROFESSOR JAMES P. FLEISSNER, 2013

PROFESSOR PATRICK LONGAN: Jim, I think what would be helpful first for the students is to have a little bit better understanding for the arc of your career. If you could tell us basically how you got started, all the different things that you have done, and then we'll go into more of the detail.

PROFESSOR JAMES P. FLEISSNER: Well, thinking about this, it occurred to me this morning that it was thirty years ago, 1983, that I was sitting right where you're sitting, which is in the first year of law school. It seems like it went by fast. Let me tell you, when I was sitting where you're sitting, I wasn't really thinking about the arc of a career. I was looking maybe for a little spark at that point. I didn't really know what I wanted to do, and I'm sure that's true for a lot of you, that you maybe came to law school with some vague notion, maybe that you're interested in litigation, and you're not really sure what that entails, or you're interested in transactional work or public service of some kind, and you're not really sure. And that's normal, and I hope you all realize that. Some of you may have a clear idea. You know, maybe you have a tax lawyer in your family, and that's what you want to do. I was always amazed at my classmates who knew for sure in the first year what they wanted to do. I always thought, well, how do they know that?

I came from a family, we didn't have lawyers in the family, I think I was the first one, so I didn't really have those kind of role models, and so one of the things I hope you're doing, as you go through this course and other things during your time at Mercer, is kind of sampling, going to talks, talking to people when you're interviewing for positions, meeting lawyers and getting a sense and trying to find some of those role models.

When I graduated from law school, which was 1986, I went to work in the US Attorney's Office in Chicago as a federal prosecutor, and I was very fortunate. The reason I got hired was that the Justice

Department at that time was growing. The Justice Department in Washington has these branch offices, the US Attorney's Offices around the country, and they were expanding, and they were hiring, at that time, so many people that there was room for someone who was right out of school. I had been an intern in that office. I did that just on a lark. I saw a sign, wrote them a letter, got an interview, and the next thing I knew I was an unpaid intern doing it for no course credit or anything. I worked in the US Attorney's Office, and that led to a job interview eventually and the opportunity to go there.

I was lucky because I didn't get pigeonholed, as sometimes can happen. There's nothing really wrong with that, to be a prosecutor with a certain type of case like a drug specialist or organized crime or something like that, but I ended up not getting pigeonholed, which was great. So I got to do a variety of things. You do a lot of routine cases that are not very glamorous, like somebody steals somebody's Treasury check out of the mail, and you prosecute them for that. But I got to do some pretty large-scale drug cases. I got to work on some police and judicial corruption cases. I got to work on a big undercover operation investigating fraud in some of the financial markets in Chicago. I had a real variety of cases that I got to try and work on appeals.

The thing that was really a gift was at a pretty early stage I got to do some supervisory work, which was a dream. If you're really interested in criminal law, that kind of position is great because what you do is you're kind of an open-door consultant. If someone is going to prosecute a case who's under your chain of command, they will write up a memo which you review. If they're going to try a case, they're going to have a conference to strategize, and you'll be involved in the conference. So with the supervisory work it is kind of like a mushroom cloud. You just see so much stuff, and usually stuff doesn't walk into your office unless there's some interesting issue. The really easy ones the prosecutors take care of on their own.

So that was a real blessing to have that experience, and it actually was particularly great because I eventually decided to go into teaching. I say decided to go into teaching, decided to put my name out there to try to get a teaching job, which I was very fortunate to get here. The supervisory stuff was a great preparation for the classroom, because it gave me a really large bank account of experiences, both firsthand that I was involved in and secondhand as a supervisor, and I think was good preparation for teaching.

Since I've been at Mercer, I've done some law practice. I've done some appointed cases on the defense side in the District Court and in the Court of Appeals, and probably I'm going to be doing some more of that. I'm hopeful the judges downtown will funnel me some more cases in the near future. With the blessing of the school, I've been able to do some government work since I've been here. I came in 1994. I did some special prosecutor work during one of the independent counsel investigations of one of the members of President Clinton's cabinet, did that for a couple of years, where I was continuing to teach full-time but was commuting back and forth to Washington and doing work out of here.

And then in 2003 the school was really very generous. They let me go on a leave of absence for two and a half years. That's almost as long as it takes to go to law school, so that's a good chunk of time, and they let me go back to the US Attorney's Office in Chicago, where I served as the appellate chief, and that was another supervisory job which was just a wonderful immersion and a whole variety of different kinds of cases. I also served as kind of legal advisor, besides doing the appellate work, which was a lot of editing of briefs and going to oral arguments in the Seventh Circuit Court of Appeals up there in Chicago. My role was to be kind of an advisor to the office on issues. So I did a lot of walk-in consultations, went to a lot of meetings, and basically got called in to participate in a lot of really interesting cases. So, again, it was a great immersion in a whole broad range of cases.

I think Pat wanted me to mention, while I was in Chicago the fellow I was working for, a guy named Pat Fitzgerald, who was the US Attorney in Chicago, got asked to be an independent prosecutor, independent counsel type of position, they call them the special counsel actually, involving this case where someone in the Bush White House allegedly leaked some confidential, classified information about a CIA operative, and there was an issue of who leaked it and why they leaked it. Pat Fitzgerald got appointed to handle that case and asked me to work on it. So, starting in January 2004 while I was still away, I started working on that, and when I came back in the summer of 2005, I got appointed to a, it's like a part-time federal prosecutor position where I stayed—I was working here teaching and working part-time for that investigation, which eventually led to an indictment of one of Vice President Cheney's staff and eventually his conviction at trial, and that work ended for me in about 2009. At this point I've cut the tether, I'm not working for the government in any capacity, which is why I expect to hopefully pick up some defense cases.

PROFESSOR LONGAN: So that special prosecutor work during the Bush administration, that's what led to the prosecution of Scooter Libby. You had a particular role in that because Scooter Libby wasn't the only one that faced consequences as a result of that investigation. There was a New York Times reporter.

PROFESSOR FLEISSNER: Yes.

PROFESSOR LONGAN: I wonder if you could talk just a little bit about your role in connection with the dispute about the sources and the government seeking the names of the sources and how—and what role you played.

PROFESSOR FLEISSNER: Well, a leak investigation, meaning someone has some confidential information and then they leaked it to a newspaper reporter, if you think about it, how will I investigate this? You don't have to be Sherlock Holmes to figure out how to investigate the case. The first thing you do is see if you can identify the person in the government, maybe through phone records or other things, who potentially had contact with the reporter. That's usually going to be a blind alley, and it was for us. Then the obvious thing is you go to the reporter. Of course, the press in the United States claims in many jurisdictions to have a privilege, which means they have the right not to disclose information in certain circumstances. In the federal system, there are limits to that privilege. One of the limits is if there's a criminal investigation that really needs to find out certain information so that it can complete the investigation to show that someone was guilty or someone was innocent, then the court can require a reporter, in certain circumstances, to turn over even a confidential source.

I was involved with litigating that involving several reporters, but ultimately a New York Times reporter, Judith Miller, resisted turning over information initially. She technically was not prosecuted, but it was a contempt action. The contempt power of a court means that they can say to someone, "I'm giving you a lawful order to turn over this information. If you refuse to do it, I'm going to put you in jail until you agree to comply with my lawful order." That's what the court's saying. The old cliche about contempt is that the person who's held in contempt has got the jailhouse keys in their pocket, because all they have to do is agree to comply with the lawful order, and they can get out. That's what eventually happened to her. After 85 days she agreed to disclose the source. Eventually there was a grand jury indictment based in part on the information that she gave, and eventually she testified at Scooter Libby's trial for false statement, perjury, and obstruction of justice.

PROFESSOR LONGAN: One of the things I know the students will be interested in is, given the kinds of things that you've done and the level at which you have practiced, is what law school did to prepare you or not, in and out of the classroom, for that experience. Full disclosure: we went to the same law school but didn't know each other at the time. But what did the law school do to prepare you, and how did you use that experience to get ready to do what you did?

PROFESSOR FLEISSNER: I think one of the really important things when you're in law school is to, obviously, you go to your classes. The curriculum is, I think, pretty well put together here. There are a lot of things that you get out of your classes. We have some things that we do here differently. This class is one of them. I didn't have a class, we didn't have a class like this, and I think this is a really great thing because it allows you, in the classroom setting, using some of your precious first-year class time, to get exposed to some stuff about the profession that you might just get in dribs and drabs or perhaps not at all.

I think it's an extremely valuable experience, and I would do it, not just in the formal setting of the Legal Profession class, but in any informal way you can get it. I mean, one strong piece of advice I give to first-year students a lot is—and I guess I'll give it to you all en masse right now—is there are a lot of things that are going on in the law school and here in Macon, which has a pretty vibrant legal community. Take advantage of those things. If there's a guest speaker, a Law Day lunch or that kind of thing, take advantage of as many of those as you can, and go and meet lawyers and listen to the guest speaker, because you never know which one of those things is going to be the one that causes the light bulb to go on that says, that looks interesting to me.

I've told Pat this story: I can trace to an exact moment when I first thought about public service and prosecution work. It was in a classroom a lot like this one at our law school, and I showed up a little late for a noontime brown bag to listen to a member of our faculty who was an older fellow. In World War II, he had been, as a very young lawyer, on the staff of the prosecution at Nuremberg, which was the war crimes trials. You can imagine for your first prosecution job prosecuting the Holocaust among other crimes. He was a labor lawyer, actually, so this was not his field, and he rarely talked about it, I think some out of modesty and some because it just wasn't his thing. He was prevailed on to come in and to talk about this, his experiences as a young lawyer.

I went there, and, of course, I showed up at the last minute, and the place was just packed. I remember sitting on the steps and listening, and it was spellbinding. I mean, he was talking about putting the prosecution together, and, of course, he portrayed his role in it as very minor. I found out years later through reading that it really wasn't so minor. I mean, he really was active as an assistant in the whole process. Like I say, it was spellbinding listening to it, and I remember thinking to myself, well, obviously I'm not going to do the Nuremberg war crimes trials or anything like it, in all likelihood, but it sounded to me kind of like a noble calling. It sounded like good public service, and it sounded exciting, frankly, the whole idea of it. Even though prosecuting someone for stealing a Treasury check out of the mail didn't rise to the same level, it was the same kind of activity, and it was something that I was attracted to, and for me that was when the lightbulb went on. If I had not gone to that little noontime speech, it could all have been different. It really could have been. So, I encourage you to take advantage of all those experiences, both here in this course and the ones that just come up along the way, because one of those very likely could shape your whole career.

PROFESSOR LONGAN: It's interesting you mentioned before, the internship you did with the US Attorney's Office. That's very common now and was uncommon when we were in law school. Could you talk a little bit about the importance of that both now and then?

PROFESSOR FLEISSNER: It was great. I had done a little bit of summertime work for law firms, and I liked it. It was litigation-type work that I was doing during the summer after my second year. The thing I liked about some of the civil cases was that they were investigations to figure out a mystery of what had happened, and that was the part of it that really attracted me. When I signed up to be an intern during my third year in the US Attorney's Office, I found out that these criminal cases, even the small ones, have that element to them, and it was very, very exciting, working on cases. I remember that I got asked to help with a trial, and at that time in the federal court in Chicago, I think it's still true, if you had a third-year permit, like a license from the state bar saying you were a third year in good standing, you could actually participate in court under the supervision of a lawyer. So, the first criminal trial I ever saw from the very beginning to the very end I was actually the third lawyer, so to speak. Of course, they gave me all the hard assignments. It was an arson case, and I had to prove that it was an arson. It wasn't in dispute that it was an arson, so that was my job.

PROFESSOR LONGAN: How did you do?

PROFESSOR FLEISSNER: I did it; I proved it was an arson. (Laughter.) But it was just fabulous experience being in the middle of the courtroom and working with two lawyers who were really good about taking me under their wing and showing me what to do, and it was very exciting. I had to miss a lot of class because I was in this trial, and I went to one of my professors, it was a constitutional law class, a specialized one, I can't remember which one it was, but I went to him and I said, "you know, Professor, I'm going to be missing a bunch of these classes." He said, "well, what's going on?" I said, "I'm actually the third chair in this arson trial, and it may take three weeks to try." He said, "you're going to learn a hell of a lot more in that trial than you're ever going to learn in my class, and so go to it. And when you're done, you come and tell me what you learned and maybe I'll get something out of it, too." So he was very generous about that. I don't know how great my grade was in that course, but that was the kind of experience that that was.

I mean, it was something that was really very exciting, so if you get those kind of opportunities through our practicum program, judicial field placement program, something you're doing during the summer, take full advantage, because that's a complement to your coursework. Some lawyers who are practicing have this attitude, "all that crap I learned in law school, I don't really need that, that's not really important. Now that I'm out I've really learned." I think that's really a skewed and flawed perspective. I think the way to think about it is that those practical experiences and some of the stuff you get in this course, that's the complement to the other stuff, and both are important, and I think if you lack one or the other, I think you're going to be at a serious disadvantage when you get out.

PROFESSOR LONGAN: Getting out is the next thing I wanted to ask you about because in law school, even a law school experience that has internships and summer employment, is not the same as being a new full-time lawyer, and so you went straight into the US Attorney's Office. I was wondering if you could talk a little bit about that. Let me phrase it this way: what surprised you when you were there full-time as a brand-new lawyer?

PROFESSOR FLEISSNER: Well, in answering the question, obviously this was my first job as a lawyer, and it was also, of course, learning about being a prosecutor, so it was kind of a combination. One of the things that I learned, and I think this is true for a lot of law jobs, if not all, is there are a lot of people skills that are involved in being a lawyer. You interact with a lot of people. If you're in litigation, you've got both people in your office, secretaries, paralegals, the guy in the mailroom, the guy in the copy room; you've got other lawyers in your office; you've got investigators from various law enforcement agencies that you deal with; you've got court personnel that you deal with; you've got witnesses that you deal with, lots of people you interact with on a daily basis, and how you do in those interactions is very important. And you talk to people, other lawyers on the phone, and you interact with them. Those are skills. I think it's the second year here at Mercer where you do this course about counseling. You're going to be doing simulation exercises. Those are very important skills, those kind of people skills of interacting with others.

I was surprised with the prosecutor job how little of it was in the courtroom. You know, you think of, like on the TV shows, the trial court scene or the appellate court scene, but a lot of what prosecutors do is outside of that context. One thing that surprised me concerned investigations. Very often, in the federal system especially, you're involved in the investigation of a case, of helping plan it. You're a legal advisor, and some of the time you're just giving your two cents about how to do an undercover scenario or something, and they don't teach that in law school, at least not where I went. A lot of it is common sense, and you learn on the job, and that was a surprise to me, being asked my opinion and then going out into the field and interviewing witnesses along with the agents. It was very exciting, and it was fun, so that was a surprise.

The other thing that came as somewhat of a surprise, although I should have known this, is that ninety-some percent of all cases in the federal system end by guilty plea, not by a trial. What it means is that a lot of what you're doing is negotiating guilty pleas, and so for those of you who are taking contracts, contract law is actually very important to that process. Pay attention in the contracts classes because those principles are very important. Essentially that's what you're doing with a guilty plea, is you're negotiating a contract, and contract principles basically apply. But that's a lot of what you do as a prosecutor, is work on investigations and then work on guilty pleas. The tip of the iceberg is the trials and the appeals and actually having cases go to court.

PROFESSOR LONGAN: I think that's all good information and good guidance, but I'm going to make you tell one story so that you can help the students know how to deal with their first day of their first trial and maybe what to do and not to do. Can you tell them about your morning the first day of your first trial as a full-time AUSA?

PROFESSOR FLEISSNER: Well, the thing to do is to have better luck than I did. It's amazing that this happened, but I was walking to the federal courthouse in Chicago, it's a high-rise building, on the day of my first trial, and we were going to do jury selection that day. I was, of course, very nervous and got up very early and put on my best suit, of the three or whatever that were in my closet, and tried to look presentable. Then I drove to the parking garage and was walking in to work. I'm going by a German restaurant called Berghoff's, which is right around the corner, and early in the morning they were offloading barrels of beer, metal barrels. You can see where this is going. What happened, they would drop them out of the truck onto a deflated tire which they would use as a pad and one of them missed the tire, hit the curbing and the seam broke, and there was this jet spray of beer. Well—(Laughter)—you can probably tell from looking at me I'm not much of a dancer, but what I did under the situation, I was able to kind of jump up and over the stream the first couple times it came by, and the third time it got me. I was drenched in the lower part of my legs with beer, and that was the day I learned that you should always have in your office an extra change of clothes and maybe even shoes in case disaster strikes.

So I went through the whole day reeking of beer. (Laughter.) The embarrassment started when I got on the elevator to go up to the fifteenth floor, and right before the elevator doors were about to close, the guy who is the first assistant, who's the number two guy in the office, gets on the elevator, and it doesn't take him more than about fifteen seconds to start sniffing and say, what the heck is that? I had to try to explain to him in my panicked state what it was, and he didn't seem to believe me very much. (Laughter.) But then all day I was trying to stay away from the judge for fear that she would smell the beer on me. She knew it was my first trial, so she was encouraging me to participate, and I was trying to stay back. It was a long day.

PROFESSOR LONGAN: There are some good lessons there. You were a prosecutor a good while and obviously you've still been involved over the years even while you've been teaching. What did you like about it? What gave you the satisfaction and joy you had in that particular kind of job?

PROFESSOR FLEISSNER: Obviously different people like different things, right? I went to school with a guy I mentioned who wanted to be a tax lawyer, and now for years he's been a tax lawyer, and he must like that, I assume. I don't think I would. I think the easiest and simplest answer is it was fun. It was challenging. There are moments when you lose sleep over difficult issues that come up. There are confrontations that occur, trials are kind of combat some of the time, and it's not like it's a stress-free kind of fun, but it was very satisfying. It's public service, which roughly means, you make a lot less money for during the same quality work as people in the big firms who are making a lot of money, but that to me was satisfying, to be able to do that.

There's a reason why people watch cop and lawyer shows, right? The reason that they have good ratings, like Law & Order, is that a lot of people just find it inherently interesting to watch the drama play out. You get to participate in some of those things, and it's fun. It's not without its challenges, and there are very difficult moments that come along the way, but that in a nutshell is why I enjoyed it and continue to enjoy it so much.

PROFESSOR LONGAN: Okay, I'll bite. Talk about the challenges.

PROFESSOR FLEISSNER: Okay. You're getting a sampling of it here this week, I mean, some of these things you've been reading about. Don't get the idea that every case turns into some huge moral dilemma, but there are ethical challenges that come up. Some of them relate to the law. You read this story, "In the Pink Room," which deals with so-called Brady obligations to turn over important exculpatory or mitigating information to the defense, and that's an obligation that you have as a prosecutor under the Due Process Clause.* If you don't do it, like the prosecutor in that case didn't do it, you're violating someone's constitutional rights, that defendant's rights. That defendant in the story you read ended up spending a lot of time in prison. In my opinion reading that story, in looking at the information there on the cases, that was really not a prosecutable case if all of the exculpatory information, the damaging information about that child witness, is known. I'm not even sure that one goes to court if all that information is on the table. So, you deal with that.

Now, I always thought that was relatively easy in some ways to deal with, because you just have to accept that's part of your job to do it, to turn that over, because you represent the government, you represent the public and you have a different role than a defense lawyer. Your role is to do the right thing, and some of the time that means you're

* Stephen Gillers, "In the Pink Room," in *Legal Ethics: Law* Stories, eds. Deborah Rhode and David Luban (New York: Foundation Press, 2005). The reference to Brady is to *Brady v. Maryland*, 373 U.S. 83 (1963).

not going to win the case that maybe you hoped and maybe even think you should win, but you have to turn that information over. In counseling and supervising people, they come to me and say, well, "I found this information, I don't think it's important information, I'd rather not turn it over." To me, that was very simple. If you really think this information can't affect the outcome of the case, if you have the courage of your convictions about that judgment, then turn it over. Why not turn it over if it can't affect the outcome of the case? If you're really afraid it hurts your case, if your gut is telling you, oh, I know how the defense lawyer could use this, this could hurt our case, then that's the barometer to tell you that you need to turn that over. Turn it over. Don't worry about whether it's necessarily going to change the outcome of the case or whether there's a reasonable probability or whatever the language is. Turn it over and know that you're doing the right thing by doing it. Then, if you believe in your case, go litigate the case and hopefully win, but you run into those.

Brady is one of the things that recur. But there are all kinds of things that come up. I'll just throw out one other example I was thinking about the other day from many years ago, and this doesn't really have to do with the law. This is just kind of a moral/ethical question related to dealing with witnesses.

I can remember a case where I had a witness who was a Chicago policeman who had gone bad. He had become corrupt, and he had some of his own mental health problems. During a leave of absence from his job on the police force, he started in with some drug dealers, and he was delivering drugs for them and carrying weapons during the transactions, and he got caught. So, he had this fall from grace. He went from being a Chicago police officer to being a convict, basically. I mean, he pled guilty, and he agreed to cooperate with the government, and he was my witness. I was going to put him on the stand. He was very fragile psychologically, and he was needy. He was a proud man, he had family, and he had had this terrible fall in his career, and he was looking for some friendship, really. I was really about the only thing on the horizon, and, of course, we weren't buddies, but he would be brought to my office when we would be working, and it was a question of keeping him in a good frame of mind so that he could testify effectively. I thought about that and worried about it. I thought about it in the sense of where is the line between being completely professional and manipulating somebody to get them to do what you want? Is it okay to be insincere of chatting up with the guy and pretending to be real interested and pat him on the back and encourage him when your interests are really selfish for your case, to make him a good witness? I struggled with that some. I mean, I'd like to think that I was extending to him human kindness, which was something that he needed at the time. But I also worried about the extent to which I might be playing the guy to get him to do what I wanted him to do, and which he did quite successfully.

Those are the kind of little things that come up from time to time where you have to sit back and think about what you're doing. It's an area of law, both defense and prosecution, where there are a lot of those little issues that come up you have to think about.

PROFESSOR LONGAN: I want to go back particularly to Brady for a minute because that's the one part of this process that the students have been exposed to. You and I both know that this has been a very hot issue over the last several years. There are a lot of high profile examples of prosecutors who have knowingly disregarded this obligation, and I wonder if you could talk about, not trying to forgive, not trying to condone, but just trying to understand what would lead a prosecutor in those circumstances, or in "In the Pink Room," what would cause them to disregard a constitutional obligation that is at the core of their job as a prosecutor?

PROFESSOR FLEISSNER: As you learned from reading that chapter, the legal standard is that you don't have to, under the law, turn over everything that could help the defense. You have to turn over what the law says is material, which means it's of such significance that it potentially could change the outcome, could change the verdict or could change the sentence in the case. I think what happens to some prosecutors is they believe in their case, they believe they've got the right person, they believe that that conviction is going to be the right outcome of the case, and when they see a piece of evidence that could help the defense, they rationalize it. They say, well, this couldn't possibly change the outcome because I know the right outcome in the case, and so it's not material, in my judgment, and so I'm not going to turn it over. Now, as I said before, my philosophy, as a supervisor and as a prosecutor, was to turn over almost everything that's exculpatory. To err on the side of disclosure on the theory that if it isn't material it's not going to affect the outcome by definition. So that was the way I did business and encouraged people to do business. Some prosecutors, I think, say no, no, I'm not going to do the defense lawyers' job for them. I'm going to be a zealous advocate for the prosecution, and so I'm only going to turn over material information, and then they have a very skewed, biased view of what is material.

Some of this, I think, comes from management and culture in an office. When you walk into a prosecutor's office, when I walk into one, I can almost tell instinctively what the culture of the office is. Is it an office where we're going to do the right thing, we're going to do it the right way, or is it an office that says, we're about locking up the bad guys, and we don't really like defense lawyers, and we're going to be aggressive, and we're only going to turn over what the law says we have to turn over and not one morsel more than that? I think if you get into that kind of a mindset, you can end up doing things like that prosecutor in the Pink Room story where they apparently had this information which was unbelievably exculpatory about this young witness and rationalized somehow, we don't think it's important enough to turn over, we're not going to turn it over, and our failure to turn it over didn't change the outcome in that story. It can happen.

In the federal system there was a very high-profile case, the prosecution of former Senator Ted Stevens, where there was a lengthy report that was done about it, and it's shocking what those federal prosecutors rationalized to do. So, you have to be kind of careful concerning Brady issues. One other thing I wanted to throw out is, I mentioned defense lawyers a couple of times, let me share with you my kind of philosophy about this. I've done some defense work. I think that if you're going to go into criminal law and you're going to do prosecution work or defense work or maybe over time some of both, I would not look at the two groups of prosecution and defense like two warring tribes, or two gangs where you have to pledge allegiance to one or the other, and once you get the tattoo of one side you can never convert over to the other. I think that's a huge mistake, a huge mistake.

I think they're both incredibly important to the system. I know people who have been on both sides, and I think the way to look at it is that both sides have a hugely important role to play. They're a check on each other. You can do both over the course of your career. I would avoid the mentality, and I've been to conferences with prosecutors and defense lawyers, and they are rah, rah for their side, and the other guys are bad, and I understand that. That's the way we motivate high school football teams, too, right? We tell them the bad guys over in the next county, they dissed us, we're going to get them, that kind of thing, you can't trust them. Well, I would try to minimize that and avoid it and try to look at both sides as contributing in an important way to the system, and to be able to do both over the course of your career if you choose to do it.

PROFESSOR LONGAN: In fact, I think in part as a reflection of your view on that, in our LLM program we train the defense lawyers and the prosecutors together in the same room.

PROFESSOR FLEISSNER: Yes.

PROFESSOR LONGAN: I think that's been an important thing for the success of that program. Don't you?

PROFESSOR FLEISSNER: Yes, that was an outgrowth of those of us who had that philosophy I just mentioned to you, that we thought, well, you know, if we're going to run a program for training federal criminal litigators, let's run it on that model where they work together. Frankly it's in your self-interest to think that way, in my opinion, because if you can, as a prosecutor, learn to think like a defense lawyer, you're going to be better at your job if you can analyze your case and really see how a defense lawyer would come at it. I know I've mentioned this to Pat, that I had a very important mentor in my career who was a prosecutor several years ahead of me in the US Attorney's Office. He was a career prosecutor. He now is in the private sector doing civil litigation mainly, but he's the best defense lawyer I ever met even though he was a prosecutor. When I had a case I would go to my friend, Dean, and I would say, Dean, what do I have to do to win this case? He would see stuff in the case, weaknesses that I never saw. He would see weaknesses that the defense lawyers never saw. He was really, really good at it. I learned that when you're a prosecutor it's such a gift to be able to think like a defense lawyer and to be able to see what's coming. If you're so close-minded and you're so wrapped up in the righteousness of your cause, you're not thinking like a really good lawyer.

PROFESSOR LONGAN: I've got a lot more to ask you, but I'm watching the clock, and I'm going to give the students a chance, so before I ask anything else, let me open it up. Any questions from you-all?

LAW STUDENT: How would you deal with an issue that there is going to be always someone that is not going to be happy? Maybe a politician, maybe someone that is bad. They can threaten to hurt you or your family. How do you deal with that?

PROFESSOR FLEISSNER: Let me deal with the second one first, and this may not ring particularly true the day after there was this report of a prosecutor in Texas getting shot. But the reality is, it is not a physically dangerous job. There are instances that arise, but there are instances that arise in a lot of litigation even in the civil side, where there's some of that. So, I wouldn't worry that it's like an armed camp where you have to be looking over your shoulder all the time. There are cases that happen where there are real threats that occur, but they usually are taken care of and investigated very thoroughly, and people end up safe.

Now, on the other side, which is much more common, you make decisions, you have to sometimes confront people, they're going to plead guilty in a case, you're delivering bad news. I can tell you, sitting across the desk from someone and saying, you're going to jail for a long time, that's delivering the bad news, right? They don't want to hear it, and their family doesn't want to hear it, and they might think, oh, you're a bad guy because you're doing it. There is some of that that happens, but it's also one of the interesting things about the job. The reason why it's a public service, is that someone needs to make the decisions and deliver the news and litigate the case, and that's something that hopefully is a benefit to the public. So in any kind of law job you're going to have some of that that happens, but it's not something that makes your life miserable, at least not in my experience.

LAW STUDENT: What does a typical workday and workweek look like as far as the amount of time you spend doing different things for your job?

PROFESSOR FLEISSNER: It varies. If you're prosecuting cases in court on a regular basis, a lot of it depends on whether you have cases coming up for trial. When you have a trial occur, it pretty much is all consuming. I mean, a lot of work, a lot of hours, and pretty much everything is devoted to that. When you're not on trial, things slow down to some extent, and you usually immediately after the trial have to return a lot of phone calls that you couldn't return during the trial, and you do a lot of routine work of drafting indictments, writing up memos for proposed prosecutions, doing grand jury work where you're bringing witnesses in to testify in an investigation, and that kind of thing.

It's also going to vary by office as kind of the culture in the office. In some offices, it's basically a nine-to-five kind of job during the week, and then when a trial comes along, it's going to be extra, and you'll be working on the weekends some. There are some offices that have a culture more like a big law firm where even though they're not billing hours like a law firm, they're working a lot. The office I was in in Chicago fits that description. So, it would be fairly rare that you wouldn't at least be working at home on weekends, and the days are often pretty long, especially when there's a trial or something that you're working on that has a deadline.

It can be a lot of work, and of course, you're making a government salary and not a private sector salary. You're not billing by the hour, so every hour that you work more than your quota, you're actually making your pay less by division. But it still is very satisfying, and it's fun work. I mean, I can tell you that I had a lot of buddies in law school who thought I was kind of crazy to go to work for the government because they wanted to work for a fancy law firm, and there's nothing wrong with that work. It's honorable work, but that's what they wanted to do, and they thought I was nuts. Then I got a bunch of phone calls one year, two years after I started working, from my buddies saying, so how did you get that job? They'd be at their law firm and they'd close the door and they'd call me and say, hey, the honeymoon is over, I'm working like a dog in this law firm, and I'm not having any fun anymore, I'd really like to do what you're doing. When you're figuring what line of work you want to go in on the pay front, it seems to me you have to factor in quality of life and how much you enjoy the work that you're doing.

LAW STUDENT: Can you talk about your process for what standard you would adopt, whether the charges were good enough or whether you were personally convinced by it?

PROFESSOR FLEISSNER: The legal standard for filing a charge is very low. It's probable cause, which if you haven't studied it already, you'll learn it's quite a low standard. As a practical matter, that's not the standard for deciding on actually filing a charge. That's because you have the burden to prove all of the charges beyond a reasonable doubt. To me, the proper standard for a prosecutor in filing a case is whether they believe that they can prevail under that standard at trial. Now, sometimes there are close cases, or maybe there's a chance of further investigating the case after the charge and finding additional evidence, but that, basically, I think, has to be the standard, because it's a serious step to bring a charge against someone. Even just the charge has a lot of consequences for people.

You read an excerpt from Justice Sotomayor's book where she was recounting an episode as a prosecutor where she didn't think the case was sufficient to prove, and she basically said, "I won't do it." I think that's the right reaction. If you really believe that the case can't be proved at trial, then you don't want to be in the position of going into the trial and arguing, "oh, ladies and gentlemen of the jury, we've proved this beyond a reasonable doubt," when you don't believe it. In most offices, if an assistant district attorney or US Attorney says, "I don't believe in this case," they will relieve you from working on that case, and they'll either get rid of the case or they'll give it to someone else. But that's something that is kind of an occupational hazard that happens from time to time, that people will say they don't believe in the case. I think only an office with a really, really bad culture would say, well, you have to go do this case anyway or you're going to get fired or your career is going to be hurt.

LAW STUDENT: As a follow-up to that, this last week we read an article about an assistant DA who was told to go ahead and prosecute a case he didn't believe in. He made it very favorable for the defense to win. In a situation where you do work in an office where they say even though you don't believe it, go through with it, what kind of advice would you give to someone like me?

PROFESSOR FLEISSNER: I know that story, the one that you're referring to and the rest of you have looked at. I don't approve of what he did there because, although you obviously want to get the right result, if you're going to court representing the government in court, the state or the federal government in court, I mean, you have to be a zealous advocate. You've got an ethical obligation to be a zealous advocate for your side. Now, prosecutors have to balance being a zealous advocate with seeking justice, and in that case I think the scales tip the other way. What he was doing was saying, well, okay, I'm getting the right result but I'm going to do it through tanking the case. It seems to me the proper thing for him to do would be to go in to the supervisor like Sonia Sotomayor did, and say, I'm not going to do this case because I really don't believe the proof is there and that it shouldn't be a conviction. Now, I think his comeback to that was, well, if I'd have done that, someone would have just gone to court and won the case. If he really believes that, what does that say? I think his proper step was not to tank his responsibility to be a zealous advocate but to go within his office and get off the case.

LAW STUDENT: You talked about how the relationship between prosecutors and defense attorneys shouldn't really be adversarial. Do you think that there needs to be even more cooperation? Is it really fair that, say, you have a defense attorney who just completely misses a piece of evidence because maybe he's a bad attorney? Should people be punished because they got a bad defense attorney?

PROFESSOR FLEISSNER: There are a couple things. One is that, although I'm in favor of civility and I'm in favor of not having a kind of tribal hatred between the two, I certainly wouldn't want to go as far as to say it's not an adversarial process, because it is. As I said before, it's combat, but it's done respectfully and as civilly as it can be done.

In terms of this issue of taking advantage, let me tell you one little practical aspect of this question of when the lawyer on the other side isn't very good. I'll tell you when this really happens. People have a constitutional right to represent themselves even if they're not a lawyer, okay? They're often really bad in court, right? And you say to yourself, well, that's my dream matchup: me, the lawyer, against the person who's not the lawyer. Be careful what you wish for, because when you try a case either with a bad lawyer or a person representing themselves, the jury will feel bad, and they'll think, well, that lawyer doesn't seem as good as the prosecutor in this case or that person is representing themselves and they're overmatched by the prosecutor. Sometimes that can hurt your chances of winning the case.

Now, in terms of just the ethics, it seems to me if the other side will sometimes make surprising judgments that you think are not all that competent, they may well have reasons for doing it, and so you have to kind of let the adversarial system work. Now, would I say you would never help them in some way if you're the prosecutor? I would say no, it's possible that you can help out the other side in one way or another. I've had defense lawyers actually tell me something that I was doing that was distracting and set me right, and they were just being nice, and that, occasionally niceness does break out even in the middle of a trial.

PROFESSOR LONGAN: Jim, we could do this all morning, but we're out of time. Thank you for being with us.

PROFESSOR FLEISSNER: Thank you.

(Applause.)

A Conversation with Dean Daisy Hurst Floyd

Introduction by Alison Myhra[*] *and Rachel Van Cleave*[†]

Life really is all about learning, and learning really is all about life. Perhaps John Dewey, one of the most significant educational thinkers and reformers of the early twentieth century, reached this conclusion first when he wrote that "education is not preparation for life; education is life itself."[‡] In his view, learning and life are inextricably linked, amounting to a social process and ultimately leading to personal growth and development.

Professor Floyd has had an innate sense of this connectedness between learning and life for a long time. At least since the beginning of her career, she has, naturally and unassumingly, blended disparate life insights gained from her experiences, both personal and professional, acquired understanding as a result, and used her new and always developing self-knowledge in positive ways not only in her own personal and professional lives but also to help others. Thus, she regularly shares her experiences with her law students to help them see that life and learning truly go hand in hand and that they, too, should seek experiences, engage in reflection, and learn as they live their lives and strive to reach their potentials. Significantly, Professor Floyd emphasizes this process to her students for the *singular* purpose of helping them grow into self-actualizing, reflective, and ethical lawyers who understand not only legal doctrine and how to make legal arguments but also the law's impact on individual clients, the public, and the institutions that govern society.

---

[*] Dean's Distinguished Service Professor of Law, Texas Tech University School of Law, Lubbock, Texas.

[†] Professor of Law, Golden Gate University School of Law, San Francisco, California.

[‡] John Dewey, *The Early Works 1882–1898* (Southern Illinois University Press 1972) 87.

We had the privilege of working with Professor Floyd at Texas Tech University School of Law (TTU) for a number of years and, not surprisingly, we have had the pleasure of many conversations with her about numerous topics and issues of the day, including her passionate interest in the learning - life educational process and what she views as the longstanding need for law schools to focus more on student professionalism, professional formation, and professional identity. During this time, she was a leader in casting light on this area of concern in legal education, and it came as no surprise to us when in 2000 she was selected as one of several legal educators nationwide to teach a Carnegie Seminar on Legal Education as part of the pathbreaking research for what ultimately became the Carnegie Foundation's widely acclaimed report on legal education, *Educating Lawyers.*[*] As a result of her outstanding work with the Carnegie Seminar, Professor Floyd was named a Carnegie Scholar in 2001 in support of a two-year project on the development of professional identity among American law students. Today, Professor Floyd is a highly regarded national authority on the topic of ethical professional identity formation in law students. She has written widely on this topic and recently has co-authored a well-received book on the subject, *The Formation of Professional Identity: The Path from Student to Lawyer.*[†] Professor Floyd also regularly presents at academic conferences on her learning and professional identity scholarship. As Dean at Mercer University School of Law, Professor Floyd supported and taught in its first-of-its-kind professional identity course for first-year law students, putting into practice her scholarship.

We were colleagues with Professor Floyd at TTU at the beginning of our teaching careers, and we have remained close friends since those days. We have always been impressed with Professor Floyd's intellect, grace, and consistent ability to remain true to her values, even under challenging

---

[*] William M. Sullivan, Anne Colby, Judith Welch Wegner, Lloyd Bond, and Lee S. Shulman, *Educating Lawyers: Preparation for the Profession of Law*, (San Francisco: Jossey-Bass, 2007).

[†] Patrick Emery Longan, Daisy Hurst Floyd, and Timothy Floyd, *The Formation of Professional Identity: The Path from Student to Lawyer* (Abingdon: Routledge Press, 2019).

circumstances. We have absolutely no doubt that we are better law professors and people because of our friendship with Professor Floyd.

In the following discussion between Professor Floyd and Professor Patrick Longan, read and consider Professor Floyd's experiences and life lessons regarding her decision to go to law school, her career choices, and how she has maintained a healthy work-life balance. Perhaps most importantly, read and consider what it was like for Professor Floyd, a lawyer, to be a plaintiff in a discrimination and retaliation lawsuit against TTU, her law school and what it was like for her to rely on another lawyer to represent her and speak on her behalf. You will not be disappointed.

DEAN DAISY HURST FLOYD,* 2014

PROFESSOR PATRICK LONGAN: Daisy, thank you for doing this. I've read a couple of things, as you know, because you shared them with me, that you wrote about your career and your life and about your experience as a client, and one of the things that caught my eye as I read your reflections on your own career was this, about your decision to go to law school. You wrote, "my decision to go to law school was not particularly well-informed. I did not personally know any lawyers nor did I have a clear picture of what lawyers did or what it would be like to be a lawyer."† Now, you've been a lawyer and a law teacher and administrator and Dean, and it's been more than thirty years since you graduated from law school. Today as we sit here, you're the Dean of this law school for the second time. How did you get from that person who didn't know any lawyers, and didn't know what they did, to where you sit today?

DEAN DAISY HURST FLOYD: Well, it's not been a straight path, I'll tell you that. It's interesting to hear that quoted back to me because it makes me sound a little stupid maybe, but in retrospect I think that I went to law school for the reasons that a lot of people go to law school: I had a yearning to do something with my life that mattered. And I had a sense that being a lawyer mattered. I knew that lawyers used their skills in a variety of ways to make a difference in the world, and I had some sense of wanting to do that. I also thought that I would enjoy the intellectual part of being a lawyer. The good student part of being a lawyer appealed to me, at least it did at the beginning.

---

* When this interview was conducted, Daisy Floyd was Dean of the Mercer University School of Law. She is now University Professor of Law and Ethical Formation at Mercer. We have kept her title as Dean in the transcript.

† Daisy Hurst Floyd, *Lessons of Hope and Pain Learned on a Woman's Journey to Becoming a Law School Dean* (unpublished manuscript, 2005).

But I think I've gotten here today by being open to things as they appeared on the horizon, trying to learn from every twist and turn of my career, using those twists and turns to learn about myself, to learn what I enjoyed about those moments in my life and what I didn't enjoy, and to learn where my strengths and weaknesses were and being open to those lessons. I did not particularly enjoy my first year of law school, and I almost dropped out of law school altogether. Ironically what I thought about doing instead was to get a PhD in political science because I wanted to be a college teacher. It did not occur to me while I was in law school that there might be a career path as a legal educator for me. I don't know why it didn't, but that was just not something that had presented itself. I think I always had this yearning to teach, but I also was attracted to the law, so in retrospect maybe it's not so surprising that I ended up with a career in legal education.

PROFESSOR LONGAN: When you say you didn't like law school, what was it that you didn't like and how did you overcome that?

DEAN FLOYD: I struggled with the same thing many first-year students struggle with, which includes that I had a hard time knowing what I was supposed to be doing, and that was uncomfortable for me as a first-year law student. The competition was something that was tough for me—I'm not somebody who really thrives on conflict, and I understand that about myself now, but that was a hard adjustment for me. Those were a couple of things and I also experienced some of the other things that we've talked about in this class. For example, the focus on the cognitive to the exclusion of other matters caused dissonance for me that I didn't recognize at the time, but I now know that that was part of my discomfort.

PROFESSOR LONGAN: When you graduated, you went into practice with what, at that time, was a big law firm.

DEAN FLOYD: Right.

PROFESSOR LONGAN: It's now a much, much bigger law firm.

DEAN FLOYD: Yes, it was about ninety lawyers then. That was a huge law firm then.

PROFESSOR LONGAN: That was a huge law firm.

DEAN FLOYD: In 1980, yeah, it was.

PROFESSOR LONGAN: You've written in these pieces that you shared with me that you were dissatisfied with that experience as you were having it, and with the passage of time and the perspective of time you have a better understanding as to why. Talk a little bit about that.

DEAN FLOYD: I think, again, it was because it was something that I was not fully prepared for. It was not anything necessarily about the environment. The people I worked with were excellent lawyers, they were good people, they were supportive, so part of it, I think, was whether I was ready for that kind of practice at that moment in my life. I think it was probably because I was not really prepared for what it meant to be a lawyer, and so I was still struggling to meet what I felt were unclear expectations. More specifically, I think some of it goes back to this notion of conflict and whether that was something that I enjoyed participating in. What I really wanted to do was litigation and I was assigned to both the litigation and the antitrust departments. What I've learned about myself, though, is that I don't thrive in situations of a lot of conflict. I don't really enjoy conflict for the sake of conflict, which can be what litigation becomes and so that was a mismatch for me that I didn't recognize at the time.

The other thing was that in that firm of ninety-two lawyers, there were only seven women, all associates. The firm had had one woman partner in its history. She had since left to go on the federal bench. That was a time of change for the profession and for this and other law firms and also a challenging time for the women who were trying to break longstanding barriers. There was a lot of adjustment going on, so there were challenges for everyone in terms of working out what the expectations of all of us were around those big changes at that time.

PROFESSOR LONGAN: Well, as you think about life as a woman in a big law firm, there came a time early in your career you found out you were going to have your first child. I was wondering if you wouldn't mind sharing with the students what the law firm's reaction was to that.

DEAN FLOYD: Yes, well, the law firm had adopted a maternity leave policy that was quite advanced for its time, and they were very proud of it, and I think that was in part because the woman partner had, after becoming partner, had her first child, and at the time she had moved the firm towards a maternity leave policy. So, as part of the firm's recruiting of young women lawyers, it had proudly invoked the availability of this maternity leave policy. But then when there were three of us who within several months of each other announced our pregnancies, and the reality hit that now it was time to implement the maternity leave policy, it became a new challenge for the firm to really live into that commitment for the first time. And for the women, well, it was new for us to be lawyers and new to be mothers; we were figuring out how to be both, much less how to combine the roles.

As an entity I think the firm worked to be welcoming. But there were some individual lawyers in the firm who didn't know how to deal with it. The way that that got communicated to me was that my decision to get pregnant at that point in my career was perceived as a lack of commitment to the firm and its work, and that was a hard thing for me to deal with. I don't want to say that that was a uniform reaction, but that was a reaction of one of my immediate supervisors, and it did lead to a difficult conversation with him at the time that I was going out on maternity leave. That was very painful. He pretty much told me, "I think you've set back your career enormously at this point," and that was tough.

PROFESSOR LONGAN: Well, you made a career change.

DEAN FLOYD: I did, yes. I decided not to go back to the firm when my daughter was born.

PROFESSOR LONGAN: And went back to the University of Georgia.

DEAN FLOYD: I did.

PROFESSOR LONGAN: You started as a legal writing—tell me exactly what your capacity was.

DEAN FLOYD: Yeah, I started teaching legal writing, which at that time at the University of Georgia, I think it still is perhaps, not a tenure-track position, so it was a staff position as an instructor. I became director of the legal writing program pretty soon after I started, still not a tenure-track faculty position, but one that gave me some administrative responsibilities along with teaching. Being hired to teach legal writing at UGA was my introduction to being a legal educator, and consistent with this theme of maybe not having my career very well plotted out, that job came about without any planning on my part.

After the birth of our daughter, we went back to Athens, where my father-in-law was a minister, to have her baptized. The dean of the law school was a member of that church. He came up to my husband and me, and he said, "you know what, we've got a couple of openings at the law school that I think you-all would be really well suited for." We had not really been thinking about moving into legal education full-time, but when it presented itself, it seemed like the right move, and at that point we did make the change. We both moved from being associates in large firms in Atlanta. My husband became the assistant director of UGA's Legal Aid clinic, and I began to teach legal writing. That was really how our career paths changed and how we got started in legal education. We both love teaching, which we've been doing ever since, so that was a really good move for us. But it was not a planned move at the time.

PROFESSOR LONGAN: That's what I wanted to ask you about because I know these first-year students hear advice from older lawyers, and sometimes that advice is plan everything, right?

DEAN FLOYD: Yes.

PROFESSOR LONGAN: Plan your career, decide what you're going to do and go for it. But your career has not been like that.

DEAN FLOYD: No, it really hasn't been like that.

PROFESSOR LONGAN: I mean, from one move to another it has been serendipity, fortuity, but also seizing of opportunities as they came along.

DEAN FLOYD: Yes, it has.

PROFESSOR LONGAN: You've been teaching ever since. What is it you like about that?

DEAN FLOYD: There's a lot that I like about it. One of the things that I like about teaching in a law school is that I am able to still have one foot in the profession and one foot in academia. That's good, because while I did not practice law for very long, I really do love lawyers, and I love the profession. So, it's been fun to be able to teach in a setting that keeps me connected to the profession, for all the reasons that drew me into the profession in the first place. Of course, the best thing about teaching is the students. Students come in with new energy every year, and being able to watch students at the beginning of their careers and then follow them throughout their careers is such a privilege. I've been doing this now over thirty years, so I've got a lot of former students whose careers have taken various twists and turns that I'm still in touch with. Getting to watch them as their careers unfold has been really exciting. Also, there's an intellectual challenge to teaching that I enjoy. There's a piece of connecting to people around teaching that I find satisfying as well. So, all of those things I've found really gratifying through the years.

PROFESSOR LONGAN: Well, as they say back in my home state and your adopted home state of Texas, you're preaching to the choir.

DEAN FLOYD: Indeed.

PROFESSOR LONGAN: But you chose eventually to become first Associate Dean at Texas Tech and then, goodness gracious, dean of a law school.

DEAN FLOYD: Yes, I did.

PROFESSOR LONGAN: And that's a totally different job.

DEAN FLOYD: It is.

PROFESSOR LONGAN: It's not just a progression from professor. It's a totally different job. Why did you do that, and what did you like about it?

DEAN FLOYD: Well, again, the associate dean opportunity came because of a dean at my law school in Texas who asked me to serve that role. It was, again, not something that I really had sought out. I had moved from being a legal writing teacher at the University of Georgia to then we moved to Texas, and actually my husband got the job in Texas first as a tenure-track member of the faculty, and then later I was hired on the tenure-track faculty of the law school there. So that was a change from one kind of teaching position to another kind of teaching position.

I say all that by way of explaining that I was still fairly early in developing that tenure-track career when the associate dean opportunity presented itself, and I had not really thought about going into law school administration before that. The dean came to me, told me he thought I was well suited for this role and that he wanted me to consider accepting the role. I did and ended up serving almost eight years as associate dean for academic affairs.

During that time, I learned that there were a lot of things about administration that I liked. Now, interestingly, because I'd been director of a legal writing program earlier, I had begun to see some of those things about what I liked in that position, and then when I became associate dean, I saw some of those things again. I liked the idea of having the big picture about curriculum, about pedagogy, about the institution. I liked the idea of thinking about how you move an institution from where it is to where it wants to be. I liked the problem-solving challenges of having a role of responsibility in an institution composed of highly educated, very smart, very vocal, very good advocates that you're working with all of the time. That presents both opportunity and challenge, and I enjoy that. I enjoy the connections with the larger university that happen when you're in that kind of administrative role; you get to see where the law school fits in more broadly with the rest of the university. So, of course, that sort of planted the seed for me to think about becoming a dean. And then at the time that our youngest child graduated from high school, it seemed a time when we might be ready to make a move, and that's when I decided to apply to several schools to become dean. Fortunately for me and my family, I ended up here at Mercer as dean.

PROFESSOR LONGAN: I'll note for the record that my greatest contribution to the history of Mercer law school is that I made the call.

DEAN FLOYD: You did make the call, that's true.

PROFESSOR LONGAN: I made the initial phone call.

DEAN FLOYD: That's true.

PROFESSOR LONGAN: At the urging of Jack Sammons.

DEAN FLOYD: Yes. In fact, I can picture where I was standing in my kitchen in my home in Lubbock, Texas when Professor Longan called to talk to me about this job. And here we are almost exactly ten years later.

PROFESSOR LONGAN: One of the things that I know the students are curious about is how you manage to do everything you do and still have a happy home life and raise two wonderful children. How do you balance all of that? Is there a secret formula? If so, please tell us.

DEAN FLOYD: I don't think there's a secret formula, and I don't know that I've always done it as well as I could. But I feel grateful to have been able to have a career where I didn't feel as if I had to sacrifice my career to do what I wanted to do to be a good parent, and I didn't feel that I had to sacrifice being a good parent for the benefit of my career, and so I've been very fortunate about that. By way of advice, my first piece of advice is to choose carefully whom you marry because that's very important. I had the good fortune to marry somebody who's been an equal partner in all aspects of my life, both personal and professional, all along. Tim and I were able to grow into that personal and professional partnership from the beginning. We married right before we started law school, and so we began our married lives with an equal emphasis on both of our careers, and then we've carried that over.

One thing about balancing family and career is to try to be in a situation where you have some control over your schedule, and as professionals we're able to do that, and that's a privilege. It carries responsibility with it, of course, but the ability to juggle happens in large part because you're in a situation where you can, for example, choose to leave the office at three o'clock and go to an after-school event, even if it means you're working after dinner or you're getting up very early the next morning to do your work. We've been able to blend, pretty successfully, our personal and our professional lives. I wouldn't hold us up as models on every single day, but I think on balance we're pretty satisfied with what we've been able to do.

PROFESSOR LONGAN: I want to shift gears now.

DEAN FLOYD: Okay.

PROFESSOR LONGAN: Because there came a time when you found yourself in need of a lawyer, and that is a traumatic event in the life of people who find themselves there.

DEAN FLOYD: Yes.

PROFESSOR LONGAN: Tell the students about what happened to lead to that, then I want to talk to you about your experience with your particular lawyer.

DEAN FLOYD: Okay. Yeah, I'll be glad to share that experience. I don't want to get into all of the detail. It's a very long story, and the details don't matter too much, but I do want to give you enough of that story so that y'all have a sense of how it felt to be in that situation and to need a lawyer, and so that you can understand the role that my lawyer played.

I was at my former institution. I had been serving as associate dean for probably five, six, maybe seven years, anyway, quite a while. I'd been in the associate dean role there for some time, had been a faculty member, had been very active in the local community and been active within the university. I was a fully tenured member of the law faculty and associate dean at the time. The dean of the law school announced that he was leaving to go take a different position, and so there was beginning the process to engage in a dean search for the law school. I was asked to serve on the dean search committee, which was pretty normal for the associate dean, and about three weeks after that process began, the dean of the law school came back from a meeting with the president of the university very upset. He told me that during that conversation the president of the university had indicated that he would not be open to appointing a woman as the next dean of the law school. And that's troubling for all the reasons that you-all will understand that it's troubling on many levels, but it was also troubling to me as a member of the search committee. I now had knowledge that that this was going to be a search that was likely to involve illegalities, discrimination, unfairness, and I had to decide what to do with that piece of information.

PROFESSOR LONGAN: May I add one little piece to this?

DEAN FLOYD: Yes.

PROFESSOR LONGAN: And that is, that as the long-term associate dean, it would be almost natural, not inevitable, but almost natural that you would step into the interim dean role.

DEAN FLOYD: Yes.

PROFESSOR LONGAN: Although I know that's not a job you were seeking, the president's statement that no woman will be the dean, and I know he didn't say it that way but that was the import of it.

DEAN FLOYD: Right.

PROFESSOR LONGAN: He said it in a much more vulgar way, that really had a direct impact on you.

DEAN FLOYD: Well, it did. And, in fact, I had decided I was not going to seek the permanent deanship there. There were reasons that I didn't think that would be a good match for me or for the institution, but I actually had asked to be considered for the interim dean position. And there is a piece of this that ends up being a little bit of a tangential piece, but that was a piece of this that had to do with that interim dean process. So, it did feel quite personal in a number of ways, because certainly that comment, I thought, reflected on my own position within the university as well as that of all women within the university. Also, as a member of the search committee, not only did I want the search to be fair, but I already had been charged with recruiting a couple of very high-profile women lawyers in the state to enter the search, and so to do that at a time when I knew that really there was intent at the top not to appoint a woman presented quite a dilemma. By the way, the president of that university denies making that comment. So, the facts were disputed, but I was convinced then and still am that what I had been told was credible and that it presented a credible threat to the search process.

PROFESSOR LONGAN: What happened next?

DEAN FLOYD: What happened next was that I decided to seek the advice of someone in the university administration who was in the provost's office, the senior woman in the university and someone with whom I had dealt pretty closely over the years. That quickly took a nasty turn because within about an hour of seeking her advice I was summoned to the president's office and to a meeting with the president and a number of other people where, well, let's just say it was an unpleasant meeting. The president was very upset. I perceived his actions to be threatening, and at the end of the meeting, we left without my having conceded that that was going to be the end of it, which is what he had been seeking to get me to concede. In other words, he wanted me to say that I did not think that what I had been told about his intent to discriminate was true and that I planned to drop the matter. During the meeting—

PROFESSOR LONGAN: Can I say—having heard the description of it, and I'm not going to put words in your mouth, but I would say, based on what I've heard about that meeting, that it looked like an attempt to intimidate you.

DEAN FLOYD: It was an attempt to intimidate me. There's no question about it. In fact, at one point one of the senior administrators in the meeting pretty much had to sort of body block, I think, an attempt by the president to get physical. I mean, he was very upset. Let me just make sure that everyone here understands that this happened before I came to Mercer. This was at my former institution. It was very clearly intimidating and threatening, and there's a record that has pretty much a reconstructed transcript of that meeting. The meeting lasted over an hour, until I finally realized it was up to me to call the meeting to a halt, and I did that.

During that meeting, by the way, the dean of the law school was summoned in, at which point he repeated his allegation of what had happened, that is, the president's comment to him that he wouldn't appoint a woman—in front of the president, and general counsel for the university, who was there, the provost for the university, and the chief of staff of the president's office. There were about eight people in the room. The dean repeated the allegation. He and the president both offered to take lie detector tests, which they never did, but it did raise that allegation to the point that now we had the dean repeating that allegation in front of a number of senior administrators in the room, which, again, is a pretty powerful allegation.

From the time that I first heard about that remark to that meeting was maybe several weeks because it took me a while to decide what I was going to do. But the meeting happened within several hours of my having gone to seek the advice of this woman within the administration. And in retrospect I probably should have been prepared for that sort of reaction. I wasn't. I did not expect that to happen so quickly. That was on a Friday, and I remember going home that evening and thinking, "I need a lawyer. I need a lawyer. I'm not going to be able to navigate this on my own." And that was a really startling moment in my life, as I'm sure it is for many clients, because suddenly I realized that although I'd been used to managing my own life pretty well up til now, not only was I in a situation where I felt like I needed to hire someone to help me, but it was a situation that involved people that I had worked closely with over a number of years and involved the institution of which I felt I was really an important part and which meant a lot to me. So it was a really dramatic moment when I realized that I needed to hire a lawyer.

PROFESSOR LONGAN: How would you characterize that moment? I think of it as a time of vulnerability, of not quite helplessness but enormous vulnerability.

DEAN FLOYD: Yes, it is a time of enormous vulnerability when you realize you've got a big problem that threatens your life in some way, and it's a problem that you can't handle on your own. And for most of us who've been pretty good at managing our own lives so far, that's really almost an assault on your identity. So, it is a sea change in how you see yourself. Ironically, I had been telling students for years that the moment somebody hires you as their lawyer, it's probably a bad moment in their lives, but I didn't really know what that meant until I experienced that moment myself. I remember being really frightened. I didn't know whether I was going to be fired over the weekend. You know, I didn't know what sorts of things were going to happen next.

PROFESSOR LONGAN: One thing that I want the students to realize from that is that being a client makes you a different lawyer; is that fair?

DEAN FLOYD: Yes, it does.

PROFESSOR LONGAN: Because you really do experience what you've been telling them all along. That they come to you at a time when they really need something.

DEAN FLOYD: Right.

PROFESSOR LONGAN: You needed a lawyer, you needed to pick a lawyer. You knew a lot of lawyers.

DEAN FLOYD: Yes, I did know a lot of lawyers.

PROFESSOR LONGAN: How did you pick the lawyer you picked?

DEAN FLOYD: I picked the lawyer I picked because at that moment my desire was to try to work things out in a non-adversarial way. I've already told you I don't really thrive in conflict. I can handle conflict, but I don't enjoy conflict. I wanted somebody who could maybe help us work through to some sort of mediated resolution. It seemed to me that there were issues about this search going forward. Number one, we needed to protect that. We didn't need this to blow up publicly because we were in the midst of wanting to hire somebody to be a new dean. And I wanted to continue to work at the institution. My husband worked there. These were people I knew who were involved; they were my colleagues.

So I hired a lawyer who was practicing in Austin who had been a former prosecutor, a former very hard-charging litigator, but who now took a different approach to resolving disputes. I think he would have described himself earlier in his career as a Rambo kind of litigator. You-all may not know that term, but it is a very hard-charging litigator. He had changed his practice in the previous decade or so, had become certified as a mediator, and had become convinced that often litigation exacerbates disputes instead of helping to resolve them. I knew that he had a real intention around trying to work things out, and I trusted him on a personal level. I had had him come speak to my classes before. I'd known him through some state bar work. I think it would be a stretch to say we were friends at that point, but we were acquaintances. We had encountered each other in a number of ways. So I did seek—

that meeting happened on a Friday. I think maybe within a few days I was down in Austin in his office talking with him about what happened and what we wanted to do about it.

PROFESSOR LONGAN: So you're in a situation where you have a lot of goals.

DEAN FLOYD: Yes.

PROFESSOR LONGAN: You want to protect yourself, and I don't mean for that to sound selfish. I mean, you've earned your spot.

DEAN FLOYD: That's definitely one, yeah.

PROFESSOR LONGAN: You want to protect yourself. You want to protect the search. You'd like to protect the university while you're at it. You'd like to protect the people who are innocent from potential collateral damage—

DEAN FLOYD: Right.

PROFESSOR LONGAN: —in all of this. An awful lot of uncertainty.

DEAN FLOYD: Yes.

PROFESSOR LONGAN: What will they do? What was next on their horizon? What if, what if?

DEAN FLOYD: Yes, lots of what ifs.

PROFESSOR LONGAN: What if.

DEAN FLOYD: I didn't have Professor Longan's what-if analysis then. I wish I had, but...

PROFESSOR LONGAN: So you needed somebody to help you chart a course.

DEAN FLOYD: Yes.

PROFESSOR LONGAN: You needed somebody to help you be wise.

DEAN FLOYD: Right.

PROFESSOR LONGAN: How did he do that? What was that relationship like?

DEAN FLOYD: He helped me a great deal, and I'm really grateful to him. As you-all may know, many people who find themselves in these kinds of situations suffer great losses personally and professionally. This did end up in litigation several years later because things went from bad to worse. So my lawyer and I had a long relationship, and he helped me through it all. He helped me, first, by really wanting to closely identify my goals. I can remember at our first meeting in his office he really wanted me to talk about my goals: my long-term goals, my short-term goals, and to keep an eye on the big picture. One of the reasons that I had hired him is because I knew that his intention was to seek resolution of issues rather than exacerbating conflict.

Another thing—I knew that he had his own committed faith tradition. It was different from mine, but I knew that he had that, so I felt like there would be space for him to take into the representation values that I was bringing into the representation about what I wanted to do. And that proved to be very true in our relationship.

He helped me the most in two ways I would identify. One is that he had come to believe during his years as a lawyer that fear accounts for most of the bad things that people do when they're in difficult situations, situations of conflict. Mark was very intentional always about identifying what I was afraid of and what we thought others who were involved in this might be afraid of. By doing that, he had a way of bringing our deliberations to a point of recognizing the humanity of everybody involved. Focusing on everyone's humanity was helpful. It is harder to demonize people when you're talking about what they're afraid of. It makes it harder to get on your high horse when you're talking about what you're afraid of. That was something that he did for me that was really helpful, and I've carried that lesson with me since. Now, if I get in a situation of conflict, or when I'm upset about the way someone else is acting, I try to ask myself what fears might be motivating that person or me in the situation. That often helps me to think differently about the person I'm struggling with.

The other thing that he did was lots of Socratic type of questioning. We would be talking about things, and you know, when you're in the middle of conflict, you're mad, you feel like you've got right and might on your side, and you want to do something out of that, and he would often get me to focus by asking questions: What's your real motivation here? What do you think is going to happen if you do this? Let's play this out. What are your long-term goals? Where do you want to be in six months? Where do you want to be in two years? And I remember he said to me one time—I was really caught up and angry and wanted him to do something kind of explosive, and he said, "we can do that, and I will do that, but I want to remind you that you told me earlier this is where you want to end up," and he said, "I don't think you'll be happy in a few months if you look back and see that this is what we've done."

Having him being willing to challenge me in those situations was really helpful. He had to bring that big picture into the decision-making that I wasn't capable of doing for myself in the midst of emotion, conflict, anger, fear, and the expectations of so many other people once this became public. It took about a year for it to become public. Once it did, then a lot of people were involved and had their own expectations about what I should do. So I'm very grateful to have had a lawyer who helped me focus on my goals, who could guide me in this way.

PROFESSOR LONGAN: There are a couple of things I find interesting about your description of that. First of all, he made no assumptions about what your real goals were.

DEAN FLOYD: No, he didn't.

PROFESSOR LONGAN: He took the time to find out.

DEAN FLOYD: Yes, he did.

PROFESSOR LONGAN: He didn't direct you?

DEAN FLOYD: No, he didn't direct me, although he certainly would offer what he thought I ought to be thinking about, so in that sense he didn't just leave it up to me, but, no, he was a really effective listener and questioner, and I know he got tired of doing that probably because that's time-consuming. He had a busy practice, and I'm sure he thought sometimes, "I've got to listen to this woman again," you know, allow her to talk over and over again. When you're going through something like that, boy, you really want to vent, and your lawyer is the safe place to vent, right? So that's another thing that I learned about being a client. The lawyers get it all. It just kind of gets dumped on the lawyer, and he was very good about that. I remember that sometimes he'd say, "okay, you're venting now, and that's kind of expensive for both of us, so maybe we ought to move on." He was able to challenge me in that way. We had the kind of relationship where we could do that.

PROFESSOR LONGAN: But he offered you advice. This was not a passive—

DEAN FLOYD: He did absolutely offer advice. And I hired him for his expertise because he had expertise that I didn't have, which is what I needed.

PROFESSOR LONGAN: I want to ask you about a particular moment in this process.

DEAN FLOYD: Okay.

PROFESSOR LONGAN: This is the moment when you see a piece of paper that says your name, plaintiff, and the institution you have served for all these years as defendant.

DEAN FLOYD: Yes.

PROFESSOR LONGAN: What was that like?

DEAN FLOYD: That was really difficult. I recall that moment quite clearly. I told you it took a while to get to the point where we filed a lawsuit, so let me give a little bit of background. One of the things that happened after this meeting with the president, and my first meeting with my lawyer, is that I decided that I should share what I knew with the search committee because this was really a problem for the search committee about how to go forward. I decided a means for doing that. We had a search committee meeting coming up. I talked to the chair of the committee and asked to be on the agenda. University general counsel knew that I'd asked about this, knew that I planned to speak. After some drama, the meeting went forward, and I spoke to the committee. The committee responded really well, and for a moment we thought that we had a process in place that was going to protect applicants and protect the university. We were satisfied with that. We thought maybe that was going to be the end.

But it was not the end. It was not the end in part because a so-called error suddenly affected my monthly paycheck that didn't get resolved for many months. In other words, my paycheck was reduced after I spoke to the search committee about what the president had allegedly said. Even though the University later called it a "clerical error," it took more than six months to get it fixed and to correct my monthly salary to the proper amount. So, a reduction in pay became the basis of one of the acts of retaliation that was alleged in the lawsuit when it was filed. I tell you all this to give you this sequence of events because for about a year this problem was completely private, very few people knew about it. The search committee knew, a couple of close friends knew, the people who had been involved in it knew, so my lawyer and I were working behind the scenes on all of this trying to work things out where the University would agree to an open and fair search and where my pay would be restored, among some other things.

There came a moment when—because of the passage of time—if I didn't file an EEOC complaint, I was going to give up some rights, including my rights with regard to my salary, so I filed an EEOC complaint. Well, of course, that's public record. Almost a year after the events began, an enterprising reporter for the university newspaper asked the university to disclose any EEOC filings that had been made against them, and mine was among those, and so he ran a very extensive story in the university paper. That's the point at which the whole thing became public. That changed the dynamics dramatically, changed what I needed from my lawyer dramatically, because now the lawyer became my public spokesperson in a situation that was getting a lot of attention locally and throughout the state. I found that hard. I have a few control issues, I guess. I don't really like somebody else out there speaking for me, and so that was a new thing for me to experience as a client.

By the way, just so you-all will know, one of the things that happened after all of this became public was a student march on the president's office. I mean, this whole thing was pretty dramatic for lots of people. (Laughter.) So, a group of law students marched on the president's office. The president ended up leaving the institution for another job. We thought things were getting better. It turns out they didn't get better. They continued to get worse for a variety of reasons that don't really matter for our purposes today. About a year and a half to two years after all of this began is when I filed the lawsuit. It was quite a journey to get from the meeting in the president's office and my hiring a lawyer to determining to file a lawsuit. Some of the reason to file a lawsuit was sheer frustration, feeling like that was the only thing that was going to help things get better.

My lawyer and I had been working together on drafting this complaint, sending documents back and forth to each other, and I remember well when the final document rolled off my printer. That's the moment you were asking about, when I see my name as plaintiff versus my institution. It made me realize what litigants go through when they become parties to lawsuits. My lawyer's name was on that document, but his name was at the end of the document, a multi-page document, right? It was not right up front, but mine was. My name was up there all by itself on that side of the "v." I had never, up until that moment in my life, felt like I had enemies in the world, and all of a sudden, there it was in black and white. You know, when you've got that "v." between your name and other people's names, that means that you're in an adversarial relationship that's official, that's public, that's known. Parties are drawing up sides to go after each other, which made me think about myself in a new way. That was a really momentous realization for me. That sticks in my mind clearly.

PROFESSOR LONGAN: Litigation is stressful for the client. I think that's clear. If you could talk a little bit about what it was like to be a client during the litigation, and then I want you to talk about the decision that eventually came along to drop the case.

DEAN FLOYD: Okay. Being a client during the litigation was hard because now all of a sudden, a lot more people were involved, either officially or unofficially. This dispute becomes public, and lots of people feel pressure to take sides. There are expectations around you. Some people think that you're going to be "the one who's finally going to clean this place up," which of course we know a simple lawsuit probably can't do that. People have expectations around what the law is going to be able to do for you that are not realistic.

Parties have a lot of tools at their disposal to make life difficult for the other party. The university spared no expense. When my deposition was taken, there were five lawyers for the university at the table: university general counsel, private counsel from a major law firm in Houston, and the state attorney general's office had representation there. It was another moment of realizing what you're taking on. Now, I want to be clear: I was the plaintiff, so I did this voluntarily, nobody did it to me, and I certainly had my eyes open going in, but it's different to think you understand what's going to happen and then actually experiencing it. Going through discovery is like just opening up your life to the world.

They were not only deposing me, they're deposing my friends, my colleagues. They want a bunch of my emails. You all know they're entitled to emails in which there's been any discussion relating to the subject of the litigation. Well, you can imagine over the course of two-plus years in an emotional event like that there were a lot of emails that people had sent me that those people did not expect at some point would be turned over to lawyers or seen by university officials. So it was really difficult for me and a lot of other people. I think workplace disputes are a little bit like family law disputes, in that they pull a lot of people in.

One of the things that happens often in these kinds of disputes is that the visible pressure on the plaintiff, or the person who's spoken up, is calculated in part for its effect on other people who are watching. There is an attempt to control the behavior of other people who are in the workplace, in addition to the one who's brought the claim. For example, there were friends or colleagues who would go to lunch with me, but we couldn't leave the law school together to go to lunch. We had to meet at the restaurant. Because they didn't want to be seen going to lunch with me. Or other people I had been friends with who suddenly didn't want to talk to me or see me at all. There were some people who stuck with me really heroically and at some real expense to their own careers. I'm forever grateful to them. But there were others who, for whatever reason, didn't or couldn't make that choice. And so it was hard. Some of those people I had previously considered to be friends.

Also, you're conscious of the fact that you're bringing this down on your workplace. Trust me, you don't really want to be in that situation of causing so much hardship. And yet I felt from the beginning that my only other choice was to not be truthful about what I knew. And I just could never—I could never get to the point where I didn't think I could be truthful about what I knew. You know, this had landed in my lap, it was wrong, and I felt like I had to speak up.

PROFESSOR LONGAN: You did, and then you decided eventually to drop the case. Talk just a minute about that.

DEAN FLOYD: Yeah. Well, I decided to drop the case after I got hired at Mercer. While all of this was going on I decided to get into dean searches. That was probably unrealistic, in retrospect. I can't imagine why I thought that would be successful, but thankfully it was. One of my damages claims was harm to my future administrative career because, as you-all can imagine, there are a lot of bad things that get said about you when you're in that kind of situation. But I decided anyway to pursue a deanship at another law school. My son had graduated from high school, we were freer to move, and it would have been the next step in my career without this incident. So, I thought, "well, I'm going to go ahead and pursue this," so I had applied to several schools, and I had the interview at Mercer. Mercer was willing to look at everything that had happened that led to my filing the lawsuit and afterwards. I don't think it was the conversation with you where I brought up the lawsuit, that first conversation.

PROFESSOR LONGAN: Not the first one.

DEAN FLOYD: But the first conversation with the representative of the search firm who was handling my search, we talked about it. Anyway, I got hired at Mercer even though I was a plaintiff in a discrimination case against my then-institution. Presidents make decisions about who's going to be dean. I was a plaintiff in a case against my employer alleging that the president had done something wrongful. As someone said at the time, that's not really a resume builder when you're applying to be a dean. But, Dr. Kirby Godsey, who was president then at Mercer, was willing to look at all of the facts, and he ultimately concluded that nothing he learned detracted from what Mercer wanted in a dean. So I got hired here to be dean, and then had a decision to make about how I wanted to spend the next few years of my life. I decided that I was ready to move on, that I wanted to devote my full time and attention to Mercer, and so I voluntarily dismissed the lawsuit.

PROFESSOR LONGAN: I know some people thought, back in Texas, that you shouldn't do that.

DEAN FLOYD: Yes.

PROFESSOR LONGAN: I won't pretend to a cause and effect here, but I do want to note that the dean of the Texas Tech law school is a woman now.

DEAN FLOYD: That's true.

PROFESSOR LONGAN: Normally at this point I would invite you to offer advice to the students, but I think what I would rather do is make sure I've got time in case they have questions for you.

DEAN FLOYD: Okay, that will be fine.

PROFESSOR LONGAN: So why don't we do that, and then if we have time I'll give you the advice question.

DEAN FLOYD: Okay.

DEAN FLOYD: Great. What's on your minds?

LAW STUDENT: I have a question. You have a great pedagogic interest in what makes attorneys and how they form their ideals in law schools. I'm wondering what really piqued your interest in that unique area of law?

DEAN FLOYD: Well, it's a good question. Two things I think piqued my interest. One was becoming associate dean for academic affairs where I saw the institution from a different perspective than I had from just being a classroom teacher. Part of the job at that institution had overlapped very closely with the dean of students role, and I was dealing with a lot of students who were having difficulty in law school. I began to see that maybe there was something systematic happening that was causing some of these problems or challenges that I was seeing.

About that time, I also had the opportunity to get involved with the Carnegie Foundation's research on legal education, and so I took that interest and was able to explore it through their support, and that started that journey. It's pretty clear, too, that my own experience of being an unhappy law student informed that interest, as well, but I think it took that experience of being associate dean to tie those threads together.

LAW STUDENT: I thank you for sharing a very personal story.

DEAN FLOYD: You're welcome.

LAW STUDENT (FOLLOW-UP HERE AND BELOW): It sounds a lot like some of the hypotheticals that we run into about, we have an administrator or senior partner in a firm and what do you do?

PROFESSOR LONGAN: What a coincidence.

LAW STUDENT: I know, really.

LAW STUDENT: How do you like my insightful analysis there?

DEAN FLOYD: (Laughing).

LAW STUDENT: One of the questions that we're always asked in our discussion groups is, "what if you had done something differently?" I mean, I'm sure you've talked a lot about it with not just your family, but thought about it.

DEAN FLOYD: I have.

LAW STUDENT: Would you have gone to that female provost official, would you have addressed the president himself personally? Would you have done it all differently if you could do it all over again?

DEAN FLOYD: It's so interesting that you ask that question because I actually don't think about it a whole lot anymore, but in the immediate aftermath I spent a lot of time thinking about those questions. And, of course, while you're in the midst of it you think about that, "what if I'd done this or what if I'd done that?" I think it's very useful to ask yourself a lot of questions ahead of time—the what ifs—and play it out as you make decisions. It can be useful up to a point to ask yourself those questions afterwards, also, as that's how we learn from experience and get better. But there's always some unknown that you just didn't know about at the time you make a decision. Where I've finally ended up is to say, "you know what, I tried to make the best judgments I could under the circumstances." I don't think every decision I made was the right one, but I tried to have good people around me helping me make those decisions at the time, and I tried to be as self-aware as I could.

I think it's clear I made some mistakes, but that's going to be inevitable. When you're acting in an environment of inherent uncertainty, it's difficult, and you're not going to get it right every time. But I did try to look ahead and do the best I could to make the best decisions I could. That's something that the lawyer did for me: you need somebody who's objective, when you're in that situation. My husband was very much involved, and he was a good counselor. I had some good friends and colleagues who were, but they were all invested in the situation in a way that the lawyer was not. He cared, but he had objectivity that none of us had. So it's one of the things that I counted on the lawyer to do, is to help me run those what ifs in a way that down the road I wouldn't have regrets. Sometimes he would say that to me, "Daisy, if we go in this direction, I think you're going to regret it." That was helpful.

LAW STUDENT: What do you think would have happened if you had not voluntarily dismissed the case?

DEAN FLOYD: I think it would have been a long, protracted and ugly process that would have been hard on me and my family and friends and distracting to my job here. I don't know that we would have gone to trial; we likely would have ended up settling, as most lawsuits do. I think we had a good enough case that we might have gotten some recovery. But part of the difficulty with the case legally was that as a tenured member of the law faculty I had not been fired. It would be very difficult to fire me, so my damages were not at the same level as many plaintiffs are when are they're filing these kind of workplace discrimination lawsuits. Because one of my major elements of damages was harm to my future career, and Mercer had just disproved that element—

PROFESSOR LONGAN: You're welcome.

DEAN FLOYD: Yes, thankfully. (Laughter.)

DEAN FLOYD: Thankfully, that's what you want. You know, we really—probably the legal aspects were lessened somewhat by my coming to Mercer, so that was part of the calculation, but also knowing that litigation gives people tools to be very destructive of each other. I think it would have gone on that way for a while, and I just wasn't willing to do that anymore. Part of my motivation had been to try to change the institution I was a part of, and I struggled with this decision at the time, but I was now going to be part of a new institution, and I decided I had to leave that struggle to those who were still at the institution. Who knows what would have happened, but I think it would have been difficult.

LAW STUDENT: Having done practice, education, and administration, are there any other parts of the legal world that you would like to participate in or maybe wish you had?

DEAN FLOYD: (Laughing) That's a good question. No, I did have a little foray into the possibility of a judicial appointment a couple of years ago and was willing to look into that and be considered for that because of my respect for the judiciary and the importance of that work and a feeling that I thought that might be a place where I could contribute. I think probably that impulse and opportunity have passed, so I don't see myself pursuing that, no. I'm really happy being a law professor the rest of my life.

PROFESSOR LONGAN: I'll tell you because she won't. The Obama administration was considering her for appointment to the Eleventh Circuit, so that's what that was.

LAW STUDENT: It seems like in a lot of our hypos doing the right thing just for the sake of doing the right thing has a lot of personal consequences, so was it worth it?

DEAN FLOYD: It's an excellent question, and I've pondered that question. Because at some point, I was motivated by lots of things, and it's easy to say you're motivated by wanting to help the institution and do all this, but there was this part of me that was just like, this is the right thing to do and, by God, I'm going to do it no matter what it takes. That's a dangerous impulse. You have to be aware of that. But, yes, I do think it was worth it in the sense that it felt all along like a choice of whether to abide by personal integrity or not. I just don't think you can give away your integrity and live with that well. I've been really fortunate that that decision has been borne out by the fact that I did have an institution that was willing to look at it and end up saying to me, as Mercer did, "we kind of like what this has to say about you," rather than it being a negative, so I'm really fortunate. Not everybody who gets in that situation is that fortunate.

But I do want you to take that lesson away, that at the beginning of all of this there were people, including my dean, who said, "do not do this. You're going to ruin your career. You're going to ruin your career." Maybe it was foolishness on my part or just an understanding that I couldn't live with myself, if I just was silent and watched this happen, that had me go forward, but fortunately it didn't ruin my career, and, in fact, I think I learned a lot through that process that made me come out better on the other end. I credit my lawyer in part for that. He allowed me to make decisions that were consistent with my integrity and allowed me to be better at the end than I was at the beginning. I don't think that would have happened in the hands of every lawyer. I am sure that there were other lawyers who could have done it, but he was key to that.

So, yes, I think it was worth it. I'll have to say I also was thinking about the fact that I tell my children, "this is the way you ought to live your lives. Stand up for what's right and for the truth and your own integrity." I'd been telling my students, "this is the way you ought to live your lives," so I thought, "well, if you're not willing to do this, you'd better just shut up about that." Right? Stop telling other people—(Laughter)—that they should do this, and stop telling people they should do things that are hard unless you're willing to do them. When it became public and my students learned what had happened, you know, that was a moment for me when I thought, "okay, I'm glad I'm not embarrassed by what they've learned." I'll just have to tell you those students kept me going for that six months or so after it became public, because that was a very difficult period in my life, and the students were unbelievable.

PROFESSOR LONGAN: I know you have a class to teach.

DEAN FLOYD: I do have a class to teach. Although I don't mind sticking around if I'm a little late to class. You-all wait for me, but... (Laughter.)

PROFESSOR LONGAN: Thank you, Daisy.

(Applause.)

A Conversation with Justice Hardy Gregory, Jr.

Introduction by Cal Callier[*]

I met Justice Gregory in 1987 when I interviewed for a clerkship. He had been on the Georgia Supreme Court for several years. When the interview ended, he offered me the position. There was one condition. I must stay for at least one year, but I could not stay longer than two. He was not looking for a long-term assistant to do his work for him. Instead, he was offering an opportunity for a young lawyer to gain experience and learn, at our State's highest court, before making his own way in our profession. I accepted his offer, we shook hands, and I promised him one year. That one year has now become a lasting thirty-five-year friendship.

I quickly realized that a twenty-minute commute could easily become an hour or more during morning rush hour. Even though I tried to arrive before daylight, I don't think I ever beat Justice Gregory to the office. He would be at his desk, in the pre-dawn hours, working on what would become *Georgia Civil Practice*, by Hardy Gregory, Jr. For years after he left the bench, he would gather, read, and organize all of the Georgia advance sheets to edit and update *Georgia Civil Practice*. The words are his, the reasoning and the analysis are his. I urge all lawyers, especially young ones, to turn first to this resource to understand and navigate Georgia civil practice. There is no better starting point than with the Georgia code in one hand and Justice Gregory's words in the other.

Justice Gregory loves the law, for its own sake, and the legal contradictions and conflicts caused by the actions of real people, along with interference from the legislature. He had a special way of solving complex issues. He would cover his desk with paper. He would draw, in Venn diagram form, the case, the parties, their arguments and authorities. Circles, squares, lines, and arrows would connect one to another. By this, he could identify the single question or conflict that, once resolved, would settle the entire board. He was fond of the word "eureka." That word was a clear

---

[*] The Callier Law Firm, Columbus, Georgia.

signal that another mess had been untangled, often at its most simple level, and an opinion was soon to follow.

Perhaps I should not say it, but it's true. Not all of the Justices paid attention to all of the cases and issues before the Court. Some would focus solely on their assigned cases. Justice Gregory paid attention to every case. He was briefed and aware of the issues in each case, even those not assigned to him. His office was a revolving door as other Justices sought his insight into whatever legal conundrum was troubling them.

When Justice Gregory says in the interview, just "quit," he's not joking. As my clerkship was ending, we talked at length, and he gave me a lot of guidance. Those discussions did not concern money, prestige, or law firm status. I got the same advice thirty-five years ago that he gives in this interview. And he lived it himself. When his service on the Georgia Supreme Court ended, he had opportunities to join, at the highest levels, very prestigious law firms. He politely declined. He wanted to again be a lawyer representing and helping ordinary people. His judicial service over, he left Atlanta and returned to private practice in Cordele and Vienna.

We always tried to have a case going together. He would join my cases and I would join his. There's hardly been a time that we have not been working together on some case or issue. That is still true today. He has not missed a beat. He is as brilliant as ever. Working with him as a lawyer, I saw a different side of him. Trial lawyers can be a pushy and bombastic bunch. Nothing unsettles that type more than a calm, confident, quiet opponent. He is a master at getting more with less. I wish I had even a portion of that talent, or the patience to pull it off.

He mentions his class action and I chuckle. Half-heartedly. That's one case he did not invite me to work on. He was "slowing down" his practice when the client called. Although I wasn't there and I didn't see it, I know in my mind's eye what happened. He had a conference table covered with poster paper. Circles, squares, and lines ran every which way. One day he looked at it, the solution became so clear and simple, the word "eureka" rang out, and the whole board and every player on it, settled! It happened just like that; I guarantee it.

So I will add for him, the one piece of advice he forgot to mention—don't ever disconnect your phone!

JUSTICE HARDY GREGORY, JR., 2015

PROFESSOR PATRICK LONGAN: Your Honor, thank you for being with us.

JUSTICE HARDY GREGORY, Jr.: Well, thank you for inviting me. I'm delighted to be here.

PROFESSOR LONGAN: I usually start at the beginning and ask how you became a lawyer, and so on. I want to do that, but I want to ask you something a little bit different to begin with. You have a military background.

JUSTICE GREGORY: I do.

PROFESSOR LONGAN: You're a graduate of the Naval Academy.

JUSTICE GREGORY: Yes.

PROFESSOR LONGAN: You served both in the Navy and in the Air Force. I know we have a number of students who are veterans, and I was wondering if you could talk a little bit about whether that background had any effect on your choice of career, or the way you practiced law, or how you conducted yourself as a lawyer.

JUSTICE GREGORY: I'd be delighted to answer that. Well, that is a part of my life. It was ten years of my life. Five in the Navy and five in the Air Force. I grew up in a little town called Vienna down the road here, and that happens to be where Senator George, whom this institution is named for, was from. And he told me if I joined the Navy, he would give me an appointment to the Naval Academy. I joined the Navy. He did, and I went. Four years later I was graduated. There was no Air Force Academy at that time, so ten percent of West Point graduates and ten percent of Annapolis graduates could join the Air Force if they wanted to. So I did. I became a navigator, and I flew on a B-52 SAC, Strategic Air Command.

I was stationed at Warner Robins most of the time, and I don't have any war stories to tell you about that, but I've got an event to tell you about that did mark my life and probably yours, too, and you don't know it. It was October 1962. Anybody know where I'm going? We just happened to be stationed at Presque Isle, Maine in our B-52s. That aircraft at the time had four hydrogen bombs in the bomb bay. I see some acknowledgment in the audience. We had two atomic weapons that were missiles under the wings that we could pickle off and go annihilate some people over here; annihilate some people over there. And our job at the time in the Cold War was to keep these planes up most of the time, so we flew these long missions, forty-two hours sometimes. We'd go the great circle route from Warner Robins up over New York out over the Atlantic. We'd get to Spain, and a KC-135 would come up, and we'd refuel, and then we'd circle the Mediterranean for two or three times, then we'd fly back, refuel, come home, forty-two hours.

But the event I want to tell you about is that in October 1962 the Russians wanted to put missiles in Cuba—as we said back then "Cuber," because that's the way the president would pronounce it, down in "Cuber"—wanted to put missiles aimed at our cities. And John Fitzgerald Kennedy said, "I don't want you to put those missiles down there. Don't do that, please." And the picture is this: we were in the work shack up in Maine watching it play out on television. And somehow, they've got the picture of the Russian vessel bringing the missiles to Cuba, and we know the president is saying to Khrushchev, "turn it around, and if you don't turn it around we're going to blast it out of the water."

They rang our bell. Now, our target wouldn't have been that ship. We had a target in Russia. We were going to go blast this city. So they said, "get on the plane." We got on the plane. We taxied to the end of the runway, five of us, five planes, ready to go. And we sat there for about thirty minutes. It dawned on me, "this is Armageddon. This is the end of the world." You know, all my life up to then I never took it seriously. I never thought we'd have a war. I said, "if we take off and we're going to do what we're supposed to do, this will be the end." We were supposed to fly to our target, do a maneuver like this (gesturing) and drop those hydrogen bombs. Then turn right, they said, and fly to Egypt, see if you can find a landing field. This is our escape route: fly to Egypt, find a landing field and see if they'll refuel you. If you get some more fuel, don't come back to the United States because it wouldn't be here. Fly to South America, see if you can make a life for yourself. More or less, that's what we were supposed to do.

But at any rate they called us down. I go back in and I watch the TV, and what happened was we were told then, here's Kennedy, here's Khrushchev, and they told us Khrushchev blinked. They had a picture of that ship turning out in the Atlantic back to Russia, and we did not have World War III, but it had an impact on me as to what I think about war.

PROFESSOR LONGAN: It will give you a certain perspective on the rest of your life.

JUSTICE GREGORY: It does. It kind of did this to me: everything settled down about it, and I just sort of felt like I was not a military person. You people that have been in the military maybe you know what I mean. I just wasn't cut out for a command. I really didn't like to order people what to do. I find that right easy from the bench because all the rules are laid out for you. But in the military, you've got to do something different. I wasn't very good at it. So, I was thinking about coming out of that, and I'm anxious to know if your experience in life is like this: I was to get out after five years. It was somewhere along about the fourth year. We land on the strip out here at Robins and pull off on the tarmac. And Glenn Mitchell, our pilot, says, "Hardy, there's a general over there in the plane next to us that sent word over here and wants to interview you to see if you'd be his aide." That was it. I either had to go over there and interview and take that job, and I would be committed to that general and to the Air Force, or I had to not do it. Have you been there? If you haven't, you will be there. Everybody gets to a place like that. I said, Glenn, tell him no. I never met the general. And so, I got out of the Air Force.

PROFESSOR LONGAN: A moment in your life that turned it a different direction.

JUSTICE GREGORY: My life has been full of that kind of thing, if I can tell one more thing.

PROFESSOR LONGAN: Absolutely.

JUSTICE GREGORY: Because what to do now? I'm not going to be a military person. What to do? So, I talked to my wife, and she helped advise me, but I decided to take a business law course that Mr. Harmon, a nice gentleman lawyer from this area, was teaching as an extension course. Has anybody here ever had business law? Probably a lot of you. That course is what brought me to be a lawyer. One moment did it, one moment in that course. Mr. Harmon is talking to us about contracts, what it takes to make a contract. Y'all had contracts yet? All right, you know what a contract is. The world out there does not know what a contract is, I can tell you. (Laughter.) I did not know what a contract was, but Mr. Harmon said, "let me explain about a contract. The law doesn't evaluate what one person does for another, what the consideration back and forth might be. It doesn't weigh that consideration, but the law requires that there be consideration." He says, "Hardy, a peppercorn would be sufficient." I don't know if they still teach that or not, a peppercorn, and that hit me like a ton of bricks. It exploded in my head. "I understand," I said, "yes, that makes sense." (Laughter.) The law is not going to evaluate the deal we make, but it's going to require some consideration. And all it takes is a peppercorn. So, I went home, and I said, Carolyn, "what's a peppercorn?" (Laughter.) She took me in the kitchen and showed me. (Laughter.) I decided I wanted to be a lawyer.

PROFESSOR LONGAN: Well, you came to Mercer.

JUSTICE GREGORY: Came to Mercer, yes, I did.

PROFESSOR LONGAN: How did we do? And what did we do to prepare you?

JUSTICE GREGORY: How did you do, Mercer Law School?

PROFESSOR LONGAN: I say we. I was very young at the time.

JUSTICE GREGORY: Well, y'all picked up with peppercorns, and you talked in some more detail about what a contract is. And you taught me something about criminal law. I like that subject. I think my favorite—I don't believe it will be yours—was property law. (Laughter.) You know why I feel that way? I understand the "ugh," but look, there's something about property law that tells you about all the law. To me, it's the history of it. You know, Professor Rehberg talked to us about livery of seisin. You go out on the ground, you pick up a clod of dirt, and I hand it to you in the face of witnesses, and that means title has passed to you. Isn't that a fantastic thought? I had that happen later in my career. I had a fellow who was a Mennonite over in Macon County, and he wanted to buy some land across the street, and we went to my office. We did all the papers and closed that out. He said, "now come with me." So, our whole entourage goes out to the farm, his farm on one side of the road. He said, "stand here and witness what I'm about to do." He gets on his tractor, drives across the road, sinks the harrow into the ground, makes a circle, comes back, says, "thank you. You can go now." For him that was title. That was the passing of title like that clump of dirt, don't you see? Anyway, y'all taught me that. (Laughter.)

PROFESSOR LONGAN: Mr. Rehberg did.

JUSTICE GREGORY: Mr. Rehberg taught me that.

PROFESSOR LONGAN: Mr. Rehberg was here when I got here. His portrait still hangs in the law school.

JUSTICE GREGORY: Yes, it is. Dean Quarles, did you know him?

PROFESSOR LONGAN: I did.

JUSTICE GREGORY: He was the dean of the law school when I was here, taught constitutional law? Have you all had Constitutional Law?

PROFESSOR LONGAN: Not yet.

JUSTICE GREGORY: Not yet?

LAW STUDENT: Next semester.

JUSTICE GREGORY: Look out. (Laughter.) He said to us, Dean Quarles said—we were talking about title, what is title to a car or to anything, what's title? And he says to us, "I don't know. I'll talk to you about due process."

PROFESSOR LONGAN: And equal protection.

JUSTICE GREGORY: Equal protection. That's the other one. "Don't ask me what a title is, I don't know." He was right. It is hard to know what title is. But he taught us constitutional law, and I liked that course. You will, too, you'll love it.

PROFESSOR LONGAN: You practiced law before you went on the bench for about ten or eleven years?

JUSTICE GREGORY: Yes.

PROFESSOR LONGAN: Before you became a superior court judge.

JUSTICE GREGORY: Yes.

PROFESSOR LONGAN: Talk a little bit about what kind of practice you had and the kinds of things that you did.

JUSTICE GREGORY: Yes, I was a plaintiffs' lawyer. We've got plaintiffs and we've got defendants on the civil side. I was a plaintiffs' lawyer. We sued people. We sued the establishment. That was our job. And I had as a mentor a man whose name has been mentioned here before because I've watched some of my predecessors. Hank O'Neal was my mentor. He was the most accomplished lawyer who ever sat at counsel table, I can assure you. Just to illustrate it: we had a case, our people were riding in a school bus that's crossing the bridge over the Ocmulgee River and it was whacked from behind by this big truck. And the defense was, "we couldn't see you because the bridge has got a hump in the middle of it." And sure enough, if you back off on the edge of the—go back up the highway, take a picture looking down the bridge, it looks like this (waving motion). And the argument made sense, you know, and kind of scared us.

Hank said, "well, let's go down, Hardy, get us a boat. Get you a boat, let's go down." We got in a little old boat and rode up the river. Turned around and looked down at the bridge. I swear to you it looks flat. You understand what I'm saying? It was the perspective how you looked at that. So, he gets an architect to build an exact model of that bridge, exactly like it is, so he could put it in front of the jury, and when George Grant says, "there's a hump in the bridge," and he's got a picture that shows one, we could say, "there ain't no hump in the bridge." And there's really not, it's almost an illusion depending on the way you look at the hump. So, I always said Hank took the hump out of the bridge and the defense from George Grant, and we won the case. He did.

PROFESSOR LONGAN: It's amazing how many people come in here and talk with me about Hank O'Neal.

JUSTICE GREGORY: Yes. He was an impressive personality, utterly devoted to what he was doing. I studied under him for five years. We would close the front door at five o'clock at the Adams O'Neal law firm. Adams, by the way, is the father of Bill Adams who's coming here.

PROFESSOR LONGAN: He was here last week.

JUSTICE GREGORY: Oh, he was? All right. His father. The Adams O'Neal law firm, we shut the front door, there were fourteen of us in there, at five o'clock. Hank would get Canadian Club—he loved Canadian Club; he had several cases of it up there—and he would wait till exactly five o'clock, and he would pour some Canadian Club in a glass. There was a drink back then called Goofy Grape. It was a grape drink, and Hank would pour that in another glass, and he would take a shot of this and a shot of this. And after about fifteen or twenty minutes—(Laughter.)

PROFESSOR LONGAN: —Hank became very congenial and conversant? (Laughter.)

JUSTICE GREGORY: I mean, seriously we would talk about—that was about the time the Civil Practice Act was passed, 1967, and we would spend hours behind those closed doors with him drinking Canadian Club.

PROFESSOR LONGAN: And Goofy Grape.

JUSTICE GREGORY: And Goofy Grape. And if I had my life to live all over again, I would have joined him in all that, but I didn't drink whiskey at the time. I've changed my attitude about that. (Laughter.) How to do it, you drink you a little snort after dark.

The thing about it was the phones were cut off, the doors locked, nobody could get in, nobody could get out until ten o'clock at night. We learned a lot, but I paid some tough—it wasn't fair to my wife and my family, so I went back down to Vienna.

PROFESSOR LONGAN: So, you left practice in Macon and went back home to Vienna.

JUSTICE GREGORY: To Vienna.

PROFESSOR LONGAN: The nature of the practice continued to be plaintiffs' work?

JUSTICE GREGORY: Yes, sir. In a little town, now, you have to draw some deeds, wills, a divorce or two, you know, to make a living.

PROFESSOR LONGAN: You got to do what you got to do. How did it come about that you first became a judge?

JUSTICE GREGORY: I was sitting in that office down there one day. This is another one of those things. I tell you, it happens that way: you got a few minutes to make up your life. The phone rang. Roy McMurray, who was the local superior court judge, had been appointed to the court of appeals, so there was a vacancy. I hadn't thought much about it. I'm sitting there trying to figure out how to win this case, a log truck had run over somebody. And the phone rings, and it's from Atlanta. He says, "how would you like to be the judge?" I said, "oh, I don't know, I hadn't thought about it." He says, "well, think about it." I said, "okay." Now, I had the impression he was speaking for the governor. It turned out later he was not speaking for the governor. He was just a lawyer up there in Atlanta who didn't want somebody else to have the job. (Laughter.) So he was trying to get me to go after the job, you see.

I said, "how long do I have to think about this?" He said, "oh, take a couple of hours." (Laughter.) So, I did. I went home, talked to Carolyn, went across the street to the Vienna Methodist Church, got on my knees for a few minutes, went back down to the office, told my partner I was going to take this job, and I did. That wound up in an election following that; thirty days later I had to run for that office.

PROFESSOR LONGAN: Talk a little bit about that transition from practice to being a judge, and how did your perspective on things change once you got the robe on and wore it up there on the bench?

JUSTICE GREGORY: Yeah, that's—so you're a lawyer, you're an advocate, and the next day they put a robe on you and say, "you're now a judge," and you're sitting there, and this is what got me: these lawyers would come in and make their arguments to the court, and I would listen to them and I would say, "my God, I don't understand that." You know, it would be some esoteric thing about law I didn't know. I thought, "well, keep talking, keep talking," you know. I said, "I don't know if I can handle this job." About six months I did it that way just fretting over it, and then I thought, "I'll just ask them some questions." And I started to asking questions, I mean, just simple questions, and I found out they didn't know what the hell they were talking about, either. (Laughter.) So that let us start from the beginning. Nobody in here—you remember what Plato said in his academy? "Nobody here speaks the truth. We all seek it together." That's a splendid attitude in a courtroom, is everybody here seeks it. We don't know what it is. Let's seek it together. So that was something I learned.

PROFESSOR LONGAN: What did you like about being a trial judge in particular? We're going to talk about the supreme court in a minute, but talk about being a trial judge.

JUSTICE GREGORY: I didn't like it very much.

PROFESSOR LONGAN: Why?

JUSTICE GREGORY: Well, you sit there by yourself, and you have to make decisions about other people's lives, and you don't really know what you're doing. You're always glad when you find a rule of law that says you must do this, but so much of the time you can do this or you can do that, and if you—that just was not fun to me, to do that.

PROFESSOR LONGAN: Just the weight of the responsibility?

JUSTICE GREGORY: Yes.

PROFESSOR LONGAN: And the uncertainty?

JUSTICE GREGORY: Uncertainty, what you were doing or not. And the nice thing about going to the supreme court was I no longer had to do that by myself. There were seven of us on the court. And so, we'd make decisions together. It took four votes to make a decision, but you had at least three people supporting you in the decision, and that's easier.

PROFESSOR LONGAN: How did it come about that you went from the superior court to the supreme court? Talk about that process.

JUSTICE GREGORY: Another one of those phone calls in the dead of the night (laughing). "How would you like to be on the supreme court?" "Well, okay." (Laughter.) George Busbee was the governor. He's also from Vienna, by the way, George Busbee is from Vienna. He impacted my life a lot. He said, "I'm going to appoint you to the supreme court." Okay. So I go up there and take an oath and everybody claps, and starts "Your Honor please," and all that stuff, I get in my office there after just a few weeks.

I'm sitting there late in the afternoon, and three people walk in, three ladies, and they have these papers. I thought they were bringing a case from the clerk's office for me to review and decide or something, so they hand me the papers, but I looked at them and, my God, I'm the defendant, it's a suit against me, so what they said was, "your appointment was not valid because your predecessor resigned at a time when there should have been a special election, and there shouldn't have been an appointment." And I said, "oh my goodness, that's a mess. I've already given up my life in Vienna and come up here." Well, so we go to court, federal district court, and the judge agreed with them, that the appointment was no good. And so, you're going to have to have a special election. And I mean, I just sank. We had a special election, and I won.

Then they go back into court and say, "that election is no good." "What was wrong with it?" "What was wrong with it was you were identified as the incumbent. You weren't the incumbent." Nobody knew whether I was the incumbent or not, really, but the judge said, "no, you can't be—you weren't the incumbent." And that question, you can see how that question came, but listen—I was before a federal district judge who said, "your appointment is no good, but in my order I'm going to let you serve on. I will let you continue to serve even though your appointment is no good." And I want to ask you by what authority did a federal judge appoint me to the Supreme Court of Georgia? I don't know, but it went to the Eleventh Circuit, and they said, "he's right."

Arthur Bolton said, "I'm going to give you the best lawyer I've got to represent you," and Mike Bowers, some of you might know Mike Bowers, was the attorney general. He took the case to go to the supreme court, and the Supreme Court of the United States granted certiorari. They wanted to look at the question of federalism, I think. And it wasn't totally clear what they were going to look at, but I think they wanted to know how a federal district judge could appoint a supreme court justice in a state. But by then two years had gone by and the regular election comes along, and I won again, and somebody told the supreme court that I'd won. They said, "well, it's moot now. We'll dismiss the case."

PROFESSOR LONGAN: Well, that's not the most direct route. (Laughter.) While we're talking about elections, and I do want to talk to you about your actual work on the court, but whether judges should be elected is and has been a long time a very hot issue. And I know you have a particular perspective on this because you had to campaign, and so why don't you talk a little bit about your politics as a judge and what that did for you.

JUSTICE GREGORY: That was like the discipline you received when you were a young child. That was the best thing that ever happened to me in that regard. This is why: here I am a big-shot supreme court justice running for office, and I'm riding around Georgia asking people to vote for me. So like everybody else, one night I wound up in front of the Lions Club in Albany, Georgia, seven o'clock at night. I make my speech why I ought to continue to be the justice, and this fellow was sitting right where you are. I'm right here and he's right over there; I'm up, and he's right there. He comes up to me like this, he says, "I want to ask you something." Nobody had done that to me in a while, you know. (Laughter.) "I want to ask you something: How come is it when I go down to the courthouse the judge says, "we do this in my court, or we don't do that in my court"? Let me tell you something: Those are our courts." (Laughter.) You know what I said? "Yes, sir." (Laughter.) I think that's a lesson that every judge ought to learn somehow. These courts don't belong to the judges, and they don't belong to the legislature, and they don't belong to the governor. They belong to you. You're going to have a job, you're going to be a lawyer, you'll have a special role in those courts, but you don't own them, either. If you think you do, go down to the Lions Club. (Laughter.)

PROFESSOR LONGAN: Were you different after that as a judge?

JUSTICE GREGORY: Yes, sir.

PROFESSOR LONGAN: Talk about that.

JUSTICE GREGORY: Okay. Well, you think about it, the governor appoints you, or the president appoints you to a federal job, you feel some obligation, you can't help but feel some obligation if you're human, to that person, and you don't want to disappoint them. Now, you hope all you have to do is do right, but there will come a case with that governor or that president involved in it, and what are you going to do? What are you going to feel and think and do about that situation? But if you know these people own these courtrooms, you think differently. "I don't work for him. I don't work for the governor." It was clear to me that I no longer worked for the governor. I guess I did at first, a little bit, but after that event I knew I didn't work for the governor. I worked for these people. So I better look at this case as though it's in their interests, as it affects this case. It changes things.

PROFESSOR LONGAN: You talked a minute ago about one of the things that you liked about the appellate work was that you had company in making these decisions.

JUSTICE GREGORY: Yes.

PROFESSOR LONGAN: Talk a little bit more about how different it is being on the appellate court versus a trial court, and what you liked about it and if there was anything that frustrated you, what you didn't like about it, talk a little bit about that.

JUSTICE GREGORY: Well, when I first sat down on that court there were seven of us up there, and I was intimidated, honestly. I didn't feel adequate to the job, and I wasn't sure of myself. So I just sat there and I listened for six months to the lawyers, and some judges asked questions and all, but I was a little afraid to ask questions. The chief judge, Bob Jordan, came to me in the hall one day and says, Hardy, it will be all right if you ask questions. I said, "Okay." So I started asking questions, and it started being fun again to ask questions and have some back-and-forth with these lawyers out there who know a lot about it. That was fun.

One day, Saturday morning, we get a case, a special emergency. There is a woman in the hospital about to have a baby any minute now. The doctor assures the local judge, and it comes up to us, that if she does not have a cesarean section the child will die, and she will probably die. We need an order, and the family—one tenet of their faith was, "we do not do blood transfusions. We do not believe in it. It's a matter of our faith, and we're not going to have this blood transfusion." And the father says to the judge and the sheriff and everybody down there, "God will provide," so he said. So they come up to us. I hope they went to God, too, because coming to us was a long way from that.

But we looked at it and thought about it one Saturday morning, and we know it's about to happen, and we decided that the state has an interest in this unborn child that's sufficient to overcome this belief, and with fear and trembling we wrote a per curiam, that is, nobody signed it, a per curiam opinion saying, "trial judge, tell the sheriff to go in there and order the transfusion, order the doctors to proceed." So we go home and sit around. At least we were all—everybody agreed on the court. There were seven of us. The next day guess what we read in the paper? The child was born by natural birth. God had provided. (Laughter.) I said, I give up. Why would we—we spent all day Saturday—(Laughter.)

PROFESSOR LONGAN: Gives a whole new definition of mootness.

JUSTICE GREGORY: But the comfort in that, it was so much easier—it was hard to make a decision about things like that, but it was easier to do it with seven people than it was with one person.

PROFESSOR LONGAN: What were the hardest kinds of cases, death penalty cases, other kinds, what were the ones that when they came to your desk you thought, "oh, boy, here we go again"?

JUSTICE GREGORY: May I ask you a question? May I ask the professor a question?

LAW STUDENTS: Yes.

JUSTICE GREGORY: What do you mean by "hard"?

PROFESSOR LONGAN: Troubling. That's what I mean.

JUSTICE HARDY: I think you probably—it's things like the one I just described or a death penalty case where human lives are involved, but if you want to say hard, it is also the cases where it takes a lot of mental effort.

PROFESSOR LONGAN: Okay, let's go there.

JUSTICE GREGORY: You want to go there?

PROFESSOR LONGAN: Let's go...

JUSTICE GREGORY: Okay. Contracts. (Laughter.) Peppercorn contracts. I really think the most difficult are these arcane statutes that are passed by the legislature on various subjects and trying to figure out what they mean and how to construe them. How do you construe this statute? What do these words mean? What does "hard" mean? Did you know that there are meanings of the word "run"?

PROFESSOR LONGAN: I did not know that.

JUSTICE GREGORY: There are eight hundred meanings, so you're there on the court trying to figure out what "run" means. You go to the dictionary, and there are eight hundred meanings of "run." Think about it a little bit and it will come to you. What you try to do is look at the context. Here's another example. A check can be a little thing you send through the mail, right? A check can be a minor investigation into a matter, can't it? A check, there's one other meaning that won't come to me right now is a check, so you have to look and see, but if the text is, "we mailed the check on Monday," you know what it is. "We went by and checked the pressure in the tires." You know what you did. It's the context. So you learn how to do that. Those are hard cases to me.

PROFESSOR LONGAN: Was there ever a time when you had a case where the law seemed to send you in one direction but justice in your mind was something else?

JUSTICE GREGORY: I wish you hadn't asked me that because that's a hard one. (Laughter.) But you did. Yes. (Laughter.)

PROFESSOR LONGAN: Would you mind commenting?

JUSTICE GREGORY: Yes. I was trying to think of an example, I didn't come here with an example in my mind, of where you feel like mercy and justice, right? Which would you rather have? Let me tell you which you'd rather have: you always want mercy. Justice can be tough. And what is justice? If you're looking at a rule—a good example of that is these mandatory penalties for drug stuff in the federal system. I guess we have it in Georgia, I don't know. Mandatory minimum sentences. So you're the judge and somebody is before you and they plead guilty, and you've got to sentence them to twenty years in the penitentiary, twenty years. And you want to say, "wait a minute, this doesn't call for twenty years. I mean, this is bad, we've got to stop this stuff, but not twenty years, not the rest of their life." But your hands are tied, you say, so therefore it leads you to try to find the person not guilty, which is not honest, either, is it, if he says—if he is guilty, so there's a lot of cases like that where it's just hard to know, hard to decide. You know, we have equity. You know what equity is?

PROFESSOR LONGAN: Yes, sir.

JUSTICE GREGORY: One way to think of equity is, it's something built into the law that gives you a little leeway. That's kind of what it is, isn't it? A judge who's sitting in equity. Have y'all studied equity? Y'all are in for a great time. Equity is going to give you a thrill when you learn what equity is, but we'll leave it at that now.

PROFESSOR LONGAN: I have a lot of questions, but there are two I want to make sure I ask before we turn it to the students. Here's the first one: you left the bench in 1990 and have been in private practice again since then. So, you have been a lawyer or a judge since 1966. How has law practice changed in that span of time? What are the changes you've seen?

JUSTICE GREGORY: The practice before I was a judge and the practice after—they were two different worlds to me, almost. One is because of the proliferation of cases, just everywhere, and different sorts of statutes you have to deal with and come to understand. I don't know if this is quite in point with your question, but this is what I want to tell them.

The experience I had in leaving the bench: when you're on the bench and people come to you and say, "Your Honor please," and they open the door for you, and if you ever start to believe that's real, you're in trouble. You've got to understand that belongs to the office and not you. I leave the court and I get in my first case and I'm talking to the lawyer on the other side, and I say to him, "this is what I think," and he says to me, "you're crazy as hell." (Laughter.) I said, "thank you, I'm back in the law practice." (Laughter.) You don't say that to the judge, you know, not if you want to win the case. So there's just a whole different world, and I like being the lawyer. That's more fun. That's just more fun. That's all I got to say. (Laughter.) You got to ask me another question.

PROFESSOR LONGAN: All right. Here's another open-ended question for you. This is the entire first-year class, and we have all the transfer students, as well. They have to be here.

JUSTICE GREGORY: I wouldn't have been here, either. (Laughter.)

PROFESSOR LONGAN: What advice do you have for them? I mean, is there anything maybe you wish somebody had said to you when you were a law student that you think that they should hear from your perspective?

JUSTICE GREGORY: Yeah, I would like to say to y'all this: here you are beginning your legal career, and I've seen so many people in your spot and then at graduation and then you pass the bar, and you get into a job that you don't like. If you get into a job you don't like, quit and get you another job, because there are so many things you can do as a lawyer, that why live a miserable life when you can have a wonderful life? It might be for you weighing peppercorns is what you need to do. For me it was the courtroom. I just liked to be in the courtroom. You might like that. But just so many things you can do. Don't be unhappy as a lawyer. Change your job.

PROFESSOR LONGAN: That's good advice. I've got a lot more questions, but I'm going to see what questions the students have.

LAW STUDENT: You said that when you started out with Adams O'Neal, that that time that you spent learning the law came at the expense of your family. Personal question: what do you think that exchange really cost you with your family?

JUSTICE GREGORY: I had a son who was diabetic at age two. He would have insulin reactions. I don't know if anybody is familiar with diabetes. I have it, too. He was just a child at the time, maybe four years old. He'd have these insulin reactions, and he would just pass out. We had one car, and I go down to the office, and I'm in there behind those doors that are locked, and the telephone is disconnected, and Greg has an insulin reaction at home, and he's got to get to the emergency room right now. Carolyn can't call me. Thank goodness Thatcher Watson was next door, aware of the situation, he gets Carolyn and Greg, and off to the hospital they go. I come home at that night, they're back home, and there's Carolyn, and I have to look her in the eye. And I could not do that very well. She told me what had happened. So I changed that. I left. I don't want to live like that, and I don't think it's worth it.

When I went on the supreme court, I told everybody around me, "if Carolyn or Greg or Liz," that's my family, "if one of them calls you, and we're in the middle of the biggest case in the world, you come get me, and I will speak to them." And what you do with your family is you tell them that. "You have access to me any time," and mean it, because you can leave. Who's going to stop you? You're free. Just get up and walk out of the courtroom and speak to your family. That's what I would advise you to do. That's what I learned in that. Thank you.

LAW STUDENT: Thank you.

LAW STUDENT: You've also talked about your faith and how it has been with you the entire time. Can you talk a little bit about how that has impacted you as a lawyer and maybe how it impacted you in school?

JUSTICE GREGORY: I won't challenge anybody about their faith. I have a faith, but I won't discuss that in that way, but here's what I would suggest; here's what I can tell you: when you become a lawyer you will not change who you are. You hear what I'm saying?

LAW STUDENT: Yes.

JUSTICE GREGORY: Whatever you bring to that will be what that lawyer is. If you go on the bench and become a judge, you're going to bring all that stuff with you. There is no way for you to be totally objective. You're going to be subjective sometimes because you are a subject. You can't help it. People ask that question about judges all the time: "how can you not have feelings about this or how can you disassociate yourself from your past, that you were a Democrat, you were a Republican, you were a something?" You can't.

LAW STUDENT: You mentioned that the first time you got called about a judgeship that the caller wanted you over some other person who was running for that position, so my question would be, would you say that politics play a certain role in terms of obtaining a judgeship, and if so, do you feel that it may interfere with your ability to, again like you said, make the court about the people and not your court or the governor's court or anything like that?

JUSTICE GREGORY: That's a great question and is right on, and the answer is politics has everything to do with picking judges, both in the federal system and the state system. Whether you run for office or you're appointed, politics—listen, what we're doing right now is politics, right? You can't take politics out of the world, and your question is more pointed than that, though, yes, if you're a judge—if you want to be a judge, you're a lawyer and you want to be a judge and you're in a—you want to be a federal judge, let's say, well, you're not going to run for office because that's not how we fill them. You're going to try to get the president to appoint you, right? That probably means you want to get senators in your state to say something to the president, right? Is that politics?

LAW STUDENT: Yes.

JUSTICE GREGORY: That's what you have to do. Is that wrong? Here's what I would ask somebody: tell me a better way. The Missouri Plan is this: first a person is selected by merit. Now, who's going to decide merit, okay? We want to pick meritorious people. Hogwash. (Laughter). But anyway, that's the theory, you pick meritorious people and put them on the bench by appointment of the governor or somebody, and they serve for two years, and then they run for that office based on the record they established in those two years. That sounds good, doesn't work, but it sounds good. It doesn't work entirely. Nobody knows the answer. If you'll come up with an answer for that that's really perfect, you'll have made your record on this planet.

LAW STUDENT: What appealed to you more about being a plaintiffs' attorney than a defendants' attorney?

JUSTICE GREGORY: It's something like this, if you're a defense lawyer and on the civil side, now, I'm not talking about criminal law, but on the civil side of the court, if you're a defense lawyer you have to keep time records and report to somebody that you worked so many hours on this case. I hate time records. That's one reason. If you're working for a plaintiff, your time is yours. It's free. You can work all you want to on it. You don't report to anybody because you're not going to be paid that way. You'll be paid based on a contingent fee. What you've got to do is win. Isn't that kind of fun? Yeah, to me it is.

It's a little bit like gambling. (Laughter.) So you're risk taking, and in order to get the case going somebody has to put up the money to finance it. The lawyer usually does. You've got all kind of escrow questions about that as supposedly advancing the money to pay for it. And experts cost a lot of money, and you can spend a lot of money on a plaintiff's case and then lose it, and somebody is just out. On the other hand, you can get a class action. (Laughter.) Let me recommend to all of you in the plaintiffs' spirit, get you a class action. (Laughter.) You've got all the advantages of representing the plaintiff plus the potential of a big lick at the end. That will cause your juices to run. And your family will be happy.

LAW STUDENT: Are there any traits or behaviors that you see in either young lawyers or lawyers in general that just rub you the wrong way?

JUSTICE GREGORY: Can I apply that to everybody I know? (Laughter.)

LAW STUDENT (FOLLOW-UP): Absolutely.

JUSTICE GREGORY: Especially judges? There are two great illnesses for judges. One is arrogance and another is ignorance, but the greatest of these is arrogance. You'll understand what I'm saying one day. Now, for a law student, I mean, a young lawyer, you're asking a different kind of question. I think that applies. You can be standing in front of the court and be cocky or write briefs that say such and such is disingenuous. Don't ever use that word. Don't use disingenuous. It's been overused. Or you write snippy things about your opponent. Don't do that. The court doesn't want to hear that. Just address the issues. Don't make it personal. And when—this is what Hank taught me: you're in the courtroom, the trial court, and you're speaking to the judge blah, blah, blah, blah, and your opponent gets up, the moment your opponent gets up, sit down. And your opponent has got to know what to do next. I mean, don't get into an argument with him, you see, don't give him any ammunition. Just stand there and look at him (folding arms). Let them squirm. It's fun. (Laughter.) Okay. Oh, yes, ma'am.

LAW STUDENT: Well, first I enjoyed you very much, sir.

JUSTICE GREGORY: Thank you. I enjoyed all of you.

LAW STUDENT: My question is when you said you were a trial judge and had the case alone and you had to make decisions about people's lives essentially, what moved you, when there wasn't a clear-cut rule to help you decide, to either be lenient or not? How did you make that decision?

JUSTICE GREGORY: That's part of the question I was asked over here: what did you bring to the bench, you know, who were you? Who was I? And I'm all these things. So you bring that to the bench, and that impacts how you make those kinds of decisions. Some people are just naturally lenient. Some people are just naturally—what's the opposite of lenient?

PROFESSOR LONGAN: Severe.

JUSTICE GREGORY: Severe. You know, I watch judges—people love to have the judge stand up there and just chew the defendant out. "You low life, blah, blah, blah, you're going to the penitentiary forevermore." That's absurd. Here's a judge who has all the power of the state or federal government behind him, all the judge ought to do is, "I hereby sentence you to so-and-so. Now, take him on, Mr. Sheriff." Don't make, I mean, these lectures, and it feels good to do that, you know, it feels good because everybody is with you, they're all mad with this guy. That's not the judge's job, to me. Don't do it. Just pronounce judgment and leave. So how do you decide whether to be lenient or strict? Which are you?

LAW STUDENT: It depends on the circumstances.

JUSTICE GREGORY: Yeah. She said, it depends on the circumstances. And it does for me. It sure does.

PROFESSOR LONGAN: Time for maybe one more.

JUSTICE GREGORY: This is the last question that will ever be asked in this venue, so who dares ask the last question? (Laughter.) Stand up to ask it. And it must be profound, deep. I don't believe we'll get another question, do you? (Laughter.)

PROFESSOR LONGAN: I think—

JUSTICE GREGORY: All right. There he is. Stand up. Wait now, wait, wait. We're about to hear the most profound question—(Laughter.)—ever asked in a setting of this sort.

LAW STUDENT: In your time on the bench I'm assuming that you got the opportunity to select your own chair, right? The chair that you sat in on the bench. What options did you go with? (Laughter.)

JUSTICE GREGORY: I think I'll give him the answer he deserves. You want me to? (Laughter.) A nice fat, soft one. (Laughter.)

A Conversation with Chief Justice Harold D. Melton

Introduction by Kevin C. Wilson[*]

From his days as the first African American President of the student government at Auburn University to his ascent to Georgia's highest court, Chief Justice Harold Melton has approached every challenge as a calling to service, and he has answered that call with faith, good humor, and a strong work ethic to meet the challenges of the day. After receiving his Juris Doctorate from the University of Georgia in 1991, Justice Melton spent eleven years in the Georgia Department of Law under two attorneys general, where he dealt with issues ranging from the creation of the Georgia Lottery Corporation to the administration of Georgia's tobacco settlement. He then served as Executive Counsel to Governor Sonny Perdue before Governor Perdue appointed him to the Georgia Supreme Court on July 1, 2005. Justice Melton continues to answer the call to serve through his current position on the Board of Atlanta Youth Academies and on the local and national board for Young Life youth ministry. Justice Melton currently resides in Atlanta with his wife, Kimberly, and their three children.

---

[*] Staff Counsel, Supreme Court of Georgia Office of Bar Admissions

CHIEF JUSTICE HAROLD D. MELTON,* 2019

PROFESSOR PATRICK LONGAN: Chief Justice Melton, why don't we start with just a little bit of your background and where and how you grew up.

CHIEF JUSTICE HAROLD D. MELTON: All right. I grew up in East Point and Marietta, went to Wheeler High School. I went to Auburn University. I went to law school at the University of Georgia. My major at Auburn was international business, and so I went to Georgia because they had a strong international law program, and I took one course in international law and decided that's not what I wanted to do. So I began to look at other options, and my interest after that was criminal prosecution. I wanted to be a prosecutor. I took all the courses in criminal law I could. I got an internship in the attorney general's office. They gave me a job offer and put me in property tax. It's one of those journeys where you just kind of go where you're told.

PROFESSOR LONGAN: Let's step back for just a minute to your time at Auburn, because you made history at Auburn. You were the president of student government, and you were the first African American ever elected to that position at Auburn University. Would you talk a little bit about that and what effect, if any, that's had on your career since then.

CHIEF JUSTICE MELTON: I got involved with student government largely because when I first got to Auburn I didn't enjoy it, didn't like it, and it took me a while to realize that I'm somebody who needs to feel connected with what's going on around me in order to feel at peace and at home. I felt too detached, so I got involved in student

---

* At the time of this interview, Harold Melton was serving as Chief Justice of the Supreme Court of Georgia. He has since retired from the Court and is now a partner at Troutman Pepper in Atlanta, Georgia. We have kept his judicial title in the transcript for the sake of clarity.

government, and every job I've ever had in my professional life has been is government. I love state government work because I like to know what's going on and who's doing it. I got involved with student government and just enjoyed it, enjoyed the campus, enjoyed campus life. Then as I was approaching my senior year, I had to figure out what to do next. I was either going to move up or out, and the only place up was the president position. It had never been done before, so I just started talking with friends, "what do you think?" And they said, "hey, it's a great idea; let's go for it." And we did.

We had three candidates in the race. This is old history. We had three candidates in the race. We got sixty percent of the vote. We had 18,600 students and 3.6% were African American at the time, and it just happened. Now, when my father asks me every now and then, he'll say, "was that experience worth it; did you get a lot out of it?" I'll say, "oh, yeah, it was the best education I've gotten." I use what I learned in that role every day. I use it especially now serving as chief. It's the same thing. It's the same blocking and tackling. It's just in a different venue. But being engaged in campus activities, working together with other people to solve problems, maybe the problems are different, maybe the people are different, but the process is very much the same.

PROFESSOR LONGAN: One of the things I often ask our guests is whether law school really prepared you for what you did, and sometimes I even asked whether people liked law school. You don't have to answer that second one, but—

CHIEF JUSTICE MELTON: I'm glad to answer that one. I did not like law school. I didn't expect to like law school. When friends and family asked me if I enjoyed law school, I said no, but you're not supposed to. It's like boot camp. You don't ask people, "did you enjoy boot camp?" You just get through it and get to where you want to be, and hopefully you'll land in a place where you look back on law school and think, "okay, that was worth it. It was worth it." There were people who enjoyed law school. I wondered about those folks. They're a different breed. (Laughter.) But did I get out of it what I wanted? Absolutely. I made some good friends. I learned how to read the law and study the law and practice law. Some of that took place in the classroom. Some of it took place outside the classroom. But the bottom line is that the law school process accomplished what it needed to accomplish. Now, the other part of that is, I was not at the top of the class. I was not near the top of the class. What I usually say is I was at the top of the bottom half. I knew some people at the top. But, you know, it's like being fiftieth place in the Miss America pageant, you're still a very attractive candidate. (Laughter.) You don't have to be top of the class to be a very good, productive lawyer.

PROFESSOR LONGAN: One of the things I know you did is that you participated in moot court. Can you talk about what that taught you?

CHIEF JUSTICE MELTON: Well, again, I guess in law school I had to find my niche, as well, and I'm not law review material. I don't even like reading law review articles. But moot court was really a nice fit for me. Judge Verda Colvin, who is a superior court judge,* was Verda Andrews at the time, and she was my moot court coach. She wore us out. She ran us through the ringer, and the one thing that she emphasized, that I didn't think about going into moot court, was the importance of writing. She painstakingly made us work through our briefs and made sure every single sentence was concise and tight. I learned a lot through that process. Then the oral advocacy aspect of it was great. I got more out of moot court than any other activity I participated in in law school. And like I said, I really didn't expect to learn to write as much as I did in that process, but that was a real strong emphasis.

PROFESSOR LONGAN: Let's talk a minute about the transition into being a lawyer from being a law student. What surprised you the most when you first began practicing?

---

*Judge Colvin was appointed to the Supreme Court of Georgia to fill the vacancy created by Chief Justice Melton's retirement from the Court after this interview was conducted.

CHIEF JUSTICE MELTON: Well, one of the hardest things that I had to adjust to when starting work was not having a nap after lunch. I used to come home after work, and I was just exhausted. It took me a while to get those muscles up and running so I could go nine-to-five or nine-to-six and go strong the whole day. The other aspect of working in the attorney general's office, it's about 100 or 110 lawyers covering the entire scope of state government, which is really not a lot of lawyers. And so when you're assigned something as a lawyer in that office, it's yours. When you're given a subject area, it's yours. There's nobody else you're sharing it with. So, when citizens called, they would call and they would look at me for an answer to their questions, but I didn't know any more than they did many times. But it was a really great opportunity to learn because if you like the sink-or-swim environment, which I did, they gave me all the responsibility I could have handled. I was able to go against some really strong lawyers, some seasoned lawyers. I learned a lot from them, as well.

PROFESSOR LONGAN: You started with property tax?

CHIEF JUSTICE MELTON: Property tax.

PROFESSOR LONGAN: How was it?

CHIEF JUSTICE MELTON: It was just like you thought it would be. (Laughter.) I really didn't want to do property tax, and I talked to friends when they assigned me to that area. This is how it worked. When you do the internship, when you accept the job offer, they ask you where you want to go, and they also ask you where you don't want to go, and they reserve the right to place you where they need to place you. There were two sections I didn't want to work in. I didn't want to do property work, and I didn't want to do tax work. (Laughter.) So, Sunday night before I started work on Monday, I got the call, and the voice on the other end of the phone said, "my name is Dan Formby. I'm going to be your boss. We're going to have you doing property tax." I said, "oh my gosh, you're kidding me." I called friends and told them what was going on, and I was kind of depressed, and they said, "well, you're going to love working for Dan Formby." I said, "yeah, but you know it's property tax, right?" "Yeah, but you're going to love working for Dan Formby."

I go in on Monday, and I meet Dan Formby. Well, Dan Formby is probably one of the least impressive people when you first met him because he looked the part and all, but he really just didn't have a lot to say. He wasn't a big conversationist. But over time I got to really appreciate the wisdom that that man had, the love for his employees that he had. I ended up loving working for Dan Formby. He's an older white gentleman from the suburbs of Rome, Georgia. For every professional decision I ever made, I always talked with him, usually first. The one exception was one occasion after I got married and I talked to my wife first. She said, "well, what are you talking to me for? You should go talk to Dan Formby." (Laughter.) So they put me in property tax, and one of the things they told me was, and this helped a lot, "if you have a question involving property tax, before you start hitting any of these books"—we used to do research in books—"before you start hitting any of these books, walk down the hall because anything that's in the books involving tax in the state of Georgia involves litigators who are on this hall. So have a conversation with these people, and that will help direct your research, concentrate your efforts," and that was a big help.

I didn't want to learn a subject matter. I really didn't even understand the big picture of how property tax worked, but ultimately over time I did learn it, and I learned that if you want to make a lot of money in this world, say bye to your friends and family for about six months to a year, learn something that nobody else wants to learn and come out and declare yourself an expert, and you can make a lot of money. I wasn't willing to do that, but I saw people who did. We hired those people as experts. But once I learned the subject matter, it's like anything else, I could move in and out of it, and I became very comfortable with it. When I had opportunities to transfer to other sections, I ended up just staying because I enjoyed the work and enjoyed the people.

PROFESSOR LONGAN: During your time in the attorney general's office, what did you like the best about that work, and what did you like the least?

CHIEF JUSTICE MELTON: There's many things I liked the best. I liked that I was able to sit in the bleachers and watch state government work. I wasn't on the field. I wasn't in the legislature. I wasn't in the governor's office, but I was advising these people, advising agency heads, and so I got to see what was going on. I liked that a lot. Great people, great people, some of my best friends, and we'd go to lunch, and we'd talk about everything that was important and mostly things that were unimportant, just have a great time. I loved the responsibility that they gave me right away. I was traveling the state doing administrative hearings on county tax digests, and it was just me, and the revenue department employee who was the client, in essence, so that was fun. I loved that the work hours were reasonable. I loved that I was able to work and do good work and then leave and do some other things that I felt were important for me and to get involved in the community and the church. It was just a perfect fit.

PROFESSOR LONGAN: Talk a little bit about the community involvement and other things that you've spent your time doing outside of work. I know that's important to you.

CHIEF JUSTICE MELTON: The main thing I was involved in was Young Life ministries. I was a volunteer leader. We worked in Grady High School and Southside High School. Southside is now Maynard Jackson, but that largely served Grady Homes and Techwood Homes, so I was walking the neighborhood of Techwood Homes. I coached a basketball team and really just hung out with kids. I hung out with teenagers, which is still what I like to do. I love hanging out with teenagers, even though I have three of my own right now. When I was at Auburn, at one point I wanted to change majors. I thought about changing majors, and I did a personality test. When I took the test, they said, "you're either going to be in law, a counselor, or a pastor." At the time I had no interest in any one of those three. And about six or seven years later I look up and I'm pretty much doing all three. I was practicing law, working in the attorney general's office, counseling kids and kind of acting like a youth pastor of sorts.

PROFESSOR LONGAN: After a number of years in the attorney general's office, you went to work for the governor.

CHIEF JUSTICE MELTON: Yes.

PROFESSOR LONGAN: How did that transition come about? Then I want to ask you about what you did for the governor.

CHIEF JUSTICE MELTON: Well, when I went to work in the AG's office, Mike Bowers, who was the attorney general at the time, hired me. He said, "come work for us. Give us four years. If you give me four years, we'll teach you how to practice law. If you leave at that point you'll leave with my blessing, but give us four." So, I planned on doing four, then seeing what else was out there. I got to four, started looking around, didn't see anything I liked better. After about ten or eleven years I'm thinking I'm going to retire at the AG's office. My boss was about to retire, and I'd begun having conversations with the front office, and they were saying I was going to be a candidate for that spot. They were looking at putting me there. I was thinking that was where I was going to be.

Then the governor got elected in November. There was a lot of media about who was going to be on his team and such. I think it was a Thursday afternoon I got a phone call from somebody from Governor Perdue's transition team, and the voice on the other end said, "my name is Bruce Bowers." Bruce Bowers is the son of Mike Bowers, who had hired me. And he said, "I'm with Governor Perdue's transition team. We want to know if you're interested in talking with us about joining the team." I said, "well, that's interesting. What position did you have in mind?" He said, "Executive Counsel." I said, "well, you've got to be kidding." Executive Counsel, as you know, is the governor's primary lawyer. The newspaper had suggested that Bruce Bowers was going to do it. I said, "I thought you were going to do it." He said, "no, I wouldn't do it." I said, "well, let me get back with you." It really took me off guard because I did not expect that call, so I put down the phone and I went to go see Dan Formby. Actually, I called my wife first. That's the time when she said, "what are you doing talking to me? Go talk to Dan Formby."

I talked to Dan Formby, and in true Dan Formby fashion, you ask him a question and he just sits, and you just wait, and then he starts off, "well, my mama used to say..." (Laughter.) So that's what he did, and he said, "well, my mama used to say it's hard to turn down a seat at the table." I talked to a whole bunch of other people. I talked to my mom. I talked to my dad. I talked to friends. I tried to find someone who knew him, who could tell me what he was about. I asked everybody all kinds of different angles, and it all came back down to, "well, it's hard to turn down a seat at the table." That's what ultimately drove my decision. So, I called him back and said, "okay, I'm interested in talking with you." That was a Friday. Over the weekend I had to work on my resume. Because I wasn't looking for a job, I didn't have a resume. Monday was my interview at ten o'clock. Monday at five o'clock was my call-back interview with the governor and the chief of staff. Wednesday was a press conference announcing I was going to be the Executive Counsel.

PROFESSOR LONGAN: That went fast.

CHIEF JUSTICE MELTON: It went very fast, from Thursday to Wednesday.

PROFESSOR LONGAN: Talk about what you did for the governor and maybe a little bit about what that did to prepare you for your judicial career.

CHIEF JUSTICE MELTON: Being the governor's counsel is almost everything you're not supposed to do as a lawyer, in this sense: what you're trained to do is to look at legal questions, analyze and research them, and work towards a final answer. When you're the governor's lawyer, you don't have any time to do that. You're drinking from a fire hose.

You have to be resourceful. At that point I'd been practicing for eleven years, eleven and a half or so, and you're traveling by instinct a lot of times. You have to know what areas you have to be careful about and when you can be confident moving forward. You have to be able to pick up the phone and call somebody in the attorney general's office and say, "hey, you deal with this. Is there anything you think I need to watch out for because we're about to jump?" You have to be able to call people in the agencies and say, "hey, what do you think about this? Are we right or is there something I'm missing?" You don't have time to do the research that you would normally do to be comfortable in the advice that you're giving, plus you're giving advice to the governor who has the highest profile of any state official in the state, and the governor is relying on that advice.

There are times when the governor would come in my office and say, "Harold, I want to make sure one last time we're right on this. Do you feel good about this?" I'd say, "yes, sir, we're good." And then he would go into his office, and in his office there's a suite of news reporters and TV cameras, and he's about to announce this initiative, and he's confident because his lawyer told him everything was just fine. I was sitting there thinking, "boy, I hope I'm right."

But it was the most fun I ever had in the workplace. It was fast-paced. When you talk about the joy I had watching the players on the field, well now I'm on the field, and I enjoyed every bit of it. I had to break myself away to go home. I'd look up and say, "oh my gosh, it's six thirty. I need to get home." You go into the office, you have this to-do list, and you would just get pulled away from one thing to the next. Good people, tough problems you're dealing with. The problems that hit the governor's office ultimately are the problems that are very, very hard to solve. Often no solutions can be found, but you're the one that—the governor is the one who has worked for the job to be able to address those questions. What I told people was I didn't have the weight of the state on my shoulders, but I had the weight of the man who had the weight of the state on his shoulders.

PROFESSOR LONGAN: Did you ever have to tell the governor no?

CHIEF JUSTICE MELTON: Yes.

PROFESSOR LONGAN: What was that like?

CHIEF JUSTICE MELTON: Well, to his credit, one of the things that I think he wanted, and he wanted to have a sense of this when he interviewed me, was whether I would tell him no. Because he had the sense that I would, he said, "okay, I need that." Now, he didn't necessarily like it when it actually happened, but he respected it, and still to this day he respects that. There are times when you don't say no, but you problem solve. One of the things about being an in-house attorney is, there's an art to it, and I had to learn the art of being in-house counsel because in that environment people want to go. They see an answer, they see an idea, they just want to go. They don't want somebody coming in and saying, "hold it, slow down" and maybe "don't do it." What I learned to do is to just kind of slide into a meeting. If I had questions and concerns, I wouldn't say anything then and there because that's how you become uninvited to meetings. I would go back and do my research. If everything was fine, and I didn't need to say anything, I just kept it to myself. If I found problems, then I would try to find alternative ways to accomplish that so when I did have a conversation with somebody, I could say, "here's a problem, but I think we can get there if we go about it this way." Oftentimes if I did it that way, that was much more appreciated.

PROFESSOR LONGAN: The time came when the governor appointed you to the Supreme Court of Georgia, I believe to replace Justice Fletcher.

CHIEF JUSTICE MELTON: Correct.

PROFESSOR LONGAN: Tell us how that came about, and then I want to ask you what it was like to make the transition to being on the Court.

CHIEF JUSTICE MELTON: There are many parts of the job of being counsel to the governor, but one of the first things that the Executive

Counsel has to do is work with the governor to create the Judicial Nominating Commission. The Judicial Nominating Commission is the tool that the governor uses to screen judicial applicants and create a short list, and the governor appoints from that short list. All that is by custom. There's nothing in the law that requires that, but it's custom, and so I helped the governor create the Judicial Nominating Commission. The chair of that was Mike Bowers, who is the attorney general who had hired me. You see how things just kind of start cycling, and you'll see that in your career, in your personal journey, you'll see that there will be some consistent trend lines. You don't know who those people will be, but you'll look back down a path and you'll see some people that keep popping up.

When Justice Fletcher announced that he was going to retire, the governor came to me and he came to Mike Bowers and said, "look, we know there are going to be candidates who are going to put in for this spot. We know who the usual suspects will be. I kind of want somebody different, and I want you," talking to me and Mike, "to brainstorm and be thinking about other people who might not put in who should put in, and we need to get behind and encourage them to give us a chance to consider it." Mike and I would talk, and we would talk with the governor and say what about this person and what about that person? Well, yes, maybe; no, maybe.

Then ultimately Mike says to me, "what about you?" And I said, "you got to be kidding." We started having that conversation, and the governor was open to it, and so I put in and I told the governor, I said, "Governor, I don't meet the profile." I was still fairly young. I was thirty-eight when I took the bench. The youngest ever was thirty-six. That was Justice Sears. One of the rules that Mike Bowers had, and all the other attorneys general had, was when you work in the attorney general's office you stay out of politics. So, I was not known amongst the political base. I was not known outside of the inner circle of government because I'd swum in that pool and only that pool. My time outside of work was with teenagers—so as long as teenagers were voting I was strong, but they weren't voting. I said, "Governor, I'm really not,

I'm not in your wheelhouse." He said, "well, that's my problem. I'll handle that. But would you serve?" I said, "well, sure." So, I put in, and we went through the process, and he appointed me and that was thirteen years ago.

PROFESSOR LONGAN: When you find yourself in your late thirties as a justice on the Supreme Court of Georgia, what was that transition like? What surprised you in that job? Then I want to know what you liked about it.

CHIEF JUSTICE MELTON: Well, the immediate thing was this, it's kind of funny. It was in June, I believe, when the governor announced that he was going to put me on the Court, and at the time the state bar was meeting in Savannah. We have about forty thousand lawyers in the state bar, and the bar's board of governors meets. That's about three or four hundred people, and so about a thousand folks down there. And the chief of staff came in my office and said, "the governor is about the make the announcement. It's going to be you. You need to get on a plane right now and go down to the state bar meeting." I get on a plane, and I go down to the state bar meeting. The announcement had been made, and people didn't know whether to congratulate me or throw me out a window because they really didn't know who this guy was. In fact, that was pretty much the theme of the response, "who is this guy?" I would walk through the hallways, and some of my friends or people I knew would come up, and they were happy, and there were a lot of folks who just didn't know what to do with me.

The good thing was that the bar, the bar leadership in particular, gave me a fair shot. That's all you can ask for. They gave me a fair shot. They didn't know if I was going to be a renegade, a cowboy, or if I even had the minimum level of intelligence necessary, but they gave me a fair shot, and then they watched. They saw that I took the job seriously, and that I treated them respectfully and took an interest in them and they in me. We developed a relationship, and they were very eager to be very protective of me, as they were of all the other justices on the court, so I'm very grateful for that. Now when I walk through the halls at the state bar meeting, it's a much different reception. They're my friends, and I'm thankful.

The transition was interesting from that standpoint. There was a lot of awkwardness. We had to get to know each other. People would say, "well, you're so young." I said, "well, I promise to get older," and I did. (Laughter.) But ultimately once I got to the office and closed the door and looked at the briefs and had the books out, it felt like any other job. The law was the same, the research was the same, the thought process was the same. It's just that when we had conversations I was talking to other justices as opposed to the folks down the hall in property tax, and when we came to resolutions, I wasn't writing briefs, we were writing opinions. But the process felt very, very much the same. That was very comforting.

The other thing, as far as transition goes, if you're going to be a judge, the Supreme Court of the State of Georgia is where you want to go. If you want to be a superior court judge, I don't know how those folks do it, because they have just wide-ranging subject matter and they have the parties right in front of them, and they're making calls right then and there. I was talking about instincts before, they're governed by instincts a lot of times. They're governed by knowledge, but the breadth of subject matter is so wide and there are so many opportunities to make mistakes. I have the luxury of reviewing their work, and we have all the time in the world by comparison. We don't have all the time, but we have a lot more time than trial court judges do. As long as we sit in the right seat and walk out in the right order, then we're generally good. That's all the orientation you need to be a supreme court justice. (Laughter.) But the trial court judges really have it tough, and I admire that they can do what they do.

PROFESSOR LONGAN: Judge Tripp Self described being an appellate judge like being in a replay booth.

CHIEF JUSTICE MELTON: Yeah.

PROFESSOR LONGAN: Is there a typical day, not as chief, we're going to get to chief in just a second, I know that changes things, but just as a justice on the court, is there a typical day? What is that like?

CHIEF JUSTICE MELTON: Well, if I have a day where there are no meetings, which really doesn't happen, the only thing that I would be doing is reading and pretty much reading, because everything comes in on the record. We have attorneys who write the briefs. I have staff attorneys who do the primary writing in my office, so I'm either reading what they're writing about the briefs and the arguments or I'm reading and preparing for the cases that we're about to hear or about to decide. So by and large if I'm working, I'm reading.

PROFESSOR LONGAN: It almost sounds kind of isolating or lonely.

CHIEF JUSTICE MELTON: It can be. That's the beauty of the job. We are elected, and you can debate whether that's wise or not, but because we're elected, we have the incentive to get out and about. Because we're elected and get out, people will invite us to events and to interact with the Kiwanis Club or Rotary Club or the law schools, and so it breaks up the day and makes things interesting. Besides that, though, we do have a lot of administrative work, so within the judiciary we have various committees and commissions and boards, and the supreme court is responsible ultimately for all of it. You serve on our commission on professionalism. You've seen the amount of work we've put in in that. You, yourself, have put in a lot of work in that for which we're grateful. Then we have all the various classes of court that work together to form the judicial council that I chair. But within the judiciary we have the municipal court, magistrate court, probate court, juvenile court, state court, superior court, court of appeals, and our court, and I may have left out one, but we all form a judicial council. We meet four times a year, and we come up with a budget for all the pieces within the judiciary. We support legislation that impacts the judiciary. We have budget hearings. I have a budget hearing today in front of a House committee at two o'clock. So, there's a lot of different things. There's a judicial qualifications committee, the commission that regulates judges; there's a technology committee, there's a commission on interpreters, there's the access and fairness committee. All in all, there's a lot of moving pieces that we're all engaged in.

PROFESSOR LONGAN: You don't think of any of that when you think of the job of judge.

CHIEF JUSTICE MELTON: That's right.

PROFESSOR LONGAN: Well, tell us about becoming chief. How was that? How did that come about, and then how has that changed your working life?

CHIEF JUSTICE MELTON: The chief has a four-year term on our court. The chief is selected by the other justices. The secret is that it generally will track seniority, but I consider it an honor to have been selected by my peers to be chief. I took over as chief in September. It's been fun. In some ways it's been a lot to get on top of, and in some ways I've been prepared for it. I'll tell you how I've been prepared for it. The last several chiefs have operated in a way where all the responsibilities that we just talked about, we engage the other justices, and so you dispatch them to liaison with various committees and commissions. Chief Justice Thompson, Chief Justice Hines both said, "well, Harold, you're going to be chief soon. We're going to give you these responsibilities." They both were very intentional in making sure I was involved in the things that would best prepare me for when I took over. In some respects, I'm probably more prepared than anybody has been in a long time in terms of just being placed in the right place. That's been good.

Following that model, I've been able to dispatch a lot of those responsibilities outward, so in some ways I'm serving on fewer committees than I was before I became chief. That said, I'm the guy that everybody sends all those, "is it okay if" memos, and so if there's somebody to blame it's going to be me. I approve all kinds of things and disapprove very few things because everything is generally well-thought-out. But I'm the guy that if something goes wrong, you blame. Then just being the spokesman for the judiciary, again, going to the budget hearings, and we have a state of the judiciary speech that will be on the nineteenth of this month, which is a week and a half or so from now. I was up till eleven o'clock last night looking over that. That probably is the scariest thing I'll have to do, is the State of the Judiciary. Y'all wish me well on that.

PROFESSOR LONGAN: Set that scene for the students because I don't think they probably know what you're talking about.

CHIEF JUSTICE MELTON: Right. So just as the president has the state of the union address and the governor has the state of the state, the chief delivers a state of the judiciary address to a joint session of the House and Senate in House chambers. You walk down the aisle just like the president of the United States and give a very stately address about the state of affairs within the judiciary.

PROFESSOR LONGAN: One of the things the students are learning about is the importance of mentors. We talked about Dan, and we've talked about Mike Bowers. Chief Justice Hines was important in your life.

CHIEF JUSTICE MELTON: Yes.

PROFESSOR LONGAN: Could you talk a little bit about him?

CHIEF JUSTICE MELTON: Yes, so Chief Justice Hines, I knew him as Judge Hines. The way I first met Judge Hines was (tearful pause). Explain why.

PROFESSOR LONGAN: (To the class) Chief Justice Hines tragically died recently. (To Chief Justice Melton) Take your time.

CHIEF JUSTICE MELTON: I was at Auburn, and Hines loved Cobb County. I grew up in Cobb County, went to high school out there, and there was an article about me in the local paper for my student government work, and his wife said, "you got to meet this guy." He reached out to me while I was still a student in college, and he said, "well, next time you're in town let's go to lunch." We went to lunch, and he gave me an opportunity to work for him after my first year in law school. I went to work for him, and it didn't feel like work. What it felt like was trying to stay awake while I was watching court happen. But all the lawyers came up to me and said, "you're going to learn a lot," and I did. I didn't realize how much I learned until I started practicing, and I saw my classmates struggle with things that seemed very commonsense to me. I'd seen what it looked like in real practice.

He and I became friends, we hit it off, and we would go to lunch. Even when he remained as a superior court judge, and I was working in the AG's office, we still went to lunch, and we've been going to lunch for thirty years. He joined the supreme court about twenty years ago, and so we were in the same building or at least right next to each other, and so we were able to go to lunch a lot more. Then we became colleagues on the same court, and he swore me in as chief this past September. He is a dear friend and will be missed.

PROFESSOR LONGAN: I have just a couple more things to ask you before I turn this over to the students and their questions. I'm sure they have a lot of questions. But one thing I wanted to be sure to ask you was whether over the arc of your career have there been any times when you think you've been treated differently because you're African American?

CHIEF JUSTICE MELTON: Well, I suppose so. I think my African American friends will attest that it's hard to know because the way I've been treated I've been treated all my life, so it's more than the norm for me. But there are situations I know when I walk into a room where everybody kind of reads each other. We all read each other real quickly. There are many times where I've walked into a room and realized, "okay, this read is taking a little bit longer than normal." And it was just fine. I play the long game. I'm used to that. I know my strengths, I know my weaknesses, and I'm pretty confident that if they give me enough time they'll learn my strengths and weaknesses. I don't need to win the room in the first five minutes. I don't need to win it in the next week. I can win it six months, over a year. And if they're still not sure, and they are not sure whether they can give me the benefit of the doubt, then my job is to make sure I don't give them any reason to say anything bad about me. Now, they can dislike me. I just need to make sure it's not for a good reason.

So that's been my approach, and that's worked pretty well. Law school was a strange place, and one of the things I noticed—one of the first things that happened in my section in law school was folks were forming these study groups, instantly, without regard to who they knew. I think it was based on who looked smart. I did not get invited to participate in any study groups, so I clearly didn't look smart. Apparently, I didn't look athletic either, because I didn't get invited to play on a softball team. (Laughter.) But again, over time we all got to know each other, and the friendships that we formed were real, and so again, I just play the long game.

PROFESSOR LONGAN: The last thing I want to do before I let the students ask their questions is to just give you an invitation. If there's any advice that you want to give this group—as you know, this is the entire first-year class and this year's transfer students, and so if there's any advice that you think they need to hear, maybe something you wish you'd have heard when you were in law school, whatever it is, this is an opportunity to do that. I'd invite you to do that.

CHIEF JUSTICE MELTON: So, a few things. One is keep your head about you. In law school it's real competitive. I know some places are more competitive. I know this is a very nurturing environment, so I think there's a more balanced approach, but it's still law school. There's a sense that everybody is doing more to get ahead of you, and they're ahead and you're behind. That sense is constantly at the back of your mind while you're here—if you're like me at least—and if you see somebody doing Con Law you think, "oh my God, they've already done everything else and now they're doing Con Law, and I've got to catch up." There are so many ways your mind plays tricks on you. I'm studying and they're interviewing. I'm interviewing, they're working their outlines. I'm working on my outlines, they're on law review. "Oh my gosh, I'm behind, I'm behind, I'm behind." Keep your head about you. You'll be okay.

A lot of what it takes to do well in the practice of law is your knowledge of the law. Just as important though, to do well, you've got to be a good person. And it's not the law school's job necessarily to focus on that aspect of it, but don't forget that part. Your primary tool as a lawyer is who you are as a person. If I don't like dealing with you, I don't really care how much law you know unless you're really, really good, and you see people like that. They're really, really good, but they're horses' rears. (Laughter.) But if they ever miss out on their game, if they ever slip in their game, they're out. If you treat people right and people like you and you make them better people, if you make the lawyers around you better, they'll want you wherever they go. They'll want you with them.

So, the other thing. My oldest son is graduating from high school this year, and I've been asked to speak at his graduation. I'm thinking what it would be that I want to tell my son as he graduates. I'm just now beginning to process this out, so I'll try it out on y'all first. (Laughter.) I think the two things that come to mind. Not to go and take on the world, and not that you can do all these great things. But how should you go about taking on the world. And how, I would say, is with grace and humility, grace and humility.

Just be humble; just be humble. You've got your law degree, but we're all in this world together, and we're all trying to get through, whether you're at the S&S Cafeteria and one of the folks behind the counter, everybody is trying to get through, so a little bit of humility as we interact with one another is important. We're not any better; we're not any worse. We just have some tools that we can bring to the table along with the tools that everybody else can bring to the table, so humility as we go about our daily walk.

And then grace. Folks do stupid stuff. I do stupid stuff. Nobody likes a hypocrite. But if we strive for high goals, high moral goals and we fail, then we're hypocrites if what we preach is right, and we don't do it ourselves. But what makes that okay is if we extend grace to those who fail, knowing that when we fail, we're going to need grace, too. The person that cuts us off in the middle of the highway, they need a little grace. Who knows what's in their mind, who knows? But a little grace and a little humility I think will go a long way.

PROFESSOR LONGAN: Good advice. What questions do you-all have for Chief Justice Melton this morning?

LAW STUDENT: I have no great philosophical questions, but as a downtown Atlanta resident I've watched the new courts building come up. What are you most excited about and what should the people there be most excited about the new building?

CHIEF JUSTICE MELTON: Well, one thing I like about the new building is air. I believe our current building is probably a sick building. It's old. The HVAC system is old, and all that needs to be gutted. And it will be gutted. All the other buildings on the hill have been substantially renovated. Asbestos, you name it. I think some offices within our old building are worse than others. When I moved into the chief's office, I had a cough for the first month or so, and it took me a while to get over it. Chief Justice Hines had a cough the whole time. I asked Justice Hines, I said, "did you notice a difference when you moved into that office?" and he said, "yeah, I absolutely did." So I'm looking forward to breathing. (Laughter.)

There are a number of other aspects. Security is a big deal. In the old building when we have court, we have court at ten o'clock, and at nine o'clock folks start showing up to the courtroom. If I show up at nine o'clock and I get on the elevator, I'm riding up the elevator with the litigants and their attorneys. That's just a bad look. The new building is beautiful. If you haven't seen it, it's right in the space of the old archives building. It's right on the interstate and Capitol Avenue. It's a $110-$115 million building, so here's why it should matter to you guys: the way it's framed, it looks directly at the Capitol. We were careful to make sure it wasn't taller than the Capitol. But it's respectfully in relationship to the Capitol, and it squarely stares at it. It defers to the legislature and the governor in terms of the presumption of constitutionality that they're entitled to have, but we're staring at them squarely to say we're ready to do our work if we have to.

Here's the other thing that's kind of important, I think, in our building. Our building is about fifty or sixty years old, and we talk about the rule of law, and the importance of the rule of law, but we've got some things that we can't really explain that have come out of our court over the last fifty or sixty years. We have a new start here, and I'm hoping that as we go into that new building that it's kind of a refresh button to say that let's make sure that everything we do in this new building is done with the mind of really doing it right. Let's make sure no opinions come out of here that we have to apologize for. That's not to say we get it right every time. We try to get it right. I'm sure something will be overruled or reversed, overruled down the line, but I don't want somebody to look at our opinions and say, "what were they thinking?" Or, "that's just backwards." "That's embarrassing."

It's a beautiful building, and what it tells me every day when we walk into it is that the citizens of this state have invested a lot of time and resources to make sure that we take our jobs seriously, the job that's assigned to us when we go in there. I had that feeling when I walked into the Capitol working for the governor, that I was going in there not just to see the two-headed squirrel but to actually do the work of the people in this beautiful building. I expect that we'll have that same sense when we walk in that building every day.

LAW STUDENT: Good morning, Chief Justice. So how do you remain connected to the people from your role currently as the Chief Justice?

CHIEF JUSTICE MELTON: You ever been married? (Laughter.) The question was, how do I remain connected? My wife's primary job is to keep my feet on the ground. My kids keep my feet on the ground. My neighbors, we have a great neighborhood, and just—my church, my own sense of knowledge of my weaknesses. One of the things that's kind of funny is that marriage has a way of teaching you about yourself, and I do believe that my wife is God's gift to me. If I ever complain about my wife does this and my wife does that, every time I do God has a way of saying, "that's pretty much how you treat me." Whenever I think that, "okay, let me slow down," and so that has a lot to do with it, just continually looking inward, just seeing all the work that's left for me to do, I think, hopefully, hopefully keeps me grounded.

LAW STUDENT: Good morning, Chief Justice. I was wondering, you're in touch with a lot of lawyers inside and outside the courtroom, what type of faux pas have you seen beginning lawyers commit?

CHIEF JUSTICE MELTON: Faux pas of beginning lawyers? So, a couple of things. One, lawyers really—this sounds obvious—lawyers really should know their case. They really should prepare. You would think, "okay, well, I'm going to the state supreme court, I'm going to prepare." Our court—maybe watch some videos. Our court is a little bit different than the way it was ten or fifteen years ago. If you're going to argue in front of our court, I would encourage you to watch some videos, they're online, and see the kinds of questions that you can anticipate. You're going to see questions about the cases that you are pointing to to support your argument. So that's very obvious, right? But that's not going to be good enough. You need to know if those cases make sense, and did those cases rely on cases that made sense. If a case that you rely on just said it, chances are you're going to be asked, "well, why should we rely on that case?" And you're going to need to have answers.

Some faux pas. If we ask you, for example, "what is the outcome that you're asking for us to provide in this case," you need to have an answer. Some attorneys don't have an answer. I've gone so far as to ask, "tell me what you want the holding to be." You need to write the holding out for us. Go ahead and tell us. Because if you can't write it, then there's a good chance there's a reason why. So go ahead and be able to articulate what the answer is. Then the follow-up question is, "how do you propose we get there?" The answer need not be, "well, you're the supreme court; you can do whatever you want." That won't work. We get that answer about once a quarter. That's not very fulfilling, is it? Those are the main things.

LAW STUDENT: Good morning, Chief Justice. Is there any one case in the time since you've been on the Supreme Court that really stands out as landmark or your probably favorite case that has had a decision?

CHIEF JUSTICE MELTON: Favorite case? Gosh, I was real proud of a good workers' comp decision we had. I say that tongue-in-cheek. There was one case that really stood out, mainly just because of the national attention, and it was the Genarlow Wilson case. Y'all are probably too young to remember, but it was about maybe six, maybe ten years ago now. How old are y'all? (Laughter.) So you could Google it.

Genarlow Wilson was a high school student who was involved at a party, I think it was a New Year's party, or something along those lines, with some older dudes. In the process there was a young lady who was intoxicated or somehow chemically compromised, and there was a videotape of these men, young men, taking advantage of her. He was prosecuted for rape. The gentlemen who were older all pled and they got, like, five years. When he was prosecuted, he was acquitted of rape but convicted of some type of aggravated sexual assault. At the time the mandatory minimum was ten years, so he got ten years. He was a high school student, B-plus student, athlete.

The national narrative was here's a young man who was acquitted of rape, so they took that to mean that it was then consensual. The basis for the conviction was the age disparity because he was eighteen and she was fifteen. I can't remember the age. But because of the age range, the age disparity was such that it made it a violation of whatever the sexual assault provision was. He got mandatory ten.

It took hold nationally because he was African American—he is African American, and it became a race issue. He's being prosecuted because he's Black, and he's getting ten years because he's Black. It resonated with me because—I'm shaking my head because he was African American, the victim, the young lady, was African American. The jury acquitted him of the most serious charge, which was rape, which told me that they gave him very strong consideration notwithstanding race. The only reason why he got the ten years was because of the operation of the statute.

The statute was not put in place on the basis of race, and, in fact, two years prior we affirmed a conviction of a white young man under the exact same statute. At least in my mind it was the exact same statute. But none of that changed the conversation. The other thing that struck me was the legislature had just ended its session and then the appeal came to our court after the legislative session. Now, you guys have studied civics. If there's a problem with the law and you want to change the law, who's the body you go to to change the law? You go to the legislature. Well, the advocates sat out the legislative session. They didn't do next to anything. But when a court hearing came, because that's when the case was front and center, everybody got engaged and became activated to try to seek change in the judicial body, which is not in my mind how it's supposed to be done. So I'm thinking, if the civics lessons have meaning in real life, folks, seek change in the legislative process.

The end result of that was we did overturn his conviction. At the time, there were seven of us on the court. I was in the minority. We determined that his conviction violated the Eighth Amendment's cruel and unusual punishment provision. Fast-forward, there was a state senator who was engaged in the legislative process and went the extra step and got engaged with Genarlow personally, and I was asked to speak at a church for the Men's Day Sunday. Senator Jones was a member of that church, and he brought Genarlow Wilson there. I spoke, and afterwards I said, "hey, let's go talk."

We went into a room, and I said to him, "you know who I am." He said, "yes." I said, "you know how I voted?" He said, "yes." He said, "I expected you to." He'd done his research. He'd researched all the cases. He knew the votes going in. A very smart young man. We had a nice conversation. I said, "how you doing?" He said, "I'm doing good." He said, "I've come home. I keep my head down and stay out of trouble. I don't go anywhere; I don't do anything. I'm good." Graduated high school. I think he went to college, pretty sure he went to college. I told him, "well, that's good, but there's a time when going home and staying out of trouble has to end. You have to put that aside, because you're not on this earth to go home and stay out of trouble. You're on this earth to go out and conquer. You've been given a break, not so you can go home and stay out of trouble. You've been given a break so you can go out and do something." I'm hoping he heard that. He's a nice young man, and I have every belief that he will do well.

PROFESSOR LONGAN: Chief, I am sorry we are out of time. Thank you very much for being with us.

(Applause.)

A Conversation with United States District Judge W. Louis Sands

Introduction by Professor Matthew Patrick Shaw[*]

United States Senior District Judge W. Louis Sands is a testimony in integrity, perseverance, grace, and as befits the judicial style, honor. One would never call him "unassuming," but if ever the somewhat paradoxical descriptor "humble majesty" were appropriate, it would be so in describing Judge Sands.

I had the distinct life-changing honor of being one of Judge's law clerks. Almost two decades later, I am still learning *now* from what he taught me *then*. As anyone who has ever served in his chambers would tell you, learning from him is the all-important fourth and fifth years of law school every law student should have. I hope to be as good a teacher to my students and mentees now as he continues to be to me.

In his interview, Judge Sands gives a glimpse into how a young Black boy from racially segregated Bradley, Georgia traversed countless spoken and unspoken barriers to a federal bench where he would preside as Chief Judge in the early 2000s. Remarkably, one never senses a spirit of anger or resentment as he recalls frequently being isolated as one of the few—and often times the first and only—Black law student, prosecutor, superior court judge, and federal district court judge. Nor is there ever any diminishment of the experiences Judge Sands and those of his pioneering cohort faced as they began the as-yet-incomplete process of improving justice within and by the legal profession. Just as importantly, there is not an ounce of pretense in Judge's understanding of his own narrative; a lesson both to those who take on airs for far lesser accomplishment and those who prematurely silence their own dreams. To paraphrase two of my

---

[*] Assistant Professor of Public Policy, Education, and Law, Vanderbilt University; Affiliated Scholar, American Bar Foundation.

favorite pieces of advice from him, "there is always room for good lawyers"; "be humble."

Judge Sands was a dreamer at a time when it was dangerous for Black men to vote in Georgia, let alone aspire to preside in a courtroom. He knew this, and he knew the limits others had laid out for him. But as he told his mother upon seeing the campus, "well, I'm going to go to Mercer." So he did, twice. For as much as he is a dreamer, he is also a pragmatist, one with a keen instinct for identifying a solution before a problem fully presented itself. As he remarks, in a generation renowned for "finding itself," he was "never lost." Whether in his decision to become a prosecutor at a time when there were none in his home district, or in venturing out in private practice, or in applying to the federal bench, it seems that Judge Sands always has a preternatural awareness of the moment. And while that is likely true, it is equally true that he always remembers who he was and on whose shoulders he stood. His is as much a story of fulfilment of his own dreams as it is fulfilment of the dreams his predecessors made possible.

It is also a story of making dreams possible for the next generation of lawyers. In the almost thirty years since taking the federal bench, Judge Sands has been a teacher, mentor, second father, and advisor to a still-growing family of law clerks not to mention countless fellow judges and lawyers. As law-firm owners, partners, counsel, prosecutors, civil-rights advocates, professors, and judges presiding over their own courtrooms, his clerks continue his legacy of making the law real for "walking people," guided by the most important attribute a lawyer can have, integrity.

UNITED STATES DISTRICT JUDGE W. LOUIS SANDS, 2016

PROFESSOR PATRICK LONGAN: Judge, thank you so much for doing this, coming all the way from Albany to be with us.

JUDGE W. LOUIS SANDS: Glad to be here. It was a pleasant drive this morning.

PROFESSOR LONGAN: I'm also welcoming Caitlin J. Sandley—your clerk, and we appreciate you both coming. I want to start at the beginning. You grew up near here.

JUDGE SANDS: Yes.

PROFESSOR LONGAN: In Jones County. I was wondering if you could talk a little bit about your upbringing and your formative years and tell us what effect that may have had on you: as a man, as a lawyer, as a judge. What about your upbringing formed who you are today?

JUDGE SANDS: Well, I was born in interesting times, as you might say. Grew up in Jones County, very near here. And I've kind of jokingly and seriously referred to that as God's country, and some people say because nobody else would love it. (Laughter.) But it was a strictly rural area. At that time, it was full of peach orchards and banana pepper crops, and that sort of thing, so most people were farmers and very rural. There was just a little bit of industrial activity, so the agrarian society, that's where we grew up. It also was during the time of segregation. I think by living in a rural area that was not quite as intensive as it may have been if I had been in an urban area. It was a time of very close community, really was a village sort of sense. Everybody had the ability to discipline whether they were related to you or not. (Laughter.) That sort of thing.

I was raised in a single-parent home, but there were other male figures that were relatives. I had an uncle and two older cousins who were more my brothers than my first cousins. Of course, church was a big deal. Everyone went to church. It was always interesting because we had a Baptist church, a Methodist church where I was a member, and we also, in the next town, had a Pentecostal church, and everybody went to everyone else's church, and there was no idea of there being a distinction. Now, being raised in a religious circumstance, of course, in an African Methodist Episcopal church, which very much emphasized education, it was an organized church, Episcopalian in style, so I got a chance to get involved in a lot of church events and things. There was a summer program referred to as the Sunday School Convention where you went around and you met people from other areas of the state, so I was able to have some contact with folk who were not in the rural area, from the larger towns, from middle Georgia and from around the area, and, of course, that gave me some opportunity to interact, to display my talents, the few that I thought I had. But it also was a time when everyone agreed that education was central and most important. My mother certainly was one of those persons that just would not abide one not getting one's lesson. So, in that environment I think I learned the habits and the values that I think have come to me this far.

PROFESSOR LONGAN: Well, you speak of education. Of course, you're a double bear.

JUDGE SANDS: Yes.

PROFESSOR LONGAN: I was wondering if you could talk a little bit about how it came to be that you went to Mercer University first an undergraduate, then a law student.

JUDGE SANDS: Yeah, if I tell the story, if anyone has heard this before I apologize, I spoke to the undergraduate graduating class this past spring. I shared with them a story of the old Mercer campus, the main campus which is away a few blocks from here. That was the campus I was first familiar with. The first time I remember seeing Mercer was—I guess I maybe was five or six, seven years old, and at that time the street, College Street, went all the way through Mercer's campus. I remember seeing this building that I described as having all these steeples. I did not understand what spires were, of course, so I asked my mom, I said, "what is that building with all those things, what church?" That's what I asked her. She said, "that's not a church. That's Mercer University. That's where kids go to college." She reminded me years later that I had said, "well, I'm going to Mercer."

Of course, this was the 1950s. There were no black kids at Mercer, and there would not be any for quite a while. What I credit to my mother was that she did not challenge me. She didn't say, no, you can't or you shouldn't. So—and she reminded me years later—as I said earlier, this was during the days of segregation and segregated schools. I think in our county, Jones County, the schools began what they called voluntary transfer in my senior year in high school, and I was not one of the transferees; I stayed where I was. At the same time Mercer had instituted this new policy that was open to integration, and they began to recruit what they felt were prepared and capable black students, and I was one of those, so I got a scholarship to come to Mercer. When my mother brought me there that fall, she said, you said you were going to Mercer, didn't you? She had never forgotten that. So that's what happened. I had applied to other schools, Georgia and other places, but Mercer was—I was familiar with it, and they offered some wherewithal to go. (Laughter.)

PROFESSOR LONGAN: That always helps.

JUDGE SANDS: So that helped, so that's how I got to Mercer.

PROFESSOR LONGAN: What was it like to be an undergraduate at Mercer at that time?

JUDGE SANDS: It was interesting. Again, you have to understand the environment. This is the end of the 1960s, beginning of the 1970s. I started at Mercer in 1967. I know all you think that is really ancient times. (Laughter.) But that's what it was. It was right after the civil rights movement was at its height, so to speak, and so people were very much conscious of their identities, you know, black and proud, and that sort of thing, and, of course, there was a certain amount of what I consider positiveness going on in society as well as, of course, the Vietnam War was really cranking up at the time. But I found the experience a very good one because Mercer was a small school and, because it was such, the small classes and the ability to get around with your classmates and the other, as well as the professors and all, was a good thing. So, to me, it was like country come to town. Here's my chance to make it. I have said to my clerks another thing that happened during the 1960s around that time was a lot of people were engaged in what they referred to as finding themselves: I have to find myself. If you go back and look at some of the movies that were made around the late '60s and early '70s, this business of finding one's true self, that was very, very popular. But growing up poor, I said I was never lost. (Laughter.) I knew what I needed to be. I needed to be out of Mercer in four years. (Laughter.) And that's what I did.

PROFESSOR LONGAN: That's funny. Let's talk for just a minute about law school. I mentioned to the class that you were a member of the class of '74.

JUDGE SANDS: Yes.

PROFESSOR LONGAN: That's a matter of great pride—

JUDGE SANDS: Yes, it is.

PROFESSOR LONGAN: —to everybody that's a member of that class. Could you talk a little bit about your law school experience and what Mercer did well and maybe what they didn't do well? Do you have any particular memories of law school?

JUDGE SANDS: Well, yeah, I look at this large class here this morning, and I look at this beautiful building on this hill. We were in the Ryals law building, and I see—I don't think I see a tie in here other than yours and mine. In those years the law school was on the main campus, and you knew who the law students were because at that time, except for maybe one or two exceptions, they were all white males, and they all wore white shirts and ties and suits, because that's the way law students dressed. So, you came to class dressed as lawyers were expected to dress up in court. Everything was very formal in terms of standing and briefing cases. The roll was called aloud, of course, and we believed that there was a conspiracy that if you were called in one class that day, you were likely to be called in another class later that day. We thought that there was a conspiracy among the professors. (Laughter.) Professor Rehberg, who died some years back, he was one of our professors that went back decades even then, so everybody knew—we called him the stingray, but he became very close to our class.

I was always the only black in my class, and I think there were three or four women in the beginning, but in the end, after the first year, there was only one. That was Ruth West Garrett, and she and I always described ourselves as "the minority." We controlled the minority class. (Laughter.) There was one white female and one black male. But our class was kind of—it was close. We really, for whatever reason, got along. Some things I remember, I guess when I say about my experience and some things that some of you may not be aware of, I think there used to be, at least, a publication in the school that was referred to as the Legal Eagle, kind of a newspaper type of setup. Well, that began as a mimeograph of, I guess, defamatory, smut sheets.

PROFESSOR LONGAN: Rag is the word you're looking for. (Laughter.)

JUDGE SANDS: That's what I'm looking for. I mean, it was just a way to spread rumors and say things and make things up about people. I mean, that's the heritage of that probably very distinguished publication now. Another thing that we engaged in doing was, of course, when we were seniors there had been for years what was called the Barristers' Ball, which was very formal. Everybody would dress up nicely, and that sort of thing, and that never quite seemed to be fulfilling to us, so we started another kind of a parallel party that was called the Barristers' Brawl. So, I don't know how much of that goes on now, but we began that thing, too. I think we were very serious about work, as far as being in class, but we had a good time at the end of the week. One guy worked part-time with the wrestling industry, so we'd go to wrestling matches down at the Coliseum. There was an ice hockey team at the time, and we'd go to Friday night hockey. There was a pizzeria on Riverside Drive that sold all the pizza you could eat and chicken wing parts, and they sold them, I think it was like a $1.65 or $2-something, so we would gang up and go to lunch, there, of course, to devastate that group.

PROFESSOR LONGAN: It's not in business anymore.

JUDGE SANDS: Not in business anymore. We had classmates that sued one of the downtown department stores who had all the fried clams you could eat, and, of course, they didn't have enough for them to eat, so they sued. Fortunately for them, we graduated in case one of them won it. (Laughter.) They didn't remain in town to prosecute their case, but it would have been wild. But we had a great time. I think because we did, it was a much smaller group, as I say, than is here, and we became close, and the way we established this class of '74 scholarship, everybody was a proud Mercerian and thought we got a great education and were part of a real good family, and as a result we set that scholarship up. Our class had a reunion every year for years starting the first year after we graduated, and we later put it into the five-year cycle, and we got together every year, and so it was a—I liked it. I don't miss law school in the sense of being abused by professors. (Laughter.) And scared to death. But in terms of otherwise I think it was enjoyable. It was an interesting experience.

PROFESSOR LONGAN: I want to ask you about a time period in your career between the time you graduated and when you first became a judge. You had a number of different kinds of jobs. You were a state prosecutor; you were a federal prosecutor; you were in private practice. Which did you like the best, which did you like the least, and why?

JUDGE SANDS: Boy, that's a difficult one because I think each one in its own way was something that I enjoyed. As far as being a prosecutor or a defense attorney, it's always been my position that a trial lawyer is a trial lawyer is a trial lawyer, only the subject of the trial changes and maybe the client that you represent, but the skill set is the same, so I saw both sides of those things as being interesting. I think I would give a lot of weight to the relative fewer years that I spent as a private lawyer because I think it gave me an appreciation for the business side of the law in a way that you don't get when you're working as a state prosecutor or even as a federal prosecutor, someone who has an office and they've got to pay the help, so to speak, you've got to pay yourself and you've got to pay them. So, you're part of the business world in that sense of being successful as well as what's the routine part that you're already aware of, as a lawyer representing a side of the case. I think probably that's unique in a way that I give some weight to because it gave me that perspective. When I became a judge, I think I had a sensitivity and an appreciation for that that I probably would not have had necessarily if I only had been in the public sector of representation.

PROFESSOR LONGAN: During those years before you became a judge, were there times when you were treated differently because of your race?

JUDGE SANDS: Well, yeah, I think so, and that's a—the way I would answer that question is maybe not the way you would expect it. Was I ever treated openly in a racist way, you know, called names in the court? No, it wasn't that. I think it was the shock of the whole idea. When I became a prosecutor here in Bibb County, there were very few—I think there maybe had been one or two African American prosecutors in Atlanta and maybe DeKalb County, I don't know, but otherwise no. At that time, it may surprise some of you to know women did not have to serve on the jury in Georgia. And Georgia had the liberal rule. There were some states that did not permit women, particularly women with children, to serve on juries until the supreme court ruled on it. Georgia's law was more permissive. It said women didn't have to serve if they didn't want to. And, of course, when the supreme court issued its decision that the jurors had to be balanced and representative, of course, a lot of women were suddenly on the jury. But before then when I began in Bibb County, they'd subpoena, say, ninety-five jurors, and you'd see about eighty-five white men and the other ten were a mixture of women and blacks.

So, for a young, skinny guy—and at the time I had been in the military for a while, so I had these horn-rimmed glasses that I would put on to try to look older—(Laughter.) I'd have my dark black suit that I would wear with the vest, trying to look serious, and to stand up and the judge would say, "call the next case," and I'd stand up, you know, and I'd call the case, and say, "I'm Louis Sands. I represent the State of Georgia." And you'd see these faces like, what, as a prosecutor? So, it's that kind of thing, that was not a role that blacks were seen in, so I guess what I had to do was to gain the credibility; I had to prove the skill set. I absolutely had a wonderful relationship with the judges, many of whom I later served with on the bench in superior court.

I wouldn't call it racist, but the idea of expecting that this is someone that has not really been in this place before in this role, can you really do it? I remember, I won't say which judge it was, but I'd work out pleas in some of my cases, and the judge would sometimes almost just talk the defendant out of it, like, you know, hey, who says you're going to get convicted? Of course, after I got a number of guilty jury verdicts, then my recommendations and proposals were taken more seriously. So, I think it was a growing thing. In other words, perhaps naively, I don't think that—obviously there are people who are racist, no question about it, but I think most people don't spend their time deciding how can I be a racist and hate people and mistreat people based on that. I think it's more of a tendency sometimes not to be sensitive to, not understanding, not perceiving another point of view, because that's not maybe an experience someone has not—one has not had or been exposed to, so that was the way it was.

Where blacks could be seen easily as defendants in the case, of course, and other roles in that courtroom, being the person in charge of presenting a case, no, that was something that had not occurred. The same as working with police officers or sheriff's deputies, there was that need to establish credibility and respectability because that's a role that had not happened. Judge Walker Johnson, who had worked in the Justice Department during the civil rights time, was an Assistant US Attorney here and later was in the DA's office. We served together, and he later became the district attorney and later superior court judge, and we worked together over the years. He and I were very close, he was very much a mentor. I had a case once where I was satisfied that the case had been charged taking race into account. There were two people who were not charged and one person who was charged, and the only difference I could see was the racial makeup of those persons, and I was quite concerned about it. I spoke to Judge Johnson, then an assistant district attorney, and he had a way of just really getting to the heart of things. I explained, "you know, this appears to me it's just not fair. There seems to be a racial aspect of this that's not proper." He really made it clear to me for the first time that I had some ability to correct what I understood to be a bad situation. He also could use some very salty language, so I won't quote him exactly. (Laughter.) He said, "you understand, you see what the problem is, then dismiss the so-and-so." Again, that was one of the reasons why I had accepted the job in the DA's office in the first place.

The late Tom Jackson, who was a very well-known African American attorney in Macon, I think he had gotten his legal training in Massachusetts, had moved to Georgia and he, as well as C.B. King down in Albany, were the handful of black attorneys who handled a lot of the civil rights cases, desegregation cases over the years. When I got out of law school, was about to come out of law school, there were very few African American or minority lawyers, period, in middle Georgia. So to have someone you could kind of talk to and hope to get some perspective of a view from where you stand was not very much available, but he was one of those persons that when I first learned that I might have a chance to be, in effect, the first African American prosecutor in this circuit, I went to talk to him about it.

If you were a young black lawyer, you were supposed to be defending people and helping get people out of jail and saving them from the system, so to speak. But having worked in the DA's office as an intern and a clerk, of course, I saw that most of the victims were African American, too, and there were a lot of things that were not receiving the type of sensitivity and attention I thought they should receive, and so in my own mind I felt that that was probably a worthwhile thing to do. But I still wasn't so settled, I guess, or comfortable with the idea. So, I talked to him, and I explained to him that I might have an opportunity. Do you think that's something worth doing? He said, "of course, it is," he says, "you understand how long it's taken to get police officers, black officers on the police force and the sheriff's departments and other agencies." He says when cases are charged, who do you think decides what gets prosecuted, what doesn't get prosecuted, and who gets what sentence? It's the prosecutor. He says, "sure, that's a job you should take." So that's kind of all I needed, the confirmation I needed and therefore went forward.

PROFESSOR LONGAN: I want to ask you briefly about your time as a superior court judge, then I want to turn to your career on the federal bench. But there came a time when you had this opportunity to become a superior court judge. Superior court judges in Georgia have a wide variety of cases.

JUDGE SANDS: Oh, yes.

PROFESSOR LONGAN: How did that opportunity come about and what did you like about being a superior court judge and what maybe was less fun?

JUDGE SANDS: Well, the opportunities came about strangely enough. The position I have now and the superior court position became open at almost the same time. I was involved in both, tried to get both, and ultimately did not get the federal position initially but got the state position. Over the years in observing what judges do and what lawyers do, I felt that I had some skill set or temperament and a way of doing things that I thought would be what I think judges ought to be able to do and how they should handle cases, and I thought that if I had the opportunity, I would go for it. So, it turned out that the superior court judge position became open first. I got that appointment. Now, what you love about superior court is, that's a court of general jurisdiction as I tell my juries now, which means basically anything that anyone wants to file can be filed in superior court, and the superior court has the authority to handle it. Judge Lawson and I often laughed about that because Judge Lawson was for a long time a superior court judge, also.

On the other hand, in federal court, that's a court of limited jurisdiction, and, of course, it's not quite so broad. So that broad jurisdiction brought in all kinds of things always interesting to me as a superior court judge. But the other thing was this almost uncontrollable beast in terms of number of cases. I tell my clerks, I say, if you want to see what an arraignment looks like go over to superior court and watch them bring two or three hundred people in and go through a long calendar call. You've never seen anything like that in federal court. And it's trying to manage that large calendar or docket of cases that are virtually every kind that you can think of.

The one thing that I liked that I don't do now was adoptions. A strange little procedure that you did every now and then because that was the only procedure that I could ever think of where neither one of the parties is angry with whatever the judge does. Some people say, if you want to do the right thing, you know, both sides should be mad with you. I don't know whether that's true or not. But adoption was where everybody was happy. You've got a situation where a child is being adopted and you gave him parents, and that's great, and the parents to be able to, for the first time they are able to have a child of their own, so it's a proceeding that the court can engage in and authorize and condone legally that has a perfectly great outcome.

PROFESSOR LONGAN: Those are happy days.

JUDGE SANDS: Those are happy days. But otherwise, none of your cases are. There were fights in the hallway. Friday was the worst day. (Laughter.) When you were what we call chambers judge, that's when everything that's non-trial, it's all of the motions and that sort of thing, and Friday morning you start at eight thirty. This morning, yeah, eight thirty, if they're still doing the same thing, they would have had URESA cases. That's the out-of-state uniform child support cases that come from other states. Do those eight thirty to nine. They have a nine o'clock calendar call for the civil docket for the temporary hearings. You call the calendar, they announce ready, call a recess, and then people go to negotiate, work out agreements. You come back in; you take the agreements. After that, for the rest of the day you hear the people who were not able to agree. So, you'd have a couple that would have a total income of three thousand dollars a month, and then they'd each prepare an affidavit showing that each of them needed three thousand dollars a month. (Laughter.) That I do not miss about my superior court. My hat's off to superior court judges.

PROFESSOR LONGAN: Well, of course, the students understand about general jurisdiction judges in state courts, and they understand about federal judges because they've taken civil procedure. The time comes when eventually you were appointed to the federal bench and confirmed by the Senate.

JUDGE SANDS: Yes.

PROFESSOR LONGAN: Could you describe that process? What was it like to be vetted to be a United States District Judge and then have the Senate vote on your nomination?

JUDGE SANDS: That is a humbling process, it really is. You can probably talk to anybody who has gone through that process successfully, that's the thing they tell you first. The first thing you've got to understand is that the way I describe it is this: all of your stars have to line up at exactly the same time. If anything is out of order, it cannot happen. There are people who would have made great judges, but the President who was elected was not the one that would be the one that they would get appointed by, you know, or the makeup of the Senate at a given time, all sorts of things could affect it. So, you realize how awfully fortunate you are to even be considered. You go through this process, of course, and you've got all this paper to fill out. I mean, it's just unreal. You've got a set you've got to do for the vetting process.

Like at that time there was a committee that Senator Nunn established, and you've got to get through that group. If you get through that group as a person who is in the final group, then the senator would interview you. I had an interview down in Warner Robins with Senator Nunn because I made the cut, so to speak, and that was a long interview and interesting process, and he and I talked about things, like some of the things I shared this morning with the group, that my background from my humble beginnings to be in a position to be considered in my life to be a federal judge is just unreal when you think about it. I mean, the odds of that are somewhere out there in the stratosphere, and I was always aware of that.

Once you finish that process, of course, and the senator makes his decision as to who to recommend to the president to be nominated, he recommended me. He called me at home one Saturday morning. I was living across the river here in Shirley Hills, and I was in the garage, and I heard the phone ring. I answered the phone, and it was the senator. He says, "hey, pardon me on Saturday morning, Judge, I wanted to call you." I said, "well, it's great that you called me at this time because you interrupted me and makes it clear to me I'm a much better judge than I am a repairer, because I was trying to relight the heater for the water heater. I couldn't figure how to relight my water heater." (Laughter.) That's when he told me that he had decided that he would recommend me. Of course, he had not talked to others who were not being recommended, so he asked that I not share it.

It was very easy for me to miss being around the courthouse, not to be available to say we had gotten it, before he announced it officially that next Monday, because I was in Jones County. Chief Justice Thompson, who's, of course, a Mercer graduate, he was on the superior court for that circuit, my home circuit, the Ocmulgee Circuit I believe it is. He had asked me, "Louis, would you like some time to come over and preside in your home county? I can arrange that, sign the documents so you can fill in for me." That Monday was the day. So, I was in Jones County in the courthouse that I had been to maybe once or twice as a kid and sat in the balcony, I remember, and so here I am presiding in superior court in my home county. No one could find me; they didn't know where I was. When they went down the list of people who didn't get it, it became clearer that I must have been the one who must have gotten it, so I didn't have to break my promise to the senator not to reveal it, because I was over in Jones County.

Of course, that's just getting through the first two rounds. Then is the White House. You've got a person assigned to you in the White House Counsel's office, and you've got another ream of paper to fill out, everything you can dream about that you may be so interested in, and do these interviews, and they try to find out things that may be a problem. Finally after that happens, at some point the president actually forwards the nomination.

PROFESSOR LONGAN: This is President Clinton.

JUDGE SANDS: President Clinton. So, my nomination gets forwarded. I had gotten a call that I'd be getting the formal notice about it. I think something was happening in Asia. Some controversy was ongoing, and the President was in a meeting of the National Security Council. I get a call from the Counsel's office, the Chief Counsel's office, saying, the president would have called you himself, but this emergency is going on. I said, oh, that's fine, that's fine. (Laughter.) I was presiding in a civil case in superior court, a jury trial involving an airplane crash, deaths in an airplane crash, and so I got this call, "you've been nominated. It's sent over to the Senate." They told me that I would be receiving a fax. At that time at the Bibb County Courthouse there was only one fax machine, near the sheriff's office over there at the courthouse, one of these old kind of Thermo fax type of machines. So this guy whose job was to watch this machine, I did not tell him what was happening, so he's looking at this machine, and here comes this letter, and at the top it says The White House. (Laughter.) It was the president's nomination. And he was like, "we got a fax from the White House." So that happened.

When that goes to the Senate now, remember you've gone through all this process, everybody wants a ream of paper, wants to know everything about you, and by this time the FBI has already done a background on you, too. It goes on and the ABA has done its thing. Then it goes to the Senate. Guess what, they have their own stack of questions that they want to ask and have you fill out a lot more paper. Ultimately, we had a hearing. Mrs. Reagan's funeral is today, and the reason I thought about that is that President Nixon died the week of my hearing, just after the hearing. The vote on us was put off for two weeks because everybody went to California to his funeral.

But you go up for your hearing, and that's when it really hit. After all of these questions, after all of this investigation, and all of the things that go on as part of the process, they put you in a hearing room. You've seen them on C-SPAN, beautiful rooms, and on the door outside of the conference room had a list of the calendar matters, it says, "W. Louis Sands of Georgia for United States District Judge." So, I'm saying, this constitutional process that I've been reading about all my life is real. When you realize that you are about to be questioned by the Senate so they can vote on you based on a recommendation from the president of the United States. I mean, it is a humbling experience to realize just what a rare opportunity that is to even have that opportunity to engage in such a thing.

So one of my children asked me why I shouldn't be a comedian, and I do kid around a lot. One of the people on the committee was Senator Strom Thurmond of South Carolina. I could do a pretty good Strom Thurmond.

PROFESSOR LONGAN: Feel free. (Laughter.)

JUDGE SANDS: No, no. Some of my children said, he's going to be at your hearing. Sure enough he was, and I'm the baby in the group. They have the hearing according to rank. The circuit court nominees and district court nominees in the order of age, so I was the youngest of the six people who had a hearing that day, so I was last. But we're all waiting, so I look and along the wall I see this kind of an orange/red plume of hair and I realize, oh boy. (Laughter.)

But I was asked one very embarrassing question that I think my supporters were more offended by than I was. Judge Cooper from the

Northern District said it really was a question for him and not for me, but somehow the senator had gotten confused. He looked at me and he asked me had I ever got arrested. Here I am sitting before a Senate committee and asked have I ever been arrested. Of course, Judge Cooper may have been arrested at some protests over the years in civil rights actions. That's what he was getting at, but I hadn't. So I said, "fortunately, Senator, no, I haven't." (Laughter.) So it wouldn't embarrass my mother on the formal record. But after the hearing he had pictures taken, and he grabbed me by the arm, and he told me, he says, "you're going to make a fine judge." (Laughter.) So, it all worked out.

As I said, the hearing itself was—the vote was delayed for a couple of weeks because of the late President's funeral. I had been invited to go to the circuit conference for the Eleventh Circuit that was being held at Sawgrass down at Jacksonville, and as a nominee you could be invited to go there. I'd been invited, so I was there. Everybody was saying, "when are they going to vote? When are you going to be confirmed?" You get these questions from everybody. My wife was going to join me later that day, and so I get a call from the Counsel's office saying, you've just been confirmed by the Senate. Like, whoa. So, after jumping up for a few minutes, then you ask about your friends, did they get confirmed, too? Yeah, everybody got confirmed. You feel good about it. But here I come for the second time, I've got to keep this secret because we don't have cell phones at that time, right? My wife is on her way there, and I don't want to tell anybody else until I tell her, and I couldn't tell her until she got there, so for a couple of hours I had to keep this secret, one of the best pieces of news of my life, until I could tell her first. But kind of squeezed down in a nutshell, that's what the process was like for me. But it is absolutely an honor to be selected and recommended and to go to this, to go through that successfully, and to see the Constitution actually in play.

PROFESSOR LONGAN: Over a couple of decades of being a federal judge you've seen a lot of different kinds of things. What's given you the most satisfaction in that job?

JUDGE SANDS: Well, I think the thing that gives you the most satisfaction is probably the thing that's most challenging. I always speak well of my friends on the state bench because I've been a state judge, and I know what the challenges are for judges who have to face election. When you realize that a judge can make a decision that's absolutely correct but is unpopular, and sometimes their careers are ended, not because they've done anything wrong, but because of what they did as a judge that was unpopular from that sense. I don't want to suggest that there's an over concern by state judges about being elected. I think the great thing is they do their jobs so well, notwithstanding that's a consequence they might face. But as federal judges we don't face that even as a possibility. So, it's an absolute requirement that the federal judges make the best decisions they can make on the law as it is and be fair to everybody and not have to be concerned about things that judges in many circumstances would have to legitimately be concerned about. You basically don't have an excuse for not doing your best.

PROFESSOR LONGAN: Judge, before I turn this over to the students, I always give our guests a chance to say anything you want to say, any advice you may have for these first-year students, maybe something you wished you had heard when you were in their shoes. You've got a free shot here.

JUDGE SANDS: Well, I always enjoyed these situations when there were people visiting who were actual lawyers and actual judges because it would kind of confirm for me one way or the other my decision. I hope all of you gave a lot of thought to why you would come to law school and serious consideration as to why you might want to become a lawyer. It's a wonderful profession. It's a very difficult and demanding one. And it's one where we're committed to this idea of law. So that is primary. If one wants an illustrious and glamorous career, I suggest there are many other more glamorous things that are not nearly so difficult as what you're facing in law school, and if one wants to make a lot of money, nothing is wrong with that, if that's your primary reason, probably you'd be better off, making a lot more money a lot easier, doing something else.

We do something that no one else can do. And that is this: we have the privilege of representing the legal interests of other people. A person in this country can do two things: they can either represent themselves in court, pro se, or they have to acquire the assistance of a licensed attorney. We hear about online law advice, you can get all the forms that you can possibly find to fill out lawsuits and those sorts of things, you can Google it and Wikipedia it. Believe it or not I have a lawyer now that will actually cite Wikipedia in a brief. I wouldn't suggest you do that. (Laughter.) But what I'm getting at is this: we have this privilege that allows us to do something others cannot do, and it requires us to do that at a very high level, with a very high commitment that means more than having a glamorous job, more than making a lot of money, because if people can get the same thing from their neighbor or from some online site as they could get from a practicing lawyer, why even have a class of people who have that exclusive right?

What I'm saying is, with that privilege comes a great deal of responsibility that we all owe to society. I hope everyone has thought about that and will continue to remind yourself of that. I think if that's the case, then we're going to be in good shape for lawyers.

The secondary thing I would say to you is this: there's nothing more important than your integrity, that is, your integrity towards yourself first, towards your clients, obviously, to other lawyers, and the court. There's nothing more important than that. Everything hinges on that situation. Obviously, you've got the character, being in law school you're going to have to prove that character. As an old friend of mine used to say, a reputation does not follow you. It precedes you. That's a more accurate word. So, that's the second thing I would indicate, that devotion to the law, married with the integrity that's required, as well as the preparation that you're getting here at this law school, should do well for you as lawyers.

PROFESSOR LONGAN: What questions do you-all have for the judge this morning? Don't be shy.

LAW STUDENT: How did it turn out for the lawyer who cited Wikipedia? (Laughter.)

JUDGE SANDS: Not good. (Laughter.)

LAW STUDENT (FOLLOW-UP HERE AND BELOW): So, you probably get resumes from every walk of life from attorneys applying to be clerks for you.

JUDGE SANDS: Yeah.

LAW STUDENT: What are maybe one or two key things that are really important to you for law school students that are applying to work for you?

JUDGE SANDS: Of course, the first thing, you want to work as hard as you can and do as well as you can to prepare yourself to do high quality work. I take the position that a good student should be able to do the practical things that are necessary in a judge's chambers; that is, to do sound research and have good legal drafting skills, but there's more to it than that. A judge's chambers, particularly federal chambers, is very small, so the ability to work with others is very important, with the idea of being a self-starter with high standards of your own to be applied in that environment is also important. I think experience is good to have. I think if you've got the opportunity to intern, I think you should take advantage of it.

I'm probably old school in the way that I don't think specialization is all that it's touted to be. I think any experience that's relevant any kind of way is a good one; that it's going to come back. Particularly for those who like to practice in a courtroom or in a trial court, every experience you've had in some way is going to come back. It's going to give you a different perspective and a deeper understanding than maybe somebody who has not had those. It's competitive. That's why I say you want to do as well as you can so to stand out there, but we're looking for people who are willing to work hard. In other words, it's not a nine-to-five. There might be some occasions, and I think C.J. can vouch on this, it's kind of like it's however long it takes, and it sometimes will take long evenings and weekends, and other times it's not so demanding. We are very busy. One of my clerks left me and went to the Supreme Court of Florida to clerk. She called me, she said, "you know, everybody wonders why do I stay after five o'clock when everybody left?" But of course, a few weeks later *Bush v. Gore* hit that court. I said, "I know there's one clerk who knows what it's like to work those long hours on something that's really hot on the press." A great work ethic and people skills are things that are also very important.

PROFESSOR LONGAN: Judge, what's the hardest thing about being a judge, whether it's the state court system or in the federal court?

JUDGE SANDS: The most difficult thing, I think, is it's a job that can be very isolating, in a lot of ways, because you've got to always be concerned about what you say, how you say it, or where you say it, and that's why my chambers family is so important. It's one of those few places you can just kind of settle down and not be concerned about that. You're removed, so it's the isolation. I think that's the toughest thing. I think it's even tougher in state court because in a way you're isolated in the same way and for some good reasons. I mean, it's not for a bad reason, but at the same time you've got to be involved because you need to maintain your necessary political matters. You've got to get re-elected in the state and stay the good graces of the electorate. So that's probably the toughest thing, is the isolation.

The other thing probably is this. I'm sure it's not true of Mercer lawyers, future lawyers, but the judge has a case to decide, and sometimes the lawyers don't help much. What should happen is the plaintiff's side brings this well-crafted, perfect, complete pleading and briefing, and the defense side brings this perfect pleading and briefing. So, Judge, all you've got to do is just decide it. I won't ask my clerk to say anything about that, but there are many times when the brief is not very complete, not very well done, at all. (Laughter.) We have to spend a lot of time looking for ourselves. So that can be kind of tough, too, doing that part. I guess it goes to the heart of being a judge. Whether there's good briefing or poor briefing, whether there are well-laid-out facts or not so well-laid-out facts, whether the science is clear or not, you've got to decide it, Judge. That's the reality that makes it so different.

I say to my applicants, if you're philosophers we can talk and say, oh, what do you think about this particular view of life and the meaning of life, and we can do like this and have a cup of coffee and we can talk. Oh, man, this has been wonderful, wonderful. We've got to do this again sometime. Of course, if you're a scientist you can just split that atom for years, trying to find that special way to look at it and be totally happy about it. But with the law and courts society can't wait to get the answer to this problem. It's got to be resolved. For that reason, it's often resolved in a less than perfect way in terms of maybe outcome, but in terms of a system that allows society to function, it is resolved.

PROFESSOR LONGAN: Judge, thank you for being with us this morning.

JUDGE SANDS: Thank y'all.

(Applause.)

A Conversation with Richard A. ("Doc") Schneider

Introduction by Chilton Varner[*]

How does a boy from Massapequa Park, Long Island, New York (population approximately twenty thousand) find his way to Mercer University Law School, where he graduates first in his class, and then go to work at Georgia's best-known law firm, King & Spalding, as the right hand—and ultimately the successor—of such storied Mercer lawyers as United States Attorney General Griffin Bell and Georgia's finest trial lawyer, Frank Jones? The odyssey of Doc Schneider is a fascinating tale.

There was a time when every lawyer in Georgia knew—or at least knew of—every other lawyer in the state. With the proliferation of law firms and Georgia offices for out-of-state firms, that is, regrettably, no longer true.

Doc Schneider is the exception. Go anywhere: Macon, Atlanta, New Orleans, Miami, Los Angeles, Detroit, New York, North Carolina, South Georgia, even Paris, France or northern Italy—anywhere. When a local resident learns that you are from Georgia, the question inevitably comes: "do you know Doc Schneider?" The interlocutor might be a judge, a former adversary, a previous co-counsel, or a staff member for local counsel who once provided trial support for Doc in some far-flung venue. The questions of all are tinged with both reverence and hope for current information about Doc.

What accounts for this abiding recognition? Doc himself has suggested that any good lawyer could and should be a better one by marrying her staunch love of the law to other outside interests that add depth,

---

[*] Senior Counsel, King & Spalding, Atlanta, Georgia.

variety, and nuance to one's approach to a jury or a judge.* Doc Schneider epitomizes the best proof of his thesis.

Doc is remembered so well because he has an appetite for *everything*—and everyone in his orbit is somehow more alive. He is a splendid cook (and trencherman). He is an oft-recorded songwriter. He is an inveterate reader. He is a self-taught guitarist. He is a graceful poet. He has the quickest wit of anyone, which he uses as a disarming tool for his extraordinary intelligence.† And he can—and does—laugh at himself. Frequently.

This interview allows all of us to learn from a master lawyer, who happens as well to be a superb entertainer. It also provides a trove of informative lessons from Griffin Bell and Frank Jones—a triple bargain.

---

* See "The Balancing Influence of Interests Outside the Law," in *A Life in The Law: Advice for Young Lawyers*, eds. William S. Duffey, Jr. and Richard A. Schneider (Chicago: American Bar Association, 2009), 31-34. "The highest calling of every lawyer is to be first a good lawyer—and to spend time developing tremendous affection for the law, the facts, and the small details that it takes to succeed and to serve our clients well....The law is everything—but it is your little something extra that ends up rounding out your life, giving you a place to unwind, and sharpening your legal skills in the balance."

† Doc's senior partner, Mercer graduate and former Attorney General of the United States Griffin Bell, once said of Doc: "that boy is the smartest person I ever met. If you could cut his brain in half, you just might have an ordinary person."

RICHARD A. ("DOC") SCHNEIDER, 2013

PROFESSOR PATRICK LONGAN: Doc, thank you for being with us. Where I thought I would start with you is to have you tell us a little bit about how you decided to become a lawyer and your background before you went to law school and then have you tell us about what brought you to Mercer.

MR. RICHARD A. ("DOC") SCHNEIDER: Okay. Well, good morning, everybody, and Happy Law Day to everyone here today. I grew up in New York, enlisted in the Navy in 1973, and, through events that I cannot recall, I ended up at Annapolis. While I was at Annapolis I met a fellow from Dothan, Alabama. I'd never heard of Alabama or Dothan, being from New York. I met a girl, as always in these tales. I met a girl in Dothan, and she's still with me. I ended up leaving Annapolis and went to Auburn where she was, and my plan had been to—I was an English major—my plan had been to write the great American novel and to teach English.

Somehow in my senior semester or quarter at Auburn, I ended up reading Anthony Burgess' book Gideon's Trumpet, about the case of *Gideon v. Wainwright*, which established, under the Sixth Amendment, the right to counsel when you were in jeopardy of imprisonment. It was a fabulous book written by, not Anthony Burgess, it's Anthony Lewis. Anthony Burgess wrote Clockwork Orange. A totally different vibe. (Laughter.) But in any event, I read that book. I was fascinated by the law and then began to try to determine what was involved in being a lawyer.

I was enrolling for a French course in my senior semester and looking at what pre-law was all about, and it seemed that I had taken most of the courses that I needed to take. So—and I realize this is not a particularly good plan of becoming a lawyer, this is very accidental and serendipitous—instead of asking about this French course, I said tell me about law school, what's involved, how long is it. Is there an admission test? He said yes, there's an LSAT. I said, well, when is that? He said it was Thursday. I said, all right, I'll take that and then I'll think about this, and I came home, and I said, "Helen, I think I've decided to become a lawyer." She said, "you're just as nutty as I thought you were."

I ended up from that then going to a law school fair at Auburn University in 1978, and I met, from Mercer Law School, one of the last hippies, a gentleman by the name of Forrest Mosten. He was this long-haired fellow with a beard, a very gentle, peaceful soul, and he was responsible for recruiting new students. I met him in a tent at a law school fair there at Auburn. What I liked about him was that he was a very laid-back guy. There was a spectacular picture of this building on the cover of the brochure that he had, but most appealing was that it was only ten dollars to apply in 1978 and I was on a limited budget. I liked him, and so I committed that I would, in fact, apply. I could at least spare ten dollars, and I did. I applied to Mercer.

A couple of weeks later I received a letter from Professor Joe Claxton saying that if I would come to Mercer, they would pay my tuition here. I said, well, this is just too good to be true. We have to go look at this Macon. We have to find this Mercer. We must take a further inspection. I'm very easily impressed. I came riding up this hill. I saw this wonderful building. I came here and met teachers, some of whom are still here, including Hal Lewis, and I met Mike Sabbath, who I thought was, like, the old man of the sea, but it turned out he's only two years older than me, and he's gotten younger since then from my perspective. But I met these wonderfully engaging people who had taken an interest—in my judgment, an unwarranted interest—in me. I was not any rocket scientist by any means. I did okay on the LSAT, and I had decent grades, but I was no stellar scholar. But nonetheless, they had reached out to me, and I said, well, let's take a chance on Mercer. I came and absolutely loved this law school, loved the education that I got here, and then loved the whole idea of being a lawyer and noodling through problems in cases.

I ended up as a summer associate at King & Spalding. I didn't realize at the time that King & Spalding didn't hire summer associates from Mercer, but I had understood that Judge Bell had gone to Mercer and Bob Steed had gone to Mercer. I'd seen these pictures and paintings around here and figured, well, that's where I should go next on this journey. I did in fact land a summer job there for the summer of 1980 after my second year of law school. I had a good summer and joined the firm as an associate in 1981, and I have been there ever since. When I got to the firm, there were about eighty lawyers. Now there's more than a thousand, and we have offices all over the world. It's been a long and ever-shifting journey, but it has been extraordinarily fun, and it all began because I walked into that law school tent at Auburn and met Forrest Mosten.

PROFESSOR LONGAN: I don't think we have any aging hippies left on the faculty.

MR. SCHNEIDER: Well, yeah, except for maybe you and I.

PROFESSOR LONGAN: Yeah, let's keep that a secret. Doc, talk a little bit, just an overview, about of your career at King & Spalding, the kind of things that you have done. As you do that, I would appreciate it if you could talk about the joy you found in that life, which I know you have found.

MR. SCHNEIDER: Sure. When I started at King & Spalding, their regimen was that after seven years you would either be elected a partner or you'd be asked to go on to your next adventure. It was an up-or-out system back at that time. Not only was it up or out, but the screening process was careful enough so that for folks who were hired, there was an expectation that they would have the right set of skills, legal intellect, energy, enthusiasm, work ethic, and personality to ultimately become a partner at the law firm. There was at least an expectation going in that that would happen. I certainly had that expectation from the moment that I walked through the door, which I think added greatly to the way in which I viewed the world.

The way in which I viewed the world when I walked into King & Spalding, was that I intended that my entire career would be there. There's a different journey there now, I think, for many students coming to law firms, but that was my vision from day one. I saw myself as part of the fabric of the firm from the moment that I walked in there. I frankly think that wherever you go, if you go to your own firm, a midsize firm, or big firm, if from the very beginning you see yourself as what you are, the lawyer responsible for the client, the lawyer responsible for thinking through the problem and not as some cog in some big machine that you feel dominated by the man, you will enjoy your adventure much more wherever you go. Now, for me, as you can see, my journey to the law in the beginning was a product of naiveté and serendipity and no planning, a complete accident. As it was with my law school, so it was with my law career in the early days.

I began working on Title VII Employment Discrimination cases. My very first case of that kind was against my Employment Discrimination Law professor, here at Mercer, Professor Hal Lewis, a genius professor, one of my favorites. He taught me very well in employment law—too well, because we went toe to toe for twelve years and I prevailed. He never forgot it, nor have I. (Laughter.) I would always feel bad when I would write, "therefore, the plaintiffs' claim has absolutely no merit whatsoever," and, of course, Hal Lewis and Charles Mathis were the plaintiffs on the other side. It was a very interesting Title VII case.

I say that took years, but during that twelve-year time period, of course, I did other things, including losing my hair, early on, maybe it was even like the first week, it just went away, and I became the bald lawyer I am today. I started on that case working on documents, reviewing documents, doing what you would think the little lawyer drone, new lawyer drone would do, and I ended up arguing the case on appeal in the Eleventh Circuit. The lawyer for the company I was representing, Brown & Williamson, then located here in Macon, was a woman by the name of Betty Foley. At first she was highly suspicious of me and would think my task was to review documents and that's about it, and she would not listen to any advice that I had to offer. She looked for guidance to Frank Jones, a partner at King & Spalding and a legend in the law. But over that twelve-year period of time, Betty began to see me learn and grow a little, get a little sense, and she began to turn to me more and more and more and more as her advocate. Finally, at the end of the case, the most important moment in the case, I ended up arguing to uphold the denial of class certification and our bench trial victory here before Judge Owens.

In addition to those kinds of cases, I participated in several large-scale investigations with Judge Griffin Bell who, as many of you know, was the attorney general under Jimmy Carter. Judge Bell was one of the great lawyers of the United States in history, in my opinion. He passed away on January 5, 2009, at the age of ninety. Judge Bell was very influential and important in my life as a lawyer. I got under his wing and worked on many high-profile matters with him for a long period of time. I have spent maybe the last fifteen years largely engaged in the defense of tobacco litigation, which is quite difficult and has grown more and more difficult, very challenging, but all throughout I served in the role of a litigator and a trial lawyer.

After my seventh year, I was elected a partner at the law firm in 1988, and I've been a partner ever since. Now, for new lawyers coming into our firm over that period of time, we went through an evolving process, and to make partner got harder and harder and harder. We moved over time to a two-tiered system with income partners and equity partners. We also created expanded opportunities for lawyers to remain at the firm for their entire career in capacities other than as a partner. We needed to find a way to do that, and we have. The firm has evolved in a number of ways so that we now have lawyers who are project attorneys, staff attorneys, associates, of counsel, junior partners, and senior partners, a whole range of opportunities for lawyers in a variety of areas. I started in a single litigation department. That department is now split into six or seven or eight different teams, and we have offices not only in Atlanta but in Washington, in New York, in Houston, in Charlotte, in San Francisco, in Silicon Valley, in London, in Singapore, in the Mideast, in Paris, in Frankfurt, and other cities around the world.

Lawyers in these various offices either do litigation or they do deals—corporate work.

The law practice has evolved. I've always thought of myself from the very beginning of the law practice as the person responsible for what I do each day, for when I come to work, for when I leave, for how hard I work, for how diligent I am, for how thorough I am, for how often I check on the client, for what ideas I think of. I think of myself as an individual lawyer inside this big law firm. I think that's extremely important for all of you whatever you do, whether you do it for a solo practice, a mid-size firm practice, a government practice, that you continue to recognize that what's happening here in law school, you're in charge of how you're doing. Whether you are succeeding on your exams, how hard you're studying, all of that is dictated by you. There's no firm telling you to do that. There's no boss telling you to do that. It's you; you're the boss who's telling you to do that. That is the attitude I have always had, and I've always told students when they've come and they've interviewed me, interviewed to come to King & Spalding, I said, you're in charge. Consider the firm as a sort of big river of work. It's your job to find what you think your niche is, find your mentor, help your mentor find you, but always remember that you're in charge. As a result, I have had an enormously fun time in the law. I can't tell you how much fun I've had. Fantastic.

PROFESSOR LONGAN: You mentioned Mr. Jones and Judge Bell, and from time to time over the course of the semester we've had occasion to talk about mentors.

MR. SCHNEIDER: Yes.

PROFESSOR LONGAN: I wonder if you could talk a little bit more about Judge Bell and Mr. Jones and about what they meant to you over the course of your career.

MR. SCHNEIDER: Yes. They were fantastically able lawyers, but they were also fantastically able people. And they had great affection for the young lawyers who worked with them if they thought that the lawyer, he or she, was giving their all, and that they could count on them and rely on them. One thing Judge Bell was known for was that he would get a matter in, and he would hand it over—we would always call his cases the children's crusade because we felt like we were like little kid lawyers—Judge Bell would get these very important matters in, and he'd just hand them to us, he'd say, here, take care of this problem. When you take care of this problem, figure it out, come back to me, tell me what you think about it. We'd go off and we'd have to figure it out.

I remember in 1981, I'd been at the firm for six months, and Judge Bell took me up to the Department of Justice. I knew Judge Bell had been the attorney general. He had been the attorney general when I was at Annapolis. Judge Bell took me up to the Department of Justice. We were there to talk about a case involving allegations of discrimination against female and black teachers in Clayton County, Georgia. I thought Judge Bell would present our defense to the Director of the Civil Rights Division, and I expected to have no role whatsoever. When we got to the Department of Justice, it suddenly hit me that Judge Bell was a true celebrity, and that these people at the Department of Justice loved him as much as I did, and I'd only known him for six months. We stopped to talk to everybody. He knew everybody. The most remarkable thing about him was he would see somebody who'd say, "Judge Bell, I don't know if you remember me at all," and Judge Bell would say, "sure, I remember, I enjoyed working with you, and your mother is from Valdosta, right? She makes those little lemon cakes." It was extraordinary, the man's mind for people and what he would remember about people. He was beloved.

And so Judge Bell and I made our way to the office of the Civil Rights Director to attempt to persuade the Department of Justice not to bring a claim against our client, the Clayton County School System. Judge Bell argued that there was no reason to bring a lawsuit. Judge Bell explained we could resolve this amicably, and then he said that Doc will tell you the facts. He'll give you a quick summary of the facts as to why that's the case. The first time Doc heard that he was going to say anything was at the end of that sentence where the period came. (Laughter.) I had no idea, so I coughed and stumbled. I had nothing, no notes, nothing, nothing, but Judge Bell knew that I'd been telling him all kinds of stuff. He knew I could tell somebody about something. And so I did. His way of measuring people was to give you a shot. It could have been disaster, and I'd seen situations where he gave people shots and they didn't do too well, and he would mumble about it. He would tell them you got to do better than that, but his way of doing it was by letting you sink or swim and being a great friend and supporter to you.

Frank Jones was the lawyers' lawyer. I have never seen a better writer, a more diligent person to marshal the facts, a more fantastically able oral advocate. When he retired, I wrote a poem about his retirement, and I tried to get the image of how much respect he commanded from clients and from judges. They would just be riveted to him. They knew he was a man of great integrity, and he taught by example.

There are two stories I like to tell about Frank. We were flying from Atlanta to Los Angeles for this case involving the placement of cigarette commercials before the running of the latest movies. Now it seems just so anachronistic. As fate would have it, some lame film house, probably with a cause in mind, ran one of these cigarette commercials before a noon showing of Snow White. (Laughter.) They got all the little kiddies packed in there, and oh my gosh, here comes a cigarette commercial. You can imagine what took place after that. Lawsuits were filed.

So, we had to go to Los Angeles to try to unravel the contracts that had been signed with Plitt Theaters to run cigarette commercials—which were never intended for underage viewers. We were getting ready for a deposition, and I'd gotten some fabulously fat notebooks together. One of these notebooks would kill you, and I had three or four of them. They were huge, they were heavy, and they had multiple thousands of tabs in there and all kinds of information. I knew the flight was four and a half hours, and the plan was to tell Frank Jones everything that was covered in my notebooks. We got on the plane. We were sitting in first class. It was on a Sunday, and I knew Frank to be the most diligent of lawyers, so I got out one of these notebooks for me, I got out one for him, and I said, I'll start explaining this. The flight attendant came by and said—now, mind you, it was about noon on Sunday—he said, can I get anybody anything to drink? Frank said, I'll have a vodka martini. I said to myself, he's having a vodka martini, I can't believe this. I had never seen Frank have a vodka martini or anything to drink ever. The attendant said, one for you? I said, no, I'll just have coffee. I'd probably been up endlessly getting these notebooks together. So, the flight takes off, I'm getting ready to open the notebook to go through it—and the movie comes on. The movie is Splash, remember this movie? I love this movie, and Frank says, let's watch this movie. I said, my God, we got to go through this notebook. But we both laughed—and I ordered a vodka martini. I realized that he was already fully prepared.

The other story is about just how much respect he commanded. Betty Foley, who I previously mentioned, went to a hearing with Frank before Judge Owens in 1981. They got done with the hearing. Betty and Frank came out onto the courthouse steps, and Frank said, I will go and get the car, and I'll come back around here and pick you up and drive you to the Atlanta airport so you can fly back to Louisville. She was with Joe Popper, also, a local lawyer. So, they're standing on the courthouse steps. Frank goes to get the car, ten minutes go by, fifteen minutes, thirty minutes, Frank doesn't come back. Betty is trying to figure out when, where. They waited on the courthouse steps for half an hour, no Frank. Finally, Joe Popper takes matters into his own hands and drives Betty to Atlanta himself. They get in Betty's car and drive to Atlanta. That was like about three o'clock. At about eleven o'clock that night in Atlanta, Frank Jones sits down on his bed to retire for the night, and he goes, holy crap, I forgot Betty. (Laughter.) So, he had gotten so focused that he got in the car and drove all the way back to Atlanta without realizing he left her on the courthouse steps. Now, she thought this was the cutest story. If I had done it, I may not be here talking to you today. So that's a little of the human aspect. Frank Jones is and was the most meticulous lawyer, the best lawyer I've ever seen practicing. He taught by example.

PROFESSOR LONGAN: You mentioned a couple of times representing the tobacco companies. That can't be easy. They're not popular entities.

MR. SCHNEIDER: Right.

PROFESSOR LONGAN: We've talked over the course of this semester about representing unpopular clients. Usually it's some notorious criminal, but in a similar sense you represent an unpopular set of clients. What's that like?

MR. SCHNEIDER: Well, it's been very interesting. I started my career working for Brown & Williamson, but I was doing employment work. It was not the defense of cigarettes. In fact, it never even occurred to me that there was this whole litigation out there swirling about product liability. I didn't even get involved in defending Brown & Williamson against product liability claims until 1994 in the so-called third wave of tobacco litigation. Personally and intellectually, I did not think that smokers, with all of the information that's out there, both through common knowledge and through the warnings on the pack, should legally be able to bring a claim. I also thought intellectually and personally that the federal cigarette labeling act preempted these state law tort claims. Those are my personal views, and of course, they happened to align with my client's defense.

We entered into a world in which a couple of significant things happened. One is a paralegal working for our company stole some of the client's privileged documents. The paralegal was an ex-drama teacher who was hired to assist in reviewing and coding various documents for analysis and possible production in litigation. He was specifically and confidentially trained on various documents, as to what issues were hot issues, what documents might be problematic documents, what documents were privileged documents. This paralegal, an ex-drama teacher working on our document project—not a paralegal at King & Spalding but at another firm, ended up stealing these documents and releasing them to plaintiffs' lawyers. That made the press. It drove a craze of tobacco litigation, and I've been involved ever since. What is required is simply focused attention on the law, making the best argument you can make, and it's been challenging but rewarding work. It happens to be done by some of the best law firms in the country.

PROFESSOR LONGAN: Obviously, practicing law is not the only thing you do. You have some avocations. The students have read your essay in the collection entitled *A Life in the Law*, published by the American Bar Association and edited by your friend Judge Bill Duffey and you. Would you mind talking a little bit about that, about how you got started doing that, how it fits into your life as a lawyer, and how on earth, as a senior partner at King & Spalding, you have time to do anything else.

MR. SCHNEIDER: Yes, that's very interesting. I grew up in the 1960s and developed a great affection for singer-songwriters. I loved that kind of music. I picked up a guitar when I was probably fourteen and began to learn to play. I wrote my first song at age nineteen or twenty or so, but then I began focusing on my studies and then my legal career. I didn't begin writing songs again until 1992. The first seven years of my life at King & Spalding were very absorbing. I worked very long hours, not because somebody was telling me to, but because I had so much work that needed to be done and needed to be done well, and it required a substantial amount of effort. I can barely remember some of those years, but I certainly wasn't picking up the guitar and writing any songs. In 1982, I did write a song called "Who Took Our Eyes Away?" It was my sort of attempt to deal with the fact that I was abandoning art and focusing on the law. I wrote that in '82 after I'd been practicing law for a year.

But in 1992 an interesting thing happened. As you mentioned, my friend and partner and the coeditor of the Life in the Law book, is retired federal Judge Bill Duffey. In 1992, we both worked at King & Spalding, and we were standing out in front of the building where we worked, and for some reason we were talking about guitars. He told me that in 1968 his father had given him a Martin guitar, which he never played, and which he put up in his attic. It had never been touched. I had never held a Martin guitar. I'd only lusted after them. I said, really, you have a Martin guitar, and it's up in your attic? Can I take a look? He said yes. I borrowed it from him. He claims that six years later he had to file a replevin action—(Laughter.)—to get it back from me. Also, my sister-in-law was visiting on one occasion, and she accidentally kicked a hole in it. I took it to Eric Clapton's guitar repair guy, and he fixed it beautifully. I mean, you couldn't tell. But Judge Duffey is the kind of guy who knows there's been a hole in his guitar, so he's always given me hell about it. But it was that guitar, the beauty of that sound, the accidental collision with music again that started me on this road to try and to write music.

I also heard the songs of a fantastically literate, brilliant songwriter, David Wilcox. I don't know if any of you have heard his music, but I would urge you to. Don't spend a minute listening to mine, listen to his. It's great stuff. I listened to it. It was inspiring. It took me back to the desire to write, to convey emotion and to convey what I was thinking both humorously and seriously, and I began writing at a heavy pace. I think in about '93 or so I would go into a studio dressed like this. There would be long-haired guys in there. There would be the scent of things that the law frowns upon. I would sit down and pull up a mic, they'd say, okay, are we going to do take one? I said, no, I've got ten songs here, we're going to record them all right in a row. Just turn the thing on. They said, no, no, you got to separate, you got to do the guitar track and—I said, I don't do that. Just straight ahead. I've got ten songs, I got four hours, let's go. I was an unusual customer for them.

I recorded at Songbird Studios in Atlanta, and David Romine ran the studio and was a great producer. He produced my first record, which was "Choices and Chances," songs I'd written over about a ten or fifteen-year period. But my real pride and joy was my second record. By the way, these—if you want a copy of these things just write to me or email me, and I'll send them to you. They're on iTunes, but I wouldn't buy them. I'd take a listen just to see if you're interested, listen to a thirty-second clip. Interestingly enough, that ninety-nine cents you pay, I as the songwriter, owner of the song, owner of the record label, the agent for the artist, the whole package, I get fifty-nine cents every time you buy a song for ninety-nine cents. That's amazing to me. I'd end up getting these checks for, you know, $14.13. (Laughter.) Or $7.06. See, it paid off; that was a good thing. (Laughter.)

But my pride and joy record is a record called "Second Chances," and my idea here was to take these songs that I'd written over this period of time and really get the pros to do them. I had a little bit of money as a result of my practice of law that enabled me to do this. I ended up hiring the best of the best. I had the piano player from Foreigner produce half the record in Chicago with artists and singers who he had, and then I had Ben Wisch from New York. He had produced Marc Cohn's "Walking in Memphis" and other records. Genius producers, who in addition to being genius producers had connections to the most fantastic musicians and studio musicians. Eugene Ruffolo sang six tracks on that record, and he and I are now very good friends. He does a masterful job—others, for example, Zev Kaz, who played bass for Elton John, plays on that first track, "Second Chances." It is a beautiful record. I hope you'll listen to it. It's good with a bottle of wine, a whole bottle. (Laughter.) And a set of headphones. There's lyrics in there, it tells a story of all this. I'm very proud of that, of the way that record came out, it sounds very professional. It's just been a joy to do.

I'm glad that I didn't start doing it when I was an associate because it was distracting. I mean, a project like that can end up taking some time, so in a year I might have spent four or five hundred hours on each of those records. We just recently did a concert at Eddie's Attic and released a live CD, double album, sort of like the White Album, Beatles album, but not quite as good. (Laughter.) It's called "Songs and Stories Live," and it has some humorous stories on there, including some of the things I've told you here today. But it's been a great joy to me.

Remember I told you I started out wanting to write the great American novel, and if I could get out the first sentence, I might get going on it. But the music has allowed me to write things that I think are meaningful in a compact way. There's a magic of the combination of words and music. The words alone could just be drivel. I try not to write drivel, but they could not be the greatest thing in the world. They're not "The Love Song of J. Alfred Prufrock," but when you combine it with the right chord changes and the right melody, it gives the words, the message, the music just some kind of mystical power to it. I've just very much enjoyed it. My firm has encouraged it. I have played at our firm retreats to just rousing applause as you might imagine. (Laughter.)

PROFESSOR LONGAN: Especially from the associates.

MR. SCHNEIDER: Yes, oh, yes, the associates just love it. (Laughter.) Or pretend to. But as a result, I've been involved in booking entertainment for our firm for various things. I give away a lot of these CDs to friends, and it's also a great thing for clients. When you come into my office, and I welcome any of you at any time to come visit, on my desk I have a series of the CDs that I've done. I actually have been involved in five or six CDs. The French, believe it or not, did a tribute album to James Taylor's "Sweet Baby James" that came out in February of 1970. February of 2010 was the fortieth anniversary of that album, and the French love James Taylor. Eugene Ruffolo and I sang on one of the tracks. We sang "Blossom" on that anniversary Sweet Baby James tribute, which is I think is a decent track. It's hard to find. You have to go online and type James Taylor and French, and you can find it out there. But in any event, clients could come to visit. It settles them down. They think, well, this guy, he's got many interests. It calms them down, and I end up giving them as gifts. People remember you by it, so in a way it advances the law practice.

PROFESSOR LONGAN: It certainly helped your practice in the Southern District when you wrote the anthem "All Across the Southern District" for the judges.

MR. SCHNEIDER: Yeah, that was a great deal of fun. That was in 2004. I was just turning fifty. David Hudson from Augusta said, "Doc, will you come and play a set of music for the Southern District judges?" I had not played a set of music since 1974, when I had hair. I mean, I'd write all these songs but in secret. I wasn't out there performing. I said, "absolutely not, I will not do it." He said, "well, Bob Steed comes to these things regularly and makes a fool out of himself, so why won't you? And we'll make a donation to Mercer. You've got to do it." I said, "all right, all right, I'll do it." So, I came up with a set of ten songs, half that I wrote, which, of course, would hit the audience totally cold. You know, you hate to go to a concert to hear all these originals. I did half covers. To spruce myself up, I did get the piano player from Paula Cole. Rakiya Diggs happened to be an associate at our firm, and she had been on tour with Paula Cole when she had done that cowboy song, and Rakiya Diggs was this great piano player. So, I knew, however it sounded, there was going to be coolness happening behind it.

I was trying to think of a song that I could write that would be about the Southern District or something, but nothing would come, nothing. It got to be the day of the event. I woke up, and I had an idea for a couple of verses. No, a verse and a chorus. I said, well, if I feel this show going down the tubes, I may bring this out sort of as a hometown favorite and say, I've got this song for you about the Southern District. And I told Rakiya basically, here's the lead, here's a chord sheet.

So, we were working along, singing the show, and about six songs in, I thought it was going okay, but I figured I should pull out this thing since I just wrote it that morning, it was fresh on my mind. I sang it. And they liked it, they clapped. Great. Get to the end of the thing, and the tape was rolling, tape was rolling, and the chief judge gets up there, and he says, I have been in the Southern District for sixty-three years and never have I been so touched. And somebody yells out, well, it's about time. (Laughter.) He said, never have I been so touched as by this song. He went through all these allusions about going to the Tick Tock in Swainsboro and having coconut pie. None of that was in the song. I had some simple stuff about Augusta being a nice place. The song was, "When you find your home in Georgia, you are Georgia's native son." It's actually not a bad little song. I think it might be on my website, which is www.legalguitarist.com. (Laughter.) Just to show you I'm totally modern. But anyway, I do the song. They said, "Doc, would you please play the song one more time?" So, we do; we repeat the same verse, repeat the chorus, Rakiya plays along beautifully.

After the fact, I listened to what the judge said, and I tried to write the images of stuff from his speech into a new verse and take it to the studio and professionally record it. So, I'm talking to the man who knows a little about everything, Judge Bell. I'm telling him, I'm writing this song about the Southern District. He said, you're not from the Southern District. He said, what do you know about the Southern District? He said, you got rivers in that song? I said, no, I don't have any rivers. You can't have a song about the Southern District without rivers. I said, what are all the rivers, Judge? He said, the Ocmulgee, the Altamaha, the Savannah, and the Oconee. I said, you got to be kidding me. (Laughter.) How am I going to get those in the song? So, I totally forgot about it.

I had a fiftieth birthday party shortly after that. Judge Bell was there, and he said, have you finished that song yet? I said, well, not yet. He says, you got the rivers in there? I said, well, no, not yet Judge. In fact, I forgot what you told me about the rivers. And he took—he was left-handed, and he always had a fountain pen, and he ripped a little piece off the menu, and he wrote on there in his little left-hand scrawl the names of these four rivers. And I said, thank you, Judge, I'll get those rivers in there. I put it in my pants pocket. About a month later, I reach in here and open it, I said, oh God, the rivers are in there. It inspired me, I wrote a little bridge, and now one of the better parts of the song is this bridge that talks about how I love these damn rivers. (Laughter.)

In any event, "All Across the Southern District," that's exactly what we did. Printed it up and sent it out there, and as a result, I'll see people from Brunswick and they'll say, aren't you that guy that wrote that song about the Southern District? I say, yeah, I sure did, and I credited it to Rakiya Diggs, I gave her credit, me, and Judge Bell. In fact, I walked into Judge Bell's office when he was eighty-five. I said, Judge, it took you a long time, but here's your first song, you've written it, and I gave him a CD of it.

PROFESSOR LONGAN: Well, I was there when that debuted. I was there at that meeting. And the chief judge had tears in his eyes.

MR. SCHNEIDER: I did not know that.

PROFESSOR LONGAN: He was very touched.

MR. SCHNEIDER: Did you ever get—did I ever send you the actual disc of the recording?

PROFESSOR LONGAN: No, but I haven't sent you fifty-nine cents, either. (Laughter.)

MR. SCHNEIDER: No, no, I need to send it to you because what I then did was, I got the layout of the Southern District, and I got a picture of some sea grass and printed that onto a CD. I have the chief judge's speech from that night, and he says, will you please sing that song again? And instead of doing my lame little guitar and voice thing, then you hear this beautiful studio recording. It sounds like—so it sounds very professional.

PROFESSOR LONGAN: Yes, I want to get a copy of that. Doc, I'm going to get out of the way and let the students ask you anything they want to ask you. I bet there are some questions.

MR. SCHNEIDER: Please do. Fire away.

LAW STUDENT: You said early on in your career when you were an associate at King & Spalding, your life was fairly consumed with the law.

MR. SCHNEIDER: It was.

LAW STUDENT: We all hear stories about how crazy life is as an associate at one of the mega firms. What was that like for you? How many hours were you working, and were the partners really as brutal as everyone hears?

MR. SCHNEIDER: The partners were not nearly as brutal as everybody hears or as everybody portrays. The pace, in my case and I think most cases, is self-imposed. It's what I felt you needed to do. I had a client's cause, I had law to be learned, I had facts to be argued. Typically, there were discreet tasks like answering interrogatories. In a complex case like the Title VII case, that took a lot of interviewing of people, compiling the information, writing out the answers in an appropriate way. What would my workdays be? Normally, 7:00 a.m. till 10:00 p.m. Then other days I would go around the clock. However, I was a big believer in, if I had done several of these long days, 7:00 a.m. to 10:00 p.m., I would just take a day off. I didn't tell anybody. I didn't make a big deal of it. I took to heart my message to you-all, that I am my own boss. Some days I would get there at eight o'clock and I'd leave at four o'clock or I'd leave at three o'clock, if I'd been working for a long time in a row.

At no point did anybody say I have to be there for regular hours at a regular time. There was no pressure put upon me to work on the weekends, although I will confess that my recollection from beginning as an associate and even years after I was a partner, was that I would work most every weekend. That's because the workload, I thought, demanded it. Let's compare a couple of circumstances. There were lawyers who did not work that hard. They were more efficient. They had another view of life. As you said, in my chapter I talk about people who were doing politics, they were doing bike riding, they were doing hang gliding, whatever they were doing. I wasn't doing any of that. But that was my choice. It wasn't because the firm was telling me, you must work this hard. Many others made partner under their model of how they got things done, they were maybe more efficient than me.

I'm now fifty-seven and I've been practicing law for thirty years. I usually don't work any weekends, ever. I find I'm very astonished at myself for this, but I don't, and I haven't for about five or six years, maybe longer than that. My typical day now is eight thirty till six o'clock. Many times, I don't get out of the house. My wife constructed a very nice office for me upstairs, and so I'll sit down there at like six thirty in the morning and start on the computer. I'll add one more thing, one more thing, and think, I'll be going to the office in a minute, in a minute. I never make it; I never make it to the office. There are still, I think, associates who get into the office late or sometimes don't make it because they're working on a brief or working on a project. It's very much, at least at King & Spalding, self-directed.

Ask yourself, what's your study regimen? How do you design it? Who controls it? Who made it up for you? I'm sure it's all come from you. You've done it yourself. That is how it is in a big firm, particularly if you insist that it be. You insist to yourself that you're not going to be run by somebody else's vision. If you think you've got all your work done and ready and lined up and don't think you need to do any work on a Friday afternoon and Saturday or Sunday, fine, that's fine, so long as you're getting your client's job done.

I tended to be an obsessive perfectionist, and I would work endlessly at things. I would rewrite and rewrite briefs till I thought that they really hummed. I took great pride in legal writing. I took great pride in trying to craft an argument that I really thought was persuasive. If you read the first paragraph of a brief that I wrote, you would know what the case was about, you would know what my key arguments are, and you would know whether you're going to rule in my favor or not on that first page. To do that takes a lot of effort. It takes writing it once, writing it again, honing it, getting rid of words, so there's a lot of that involved.

But I worked a tremendous amount, I would say on average of 2,400 hours a year. Some years 3,000. In my partner years, last year I worked 2,200, but there were a few years ago when my workload slowed due to various factors and I only logged 1,300 billable hours. I did other work as well—and 1,300 hours should never be your target! You have cycles within your practice. But I think an average today, no matter where you go, whether you're a solo practitioner, you go in a mid-level firm, big firm, about 2,000 hours a year billable is what is expected. That's going to take you probably around 2,400 hours in the office to get there. It's manageable, especially if you have something important and exciting to do and you're charged up about it, and you don't feel like it's some chore. You're really charged, you're trying to write the best brief you can possibly write. You're trying to make the best deposition outline you can take. You're getting ready tomorrow to make an argument that is so powerful, so persuasive, so compact, so well thought through that you're energized by it. The hours fly by. You have fun with this.

Yes, we're going to make money from the law, it's going to be our livelihood, but my view is you should embrace it and say, this is a challenge; I love doing this. Now, if you say, I can't stand doing this, if that's what you say every day, then let's get a new gig. If you don't love it, if you're not passionate about it, you'll find it to be a strain on you. But if you are passionate, the hours will fly by. I guarantee it. They will fly by.

While we are talking about balance-of-life things, I have two daughters and four grandchildren. My two daughters were young in my early years in the law, and I can barely remember their early years as little souls. Now, I have a granddaughter who lives with me, and she is ten, and I remember everything about her. I could tell you what pants she wore when she was one and two and three and four and five and six, but I can't remember those details about my own daughters, from the pace that I was keeping. I think that was a little too crazy. You've got to find the right balance. If you believe me that you're in charge and insist that you're in charge and be passionate about your assignments, and if the one you're working on is boring, okay, well, look for the next good one that's coming out there. What else is in the firm? What other work is in the firm? What else is out there to do? Keep yourself engaged. You'll find the time will fly by.

LAW STUDENT: Since you work so much, what's your best advice for maintaining your personal and family life?

MR. SCHNEIDER: Well, you have to marry a very good girlfriend or boyfriend, and Helen has been a very understanding soul. As demanding as you have to be about doing your work and getting your job done, you have to be able to say, no, there are certain limits. If you really think you need to spend another twelve hours on getting ready for this deposition, but it means you're missing the father/daughter dance, well, you're not missing the father/daughter dance, period. There are some things that are not negotiable. My kids didn't do a lot of sports. I think I was at everything important, I hope, but I know guys whose sons or daughters were great athletes, played softball, soccer, and they were leaving the office at four o'clock every day and finding the right balance. I think the great mis-message about law practice and law firms is that you somehow are going inside of an organization, and you will lose yourself and you have to fall victim to a set of rules that you don't want to abide by. There will be some rules, but there's ways to find your way around them, to be your own boss. If you're your own boss, then you decide what's important and find the right way to balance it.

LAW STUDENT: What about maintaining good health? When you're busy you don't always eat the best things and if you're stuck sitting and typing and researching, you're not always up and moving around.

MR. SCHNEIDER: A very good, very good question, particularly to me. I probably eat too many snacks, but I think daily exercise should be part of the regimen. For a period of time, in keeping with my extremist personality, I was playing squash with a guy, we would play every day, we'd play thirteen or fourteen games of squash. We'd be completely exhausted, but, man, we were in great shape, and we did that for five or six years, and that kept me in shape for a while. But eventually, you're exactly right, if you're on the road, you're eating fast-food or you're eating too much at dinner, you're having a little bit too much wine, etc., that's another area. It would be a good idea to put down a list that would identify family life, health, and work, and ask what am

I going to do to be in charge of all these? I have tended to let everything happen accidentally, and that's not good. I think you should have a plan. I see people in my firm who I greatly admire, who are fantastic lawyers, great family people, who run, ride bikes, are in great shape, that's the ideal model. I would not follow me on the health and exercise regimen, but I'm working on it. It's very important to do that, and hard to do when you're on the road.

PROFESSOR LONGAN: Got time for one more.

MR. SCHNEIDER: Yes.

LAW STUDENT: I was going to ask, during your career how many times have you had to face serious ethical challenges or limits that you thought you had to seek advice or maybe even a family member to help you decide how to handle it?

MR. SCHNEIDER: A number of times. Most often they are conflict issues. Because we're such a large firm and represent so many different clients, there's a possibility of conflicts, particularly between maybe a company we represent and their affiliates and their subsidiaries, and is that a conflict and can we take the matter? Then sometimes we have one client, and another client hires us. There's not really an adversity between the two, but there's an adversity of position. This client is asking us to articulate a legal position on a legal issue that probably this other client wouldn't want us to do, although it's not technically adverse, and what to do in those circumstances. We have in-house ethics experts that we turn to, but from time to time we've had to turn elsewhere.

In terms of cases, the casework where there's been issues of perjury or not producing documents you should produce, I really haven't run across that. I had a deposition of a client one time in New York, and we were talking about things, and I said, you know, they just asked you did you get notice of this, and you said no. I said, are you sure of that? Don't you think you got notice of that? He said, oh, yeah, I did get it. I tell you; I'm not going to tell them. I said, no, no, that's not how we run things. God Almighty. (Laughter.) So, when you go back in there, the first thing you say is you have something to correct on the record, and happily, this person complied with that, complied with the instructions. So, I've had semi-run-ins with issues like that. You're going to have ethical issues all the time.

You're also going to have times in a law practice when you make mistakes. You know, I've had a document project for a client, and one of our principal jobs is to stop privileged documents from being produced. We had a good team, a trained team, and they produced a critical privileged document through error, probably an error of failing to instruct them sufficiently about what should be screened out. This was a major problem. We had to go through the process of trying to get it back, and had to go before the client and say, you know, I've screwed up here, but here's what we're going to try to do to turn it around and get it to happen. It's not all as rosy as I say it is, but I think ninety-eight percent rosy. But there are little moments of thorns like that, either ethical thorns or mistakes that you make. That's just all part of the journey.

PROFESSOR LONGAN: Well, Doc, we're out of time. I appreciate you coming today. Thank you.

(Applause.)

A Conversation with Judge Lamar W. Sizemore, Jr.

Introduction by Manley F. Brown[*]

I came to know who Lamar Sizemore, Jr. was when he appeared as a student in my Trial Advocacy class in 1972. I was just beginning my teaching at Mercer Law, which lasted forty-four years.

Lamar is the eldest son of a famous Georgia, and Mercer, lawyer—Lamar Sizemore, Sr. Every lawyer in Georgia knew who he was. I knew about him from seeing a nationally televised speech he made as the leader of the Democratic Party of Georgia. One of his law partners was the also-widely-known sage, Bob Hicks, another prominent graduate of Mercer Law.

When I saw Lamar's name on my class roll, I wondered what he would be like. At my first class I called his name, and a handsome face with a big, black moustache answered, "here!" My first thought: What a moustache!

As I came to know Lamar, I realized that he was destined to be someone special in the law: intelligent, likeable, with a name that gave him instant recognition by the Georgia Bar. My intuition about Lamar proved accurate; he came to fulfill my every expectation, and then some!

It was my great privilege and pleasure to practice with Lamar for many years; he was steady, reliable, and the best dealmaker I ever knew. Those qualities are why everyone seems to want him as a mediator to help them settle their cases. He is an experienced plaintiff's lawyer, a highly respected retired Superior Court Judge, and a highly ethical master of mediation skills. It is no wonder that, in my opinion, he is the best!

Young aspiring lawyers would do well to listen closely to Judge Lamar Sizemore, Jr. He is gifted with innate wisdom and ability earned on the legal battlefield. He can and will help you become the lawyer you hopefully want to be.

---

[*] Retired Partner, O'Neal & Brown, Macon, Georgia.

JUDGE LAMAR W. SIZEMORE, JR.,* 2014

PROFESSOR PATRICK LONGAN: Thank you again for doing this. You're very kind to do it. As I mentioned when I introduced you, you've really had more than one career. You are, as I think you put it, in phase three. But I want to go back to phase one and start with your time as a practicing lawyer. In that phase of your career, which lasted a number of years, you represented plaintiffs. You represented actual human beings.

JUDGE LAMAR W. SIZEMORE, JR.: I did.

PROFESSOR LONGAN: Could you talk a little bit about that practice and what you did and what you liked about it and didn't like about it.

JUDGE SIZEMORE: I loved it. I did that for years, practiced with Manley Brown who, if you don't know Manley, surely you will before you leave law school. Terrific lawyer. I mean, one of the best I've ever known. My mentor right out of law school, my adjunct faculty member when I was a student. I think he started teaching in '72, so he's got me by eight years teaching here. We had a plaintiffs' practice. We also practiced with Hank O'Neal. There's a scholarship here named in Hank's honor. Probably the finest trial lawyer I've ever known. I quote him almost daily and probably will before this session is over.

I really enjoyed representing people, and in a personal injury practice, that's who we represented. We didn't represent insurance companies; we didn't represent corporations. Most of the people we represented were not well-educated. Most of them were not well-placed in society. Most of them would not be able to begin to address their legal

* At the time of this interview, Lamar W. Sizemore, Jr. had recently stepped down as a Superior Court Judge for the Macon Judicial Circuit in Macon, Georgia and was Of Counsel with Sell & Melton. He is now Of Counsel at Clark, Smith & Sizemore in Macon. We have used his judicial title in the transcript as a matter of custom.

problems without somebody's help, and generally they were very appreciative of what you did for them, and I always liked that. I enjoyed talking with people. That's not to say there's anything wrong with representing corporations and insurance companies, and the law firm I'm with now does that, and I'm engaged in some of that. But when it's everyday business like it is with insurance adjusters and claims people, it's just one more case.

But to the plaintiff it is the only case, and generally the only case they'll have, their only involvement with the legal system, and I always treated that as kind of a special relationship, and I would encourage you to do the same thing. If you become a plaintiffs' lawyer or you are representing individuals and they call and make that first appointment, set aside an hour on your calendar, at least an hour to spend with them. A lot of firms, they'll have a paralegal sit down with this new client and spend minutes taking down information. It may be an hour or so, may be another day that they finally see a lawyer, but when that person comes with a crisis in their life and they need advice, don't brush them off, don't cut them short on time.

We had a lawyer I remember in our firm who was an of counsel lawyer, and I would get him in an interview with a new client, so that maybe this could become his client. The first two times he got up midway through the interview and walked out, and finally after that, I said, "where did you go?" He said, "I've heard you give that spiel about how we handle these cases before. I didn't see any need to sit in there." I thought, you missed the point. This hour is about getting to know this client and letting this client get to know you and develop some sense of confidence in that client toward you. If you just get up and walk out, the client doesn't know you. They haven't heard you say anything; they haven't had an opportunity to have some interaction with you.

So set aside an hour to meet with a client. It's not responsive to your question, I know, but I got to thinking about that experience. It's important in dealing with people to give them the time they need to understand what this process is about, what you're going to be doing. It was rewarding to me because they always seemed to be grateful. I have a former client. He used to bring me a bushel of sweet potatoes every year around Thanksgiving, never forgot. I have another former client who either brings a ham or a cake or a pork shoulder every Christmas, and no matter how many times I say, "we're even, you don't need to do this, thank you, have a merry Christmas," they still come back every year. So, I think individuals who you help are appreciative. Large businesses, insurance, other corporations, it's business, not personal.

PROFESSOR LONGAN: You don't think the insurance company is going to bring you a bag of sweet potatoes, then?

JUDGE SIZEMORE: Not likely.

PROFESSOR LONGAN: Obviously I've got a list of questions I want to ask you, and I sent them to you ahead of time, and you know the order that I put them in. But I'm going to go a little bit out of order if that's okay.

JUDGE SIZEMORE: Sure.

PROFESSOR LONGAN: Because you mentioned Mr. O'Neal and you mentioned Manley. One of the things in this class we talk about, although we haven't talked about it much yet, is the importance of mentors, and I was wondering if you could talk a little bit about your mentors, what they meant to you, what they actually did, and what difference they made in the arc of your career.

JUDGE SIZEMORE: I think finding the right mentor out of law school is probably the single most important thing you can do to further your career. I was blessed. I grew up with a lawyer for a father, and so I saw how he dealt with this, and I'll just take each of these mentors and touch on it just a minute to give you an idea of what they did and how important they were to me.

I can remember my dad, he was so dedicated to his clients that, when I became a teenager, he put in a phone, a separate number for this phone beside his bed in his bedroom. Nobody was allowed to touch it unless he was not at the house. If he was in the house, nobody touched it, because that's how his clients knew to get in touch with him at night. I mean, all hours of the night. He had more of a corporate practice, but he'd get calls from all over the country, and we knew not to touch that phone. That was his dedication.

He had an opportunity to be on the Georgia Supreme Court. He had an opportunity to be a United States district court judge, but he always carried around a little note in his wallet, something he'd clipped, a quote, and I don't remember the exact quote, from Abraham Lincoln. It dealt with the importance of the lawyer's responsibility to his clients, and he always felt like his clients depended on him so that it wouldn't be fair to those clients to leave them and go do something else, and so he turned down those opportunities. That was back in the day when the senator, the tenured senator in your state, just offered you the job, and that was how you got it.

I can remember Dad sitting on the patio in the evening and neighbors coming by to sit and talk and ask legal questions, and I always thought about Atticus Finch, folks coming in and asking him advice. I never got to practice law with Dad. He died six weeks after I graduated from law school. Wasn't but fifty-four years old. But I have never forgotten the example that he set in connection with his dedication to his clients, the sense of responsibility that he had for those clients.

I was fortunate enough to have Hank O'Neal as an adjunct faculty member during my law school days, and Manley Brown, both of whom had tremendous impacts on me. Manley, for whatever reason, took me under his wing. I had his course in my second year during the spring of '72, and I remember talking with him about trying to find a summer job, and I wanted to be with a law firm. I had been with a governmental agency the summer before, and he called me and said, go talk to Floyd Buford at Byrd, Groover & Buford. I didn't know anything about Floyd Buford, but I did go down and he hired me. He knew my dad, and Garland Byrd knew my dad, and Denny Groover knew my dad. They were contemporaries. Some were in law school together here at Mercer with Dad. Then I began to learn, as I went down there in the afternoons and during the summer, what kind of lawyers these guys were. Garland Byrd had been lieutenant governor. In fact, as probably a ninth grader in high school I was a page for Garland Byrd, though I didn't know who he was, and I'm not even sure I met him when I was at the capitol that day as a youngster. But he served as lieutenant governor, one of the foremost trial lawyers in the state. He could give a closing argument that was just, everybody was enthralled by what he was saying.

Denmark Groover—now, y'all probably never heard of Pappy Boyington's Black Sheep Squadron. Anybody here have a clue who that is? During World War II, the Marine Corps had a number of fighter pilot squadrons, but they put together one with a Major Gregory Boyington, I think it was, Greg Boyington. They nicknamed Pappy because he was so much older than the eighteen and nineteen-year-olds who were flying these fighter planes. Sent them to the South Pacific to fight the Japanese. Denmark Groover was one of those fighter pilots. He was wounded while he was over there but was able to get his plane back to the island and land it, thank goodness. He lived with shrapnel in his leg and back all through his life. But semper fi meant something to him.

He came back, went to law school, became a legislator, served off and on over four decades in the Georgia legislature. The last years that he was there, no matter who you talked to who had anything to do with legislation in Georgia, they would agree that before a bill was passed in the capital, in the legislature, it had to be "Grooverized" first. He was such a terrific lawyer and such a parliamentarian. I mean, he understood government and how things worked in the legislature, but he would help people who were his opposition on the bill to get their bill right. Republicans would come to Groover to see how to best present their bill. Now, he might oppose it, and he'd tell them, but he would share "this is the way I would do it if I were you" kind-of-thing. He was well-respected. Terrific trial lawyer. I mean, he and Hank O'Neal were the two best, and there were a couple of occasions when there were jury trials with Hank representing the plaintiff and Groover for the defense, and law students left class and went down to watch the trial, down at the courthouse. I wished we'd had video back then or had thought to do video, what a learning experience that would be for generations of lawyers to watch that. Terrific lawyer.

And then Floyd Buford. Floyd grew up out here in the country, really, on a dirt road, outside of Macon. The Howard community. He grew up working on roads. His dad was a road building contractor. He went to law school after the war. Groover and Byrd went after the war, as well. Floyd became an Assistant US Attorney and then later was appointed by John F. Kennedy as the United States Attorney for the Middle District of Georgia, and what a formidable adversary he was in the courtroom. He knew how to talk to country people. He grew up in the country, and he tried some of the most famous civil rights criminal trials, including one that ended up in the United States Supreme Court. They made movies about some, and he was just a tremendous lawyer.

So those were terrific mentors for me in law school. And I will say this: Manley, when he told me about this job opportunity, he said, you're going to learn more than you'd ever learn anywhere else. And he's right. I was drawing petitions for writ of certiorari to the US Supreme Court in cases that had been tried in the Middle District, then to the Fifth Circuit, at that time it was, and up. I also, just about every day, went to the Nu-Way to get lunch, so the highs and lows of being a law clerk. I was an errand boy, too.

Manley also said, promise me one thing: promise me you will not adopt any of their personal habits. That was pretty good advice. Friday afternoon three o'clock they'd usually lock the door and bring out a bottle of Scotch whiskey, and we'd sit around the library table and tell stories, or I'd listen to stories. I remember Groover one time caught me researching, and he said, "Lamar, what are you looking for?" I told him what the facts were, and I was looking up something for Mr. Buford. He stood up there at the bookcase like a great, big bear scratching his back and he said, "I don't remember the page number, but if you'll look at 122 Appeals, *Jones v. State*, I think that will help you." Sure enough, there it was. I mean, that was the case that was on point. The only other person I ever saw that could do that was Hank O'Neal. Hank could give you book and page number off the top of his head. I just was amazed at that.

But I then practiced law with Manley and with Hank, and I could not have had better mentors. I mean, I learned, not just the tricks of the trade, if you will, or good habits, but I learned about ethics. Every time something would come up and you'd think, gosh, is this really an issue, is this something I ought to be concerned about? It smells a little bit, but I mean, does it pass the smell test with you guys? They would analyze it and give you an answer. They'd give you the quick answer because they knew how they'd handle it immediately, but then they'd explain to you why. I don't pretend to be an expert on ethics and professionalism, but I learned an awful lot from those guys. I also learned all about law practice, how to treat clients.

But pick the right mentor. I was on the disciplinary board for years, and so many of the bar complaints that we had to deal with, people who were in disciplinary trouble, people about to be disbarred or reprimanded or suspended from the practice of law, I came to realize were people who had no mentor when they got out of law school. They got out, hung a shingle, and used the "just do it" rule. Did whatever sounded right, felt right, without asking somebody who could give them good advice. The odds of failure are high in terms of ethics if you don't have a mentor who can give you advice.

So, if you go to a big firm, you'll probably be assigned one, like in our firm, associates are assigned an experienced lawyer as their mentor. The state bar has a mentor program, and they can assign mentors to people. The single most important thing you can do after graduation and passing the bar is get the right mentor. If you can't find one, call me and I'll do what I can to help you find one. Then remember, as time goes by, and you become an experienced lawyer, the second part of this is, be a mentor. We all stand, you know the expression, on the shoulders of the people who came before you. Well, every lawyer practicing law does that, and I think we have an obligation to return that or pay it forward, as another expression goes, and mentor others, and so bear that in mind. Just a suggestion from me.

PROFESSOR LONGAN: Well, it's a great suggestion, and if you talk to experienced lawyers and judges and say, who was your mentor, they can all say it right away.

JUDGE SIZEMORE: Yes.

PROFESSOR LONGAN: One of the things, of course, the students are learning about this semester is how professionalism can be challenged when you're out there in practice, in the deposition room or wherever, and how that comes about and how you have to deal with it. You were in a particular kind of practice. You were in a trial practice, personal injury practice. What kinds of things did you see that you would classify as professionalism issues or lack of civility? Tell them a story or two.

JUDGE SIZEMORE: Yeah, okay, I can do that.

PROFESSOR LONGAN: I can give them the theory. You tell them the story.

JUDGE SIZEMORE: When you've practiced law for forty years, you've got a few of those stories. The simple one I remember, right out of law school a partner gave me a case, small case, a fender bender. The client took his car to get fixed and discovered that rather than putting a new fender on there like he had said he wanted and what he paid for, he discovered they'd used Bondo, a filler. He just took a magnet, ran it across the fender and realized that it wasn't sticking. You know, that the magnet was failing. So, they sued him because he refused to pay them. I get this case with about two days to go from our days to answer this lawsuit, and we needed to file a counterclaim. I called my friend and classmate across the street who was representing the other side, and I said, "look, I just got this, and I need to do some research and get an answer. I'm in the middle of a bunch of stuff, can I have an extra five days or an extra three days?" He said, "oh, no problem, but I'll have to run it by my client." And I said "okay," and asked him to call me back. "No problem,' he said.

So about five hours later as the day is getting on, I call over and leave a message. They tell me, "yes, he's gone over to the courthouse; I'll have him call you as soon as he gets back." Well, five o'clock came and I thought, do I bug him again? I'll wait till in the morning. Next day is the last day. Called at nine o'clock. They said, "yeah, he was here, but he's run over to probate court, and I'll get him to call you. He did get your message, and he'll call you back." Well, about lunchtime I called again. She said, "yeah, he got your message, but he had to run out to Jones County. But he says he's going to get back to you." I said, "well, thank you." I had to cancel everything I had in the afternoon because I couldn't wait any longer.

I went ahead and prepared the answer and counterclaim, did the research, got it filed just barely by five o'clock, and to this good day he has never returned that phone call. (Laughter.) The sad thing is, that lawyer and classmate of mine who I've known a long time—in fact, when he died his wife called me to go with her to pick out his casket. I mean, I had that kind of relationship with them. But now as I think about this lawyer, what do I think about? I think about the way he took advantage of me, trying to get me into a bind. He wanted it to go by so that I'd have to have my client pay costs. It was really just a trivial thing.

I will tell you any lawyer who tells you he's got to talk to his client about extending the time to answer a lawsuit or extending the time to answer discovery, you be careful of that lawyer because that's not lawyering. I mean, you're in charge of that sort of thing. I've never—I've just told clients, you know, it may come around to where I'm the guy who needs the extension next time. I'm certainly going to give the other side extensions—that's for me to decide. I didn't appreciate that. I realized what he was doing, and I saw him many times after that, and he never mentioned all of those messages there.

I have another lawyer friend, not social friends necessarily, but certainly professional friends, for whom I have a lot of respect. I'm still very cordial with him, but we had a case against each other. I had a brain injured client, he had a truck driver and trucking company, and I received in the mail one day a deposition subpoena to the registrar at Fort Valley State College for the entire file of my client, including transcripts. Well, that file could contain some things that are not subject to being published: confidential, privileged information.

So, I did what I typically would do if I've got something like that. I called over there and said, "look, I tell you, I don't know what's in there any more than you do, why don't we do this: why don't I go ahead and get the file, because I can get an authorization from my client and run down there and get it, and I'll look through it, and if there's anything I think is privileged or confidential, I'll put it in an envelope, send a cover letter with it over to the judge, send you a copy of the letter letting you know that I have sent some stuff over there, and we'll let the judge decide whether this is privileged or confidential. And that way there won't be any disclosure of stuff prematurely, and I'll give you everything else and may not have an objection to any of it, but I need to see the file first."

He just started laughing. I said, "what's so funny about that?" He said, "we've already got the file." I said, "what do you mean you've got the file?" He said, "yeah, we went to the clerk's office, got her to sign the subpoena, jumped in the car, went down there, told them the deposition was next Tuesday or they could give us the file. They gave us the file, and we came on back to the office." I said, "and then you put my copy of it in the mail so I would get it the next day or so." He said, "well, yeah, when we got back, we mailed you your letter." I said, "did it ever cross your mind that when you do that, there's no way for me to object in a timely fashion? You've got the file already, and I had no notice and no opportunity to object."

Now, let me think about this a little bit. I knew that the state bar's advisory board had issued an opinion in 1980 that said to do what they did was to, in fact, commit a fraud on the clerk, on the opposing counsel, on the opposing party, and on the judge that caused the subpoena to be issued. They didn't have any intention of doing a deposition. This was their way of getting the file without having to deal with an objection from anybody. So, I wrote them a letter, and I said to my friend, "here is Advisory Opinion 40. I want you to take a look at it, see if you agree with me that what has been done here is not in accordance with this opinion. If you tell me that you're just going to take the file, seal it up, and never make reference to anything in it, as far as I'm concerned that's the end of it. I'm not going to say anything, no need to say anything to the judge or anybody else. We'll just go on as if that file doesn't exist." He got back in touch with me a day or two later and said, "no, I think I'm going to need that file; I think I'm going to use that file." So, when we started filing motions in limine, I called it not just a motion in limine but a motion to suppress evidence. I was so mad I wanted to put an exclamation point on it to make it sound like a criminal motion. I mean, I was so mad.

When we got over there with about seventeen motions in limine to argue with the judge, and I had already sent my motion to the judge with my letter attached to it as well as the Advisory Opinion. I jumped up and said, "Judge, I'd like to start with this Fort Valley"—he said, "no, Mr. Sizemore, let's just save that one for last. I'm going to go through these others first." So, we go through the others, and he rules this way and this way. You know, we get down and I said, "now, Judge, I want to get to talk about Fort Valley." He said, "sit down, Mr. Sizemore. I know your position." This is Judge Tommy Day Wilcox, if you can picture this. He looks over at the other lawyer and says, "stand up, Mr. So-and-So. I want to hear what you have to say about the suggestion Mr. Sizemore made in his letter: are you willing to put that in an envelope, seal it up in your file and never make reference to it during the course of this trial?" He said, "well, Judge, we really think we need to use this. We just think it's going to"—Judge Wilcox interrupted him and said, "let me tell you—you're not going to use that, you're going to put it in your file, you're going to seal it up, and I want you to go back to your office and you tell every lawyer in that office that if they pull a stunt like this, even though Mr. Sizemore didn't ask for sanctions to be imposed, you tell them that the next time it happens, I'm imposing sanctions whether the lawyer asks for it or not. That's improper. It ought not to be done. You ought to be embarrassed about it and ashamed of what you did. The ruling is none of that is admissible in the course of this trial."

Boy, I was just pumped up. (Laughter.) I didn't have to argue a thing, didn't have to open my mouth, really. But that's really what should have happened. Now, that lawyer, despite being a friend, and again, not social acquaintances necessarily, but certainly professionally, I have a lot of respect for him, he is on my "list." Hank O'Neal used to say when I'd say, "we need to do something to this guy, I can't wait to get him in the crosshairs," O'Neal would say, "now, Lamar, don't worry about that. I mean, don't be worried about getting revenge. All you have to do is just remember to put him on your list." I said, "what list are you talking about?" He said, "I mean the list up here (pointing to his head). You put him on the list—he can move up, he can move down, but he doesn't ever come off the list. (Laughter.) I mean, they never come off the list. That means that when you deal with that person next time, there are certain precautions that you have to take. You don't treat him with the same liberal approach to things that you might another lawyer." I'm happy to say that after forty years I can count five lawyers that are on my list, and maybe a judge that offhand I can think of, but no more than five lawyers in forty years. Remember that. I mean, he can move up, he can move down, but he never comes off the list, and those are people that you deal with on a little different basis than you do everybody else.

PROFESSOR LONGAN: Like with mentors, I think every lawyer I know has a list.

JUDGE SIZEMORE: That's right.

PROFESSOR LONGAN: I can tell you the ones on mine, and I haven't practiced in twenty-four years. I want to turn in just a second to your time as Superior Court Judge, but you've got to tell one story, and that is the deposition in Tifton.

JUDGE SIZEMORE: Oh Lord.

PROFESSOR LONGAN: And then I want the students to hear what it was like to be a judge.

JUDGE SIZEMORE: This goes in the category of professionalism, I would think, not an ethical thing. A friend of mine from Tifton asked me to associate on a case with him, help him in a life insurance policy case. The question was whether it was a suicide or a homicide or an accident. If it was suicide it was still within the period that wouldn't allow a recovery. If it was accident or homicide, then certainly the policy would pay. Our client was the widow. We actually did it here in Macon in our conference room, but my lawyer friend was from Tifton, and the other lawyer was from Atlanta. He's a guy that's on my list, one of the few. And he's on my friend's list, big time on my friend's list.

They were taking the deposition, the defendant was asking questions of our client, and my friend, who was kind of a big guy, kind of a bulldog personality, he didn't like some of the questions, so he objected and said, "I don't understand the question." The lawyer on the other side, just to provoke him a little bit, said, "frankly, I don't care whether you understand the question. It's the witness I want to understand the question, so I don't care whether you do." My friend said, "well, by God, she's not going to answer a question unless I understand what you're asking her. I'm going to instruct her not to answer."

Well, all right, so the other lawyer tries to explain the question. My friend said, "I still don't understand it. I'm objecting." The other lawyer said, "well, by gosh, I've explained it to you in English, I'll do it in German if that helps," and then my friend stands up and says, "well, by God, I'll sprechen with you." (Laughter.) The next thing I know, they're shouting at each other in German. (Laughter.) The court reporter is trying to take it down phonetically, and finally just quit (throwing his hands up), and my client, her eyes were that big. I said, "time out, time out. We're going to take a break." I had to take my friend, I had to get him to quit speaking German and come with me to my office along with our client. I guess would go in the category of: it's not really professional to threaten and then to break into German. (Laughter.)

PROFESSOR LONGAN: I need to learn what the German form of professionalism is.

JUDGE SIZEMORE: Yeah, yeah, that's right. I actually have that videotape. We were—the lawyer who was on our list was on our list for a reason, and we thought having a camera there and videotaping this would sort of tone him down because he'd know we could play it and hear the snide tone of his voice and see the sneer on his face and that kind of thing. But I now have it, and I've threatened my friend from Tifton about showing it sometime, and I haven't done that yet.

PROFESSOR LONGAN: Oh, I would love to have that.

JUDGE SIZEMORE: I'll have to run you a clip.

PROFESSOR LONGAN: Let's change gears. After all those many years of representing plaintiffs, you had the opportunity to become a Superior Court Judge and spent years doing that.

JUDGE SIZEMORE: Ten years exactly.

PROFESSOR LONGAN: Ten years. And I wonder if you could talk about what you liked about that, what you didn't like about it and maybe about why you stepped down. It's unusual for judges to ever give up that robe, and you did, and I was wondering if you could just tell us about that experience, pro and con.

JUDGE SIZEMORE: Sure, I'll be glad to. On January the 3rd of 2001, Governor Barnes swore me in to become a Superior Court Judge. We have five here in Macon for our circuit, which includes Peach County, Crawford County, and Bibb. I'd practiced law for twenty-seven years, all of it personal injury work, insurance work, and I really felt like I just needed a change professionally, needed to do something different. And this opportunity came up. I loved the variety of work. I mean, I was also very apprehensive. It had been a long time since I'd handled criminal cases. Never dealt really with domestic relations cases, but I enjoyed learning them, and I had lots of hornbooks around my desk, and code books. My rule became always, always read the code section, don't just try to remember and go off of that. I mean, every time I'd pick up a foreclosure confirmation case to deal with, I'd have to go to the code, and I'd read the code sections again. But it was interesting. It was new. It was different.

I felt like I was really serving the community. I'd never really done any public service work before, and I'd always felt like everybody owes a duty to their community to do some sort of public service, whether it's Red Cross or United Way or Boy Scouts or whatever it is, and if you had the opportunity to serve your profession, I just felt like this was an opportunity for me to do that. When I went in, I didn't know whether I'd do it forever or not.

I enjoyed the jury trials. That was my favorite part. I had 124 jury trials to verdict or mistrial in those ten years, and that was, to me, really the highlight. That's what it's all about. Talking to the jury, helping the jurors understand what was going on and why, helping them, I hoped, develop an appreciation for the system and the importance of what we were doing, the significance of it to the community.

I enjoyed the people in the courthouse. Great people working over there. I enjoyed the lawyers, the interaction with lawyers. I had been mediating cases as part of my law practice since 1988, so from '88 through 2000, and I loved that interaction with lawyers about cases, and so that was part of what I enjoyed about being a Superior Court Judge. I loved pretrial conferences, sitting, talking about issues and motions in limine and discussing, well, what about this and why do you think this will work and you can do that? It was challenging.

I hated deciding who was going to take the children home in a child custody case. Those were tough, tough cases. And, as my wife likes to quote me as saying, there were many times when my view was, I wanted to take the kids home because I didn't think either parent was fit to have them. And those are just tough, tough decisions.

I will tell you, a lot of people will say, "ah, he's a Superior Court Judge, he just went over there to retire." That is the toughest job in our profession, being a trial judge. Bar none, the toughest job in the profession. I mean, supreme court justices will tell you that. I had several tell me, "you've got the hard job. We sit up here and read cases and write opinions and proofread. You have to deal face-to-face with the people who are losing the children or who are fixing to go to the penitentiary."

You start thinking about the ripple effects of those decisions. Every day you make hundreds of decisions, and it may be just signing orders, but you make literally hundreds of decisions, and in the courtroom when you're sentencing somebody, and you've got the defendant standing in front of you and his family sitting over here, over here you've got the prosecution sitting at the table, and behind the prosecution is the victim's family. This person who's gone who they'll never see again, and you're having to impose sentence on this person who's got a family, a wife and kids and all this, I mean, those are tough decisions. If you sit there you can be—and this is one of the things a judge can never let himself be—paralyzed by the weight of the decision. I can see how judges can get paralyzed by them. I mean, to pronounce a sentence that has the sort of impact it does on not just those people sitting there but the extended family or the employer he works for or others, I mean, every decision just sort of spreads across the community, at least to a limited extent. Tough, tough job.

PROFESSOR LONGAN: If you did it long enough, I would think some people would become desensitized to it and it wouldn't bother them—and that should bother us. Did you see that?

JUDGE SIZEMORE: I did.

PROFESSOR LONGAN: Not that it happened to you, but—

JUDGE SIZEMORE: Yeah, I did see that. That was one of the reasons after ten years I thought, well, I miss law practice, I miss the camaraderie of the law office, I miss mediating cases, and now is better than four more years from now, and so I'll have phase three, mostly mediating. But, yeah, I did see that.

I remember a judge from my youth who would, on calendar call, in a major felony criminal calendar, get all the lawyers, all the parties in the courtroom, and call the calendar. They were going to take pleas that day, with jurors waiting, and the judge would make everybody stay in the courtroom while pleas started. The judge would start taking the pleas, never tell anybody in what order these pleas are going to be taken but not letting anybody leave the courtroom. So, the prosecutors who needed to be preparing for a jury trial tomorrow morning are having to sit there all day, waiting—not knowing when the case would be called. And the judge might go in and eat a quick salad or half a sandwich, but nobody else could leave the courtroom. The judge would come right back and go on with the calendar—and then pick a jury at seven o'clock at night. I mean, jurors have been sitting there all day long and into the evening, not planning to be there past five or six o'clock, and you pick a jury.

Now, that's a judge who has forgotten what it's like to practice law. Forgotten that you've got other clients, you have other responsibilities. Time spent sitting through another proceeding, somebody else's proceeding, is wasted time for a lawyer. This judge was otherwise a terrific judge. Smart. You knew the opinion written by that judge was the right opinion, and nobody ever really questioned the rulings of that judge, they were so good, so precise. But that judge forgot what it was like to be a lawyer, and when you do that, you become a tyrant. A judge can become a bully. I mean, who's going to cross the judge, right? You can sit there and talk just as mean and harshly to people, you can be like Judge Judy. When I went over there, that was one of the things that used to drive my wife crazy, is her friends would say, "is Lamar going to be like Judge Judy?" You know, the image people have of judges, but there are some who are like that. It's unpleasant for lawyers. It's embarrassing for lawyers.

Some judges will embarrass lawyers in the presence of their clients. I just think that's awful. Or in the presence of the jury. I think the better practice is if somebody does something wrong you call them up to the bench and you have a little private conference with them.

I'll never forget a guy in the middle of a trial, the prosecutor objected, and I sustained the objection. He took his legal pad and went over to his table, his counsel table, threw that pad down and it hit, I mean, I don't know how you could ever again repeat the way it hit, because it hit perfectly flat, but it went "kapow" when it hit. I mean, it didn't just lay down on that table, and then it started sliding across the table. And as it slid across the table, I mean, time stopped. Nobody said a word, but everybody watched that pad slide across that table. It slid right in front of the defendant. Did he reach out to stop it? Uh-uh. He wasn't touching that pad. And it slid till it was stopped finally hanging over the other end of the table. The lawyer looked at me. I did like this (motioning with finger), and we had a little talk up at the bench. But I didn't chew him out in front of the jury or in front of his client. He said, "Your Honor please, I'm sorry, sorry, sorry, won't do that again, sorry, sorry, sorry." You know, that's not professional, by the way, to throw your pad down in response to a ruling by the judge, but the judge shouldn't chew him out, I don't think. Anyway, it's just one of those things.

PROFESSOR LONGAN: I'm going to ask you my last question, which is, as you know, an open-ended question. You have the whole first-year class here. I was wondering if there's anything that you want to make sure that they hear, maybe something you wish you had heard, and then I'll turn it over to the students for their questions.

JUDGE SIZEMORE: Well, I don't know that I've got anything so profound to say that I wish I had heard it before. I will say this, though, just a piece of advice: we were talking about lawyers on the "list." Whatever you do don't become the lawyer you hate. I don't ever want to be like the lawyers on my list. I mean, if I find myself in a deposition getting so worked up that I'm fixing to figuratively, break into German, I know I've got to stop and take stock of what I'm doing. So, one piece of advice: don't become the lawyer you hate. Don't repeat the practices that make you so angry at this lawyer.

Advice I give to young judges consists of three things. The first one goes back to the judge who forgot what it was like to be a lawyer. Number one, remember that first you were a lawyer. If you ever forget that, you become a tyrant. You've got to remember what it's like. You serve lawyers, I think. I mean, I realize the community, that's your constituency. But you're there to help lawyers get their cases handled and their clients looked after as fairly, equitably, and expeditiously as you can. I mean, do things to make the business of the court convenient for lawyers. Number two, criminal cases, err on the side of mercy. That's what I told every new judge that came to the courthouse: err on the side of mercy. And finally, just rule. One of my dad's law partners, who's like an uncle to me, I've known him all my life, Bob Hicks who's in Atlanta, Bob said that the raison d'être, the reason for being a judge, is to rule. If you can't rule, you ain't got any business being a judge. So, as hard as it is, don't be paralyzed by the difficulty of the issues, the weight of the issues, the people who are going to be affected by your ruling. Rule. They can't go anywhere else until you rule. I mean, time is literally standing still for them. Justice delayed is justice denied. I mean, that's real. Just rule.

I guess—one other piece of advice. For the ten years I was at the courthouse I was blessed through Professor Longan and Professor Floyd to have interns, and we had law clerks, and in ten years I had thirty-four interns and law clerks. Everyone received, at the end of their little time with me, a hardbound copy of To Kill a Mockingbird with a note in the front to read this book every five years or so during your legal career, to remind yourself of the example of Atticus Finch. I realize he's a fictional character, but there's a book out, that came out during the anniversary of *To Kill a Mockingbird*, and Scott Turow wrote one of the several essays in this book. He pointed out that just because there aren't many (if any) people in the world like Atticus Finch does not mean that you can't aspire to be like Atticus Finch. As idealistic as that sounds, I think you need to have a little idealism about practicing law. You have to think about the ideals of our profession and the good of the community and read *To Kill a Mockingbird* every five years or so just to remind you of that example of Atticus Finch. That's just sort of my role model.

PROFESSOR LONGAN: Good advice. What questions do you-all have for Judge Sizemore?

LAW STUDENT: I have a question. Thank you for joining us today. You talked a lot about finding a mentor, and I'm sure we all have people in our lives that we look up to, and some of us have parents who are lawyers or close friends who are attorneys, but the problem I find with finding mentors: when to know that you've found the right one. Some of us have very different interests in law, and if Mr. O'Neal or Manley Brown was interested in a certain aspect of the law that you weren't, would they still be appropriate mentors? How do we know when a mentor is an Atticus Finch or something much lesser?

JUDGE SIZEMORE: You really need to talk to folks in the community, talk to some lawyers or law professors. I mean, Professor Longan and other faculty members, they know the lawyers in town. They're involved in the Bootle Inn of Court, the Macon Bar, and they know who's interested in law students and interested in helping law students, and certainly they can help you identify people, and they can direct you to people who are familiar with lawyers in Macon. I've dealt with, met with several people in law school who when they were graduating said they were going to be practicing in Macon. They thought they were going to be practicing solo, and I have suggested names and talked to lawyers about whether they would be willing to serve as mentors for others. That's one way to do it.

If you're in a firm like our firm, Sell & Melton, you've got a lot of experienced lawyers, ethical lawyers, and the firm typically will assign somebody. I was never assigned to Hank O'Neal as my mentor. I just worked with him; he was my mentor. Manley is the same way. Byrd, Groover & Buford—I didn't go over there at the time looking for mentors. They just turned out to be, and I had somebody like Manley directing me to them. Why Manley Brown took an interest in me as a law student, a second-year law student, I'll never know, but I'm forever grateful for it because it had such an impact on virtually all of my career, not just practicing with him: the area of law, the teaching at the law school, he and Hank did that. You know, working in Georgia Trial Lawyers Association. He did that. He was on the Board of Bar Examiners, here I am on the Board of Bar Examiners now all these years later. So, sometimes you just luck into a mentor, but my suggestion to you is that you talk to professors or somebody like me who's been around a few years and has gray hair enough to know who's in the community and who would be a good mentor.

LAW STUDENT: Do you still adjunct here at Mercer?

JUDGE SIZEMORE: I do. This is my thirty-fourth year of teaching my Problems in Insurance Litigation. Wednesday morning, assuming the snow is not covering the ground, we'll be here at eight o'clock talking about automobile insurance.

PROFESSOR LONGAN: Judge, I know one of the things that comes up is students say, well, you talk about incivility and the yelling in German. One of the hard things for students to imagine is just dealing with that, and in the one minute left to us—this is totally unfair to you—could you talk a little bit about that? I know you've used the phrase before with me "observing the formalities." Could you tell them a little bit about that, and then we'll close.

JUDGE SIZEMORE: Sure, a quick example of this, my daughter's automobile was damaged. A young lady ran a stop sign and ran into her. I was dealing with an insurance adjuster, could just as easily have been a lawyer, same kind of setting, and I knew that I was entitled to the difference between the value of the car before it was damaged and the value of the car after it was damaged. That's really what the measure of damages is on a property damage claim. We're always thinking about repairs, but repairs usually are not as expensive or not as much money as the difference in fair market value.

Well, it's an older car. They wanted to just replace the fender and paint the fender. Well, then you'd have a pretty, shiny, blue fender here and a dull blue everywhere else. So, I said to the adjuster over the phone, "I tell you, rather than asking for the difference between fair market value, which would be greater than this amount, I've talked to the body shop, and they can paint the whole car and do the fender for this lesser amount, and I'm perfectly content to do that, and you don't have to worry about the difference."

Well, he starts cussing at me and calling me a shyster and various other things. I said, "wait a minute, we don't have to have this conversation." He said, "well, by gosh, we do, too, because I'm the guy making the decision on this." I said, "I don't ever have to talk to you again. We're going to end the conversation." He said, "yes, you are going to talk to me." I said, "look, all I have to do is sue your insured, and from now on I'll talk to your lawyer," and I hung up the phone. The next day he called back very sheepishly and said, "all right, we'll pay to have the whole car painted." Because he knew it was a better deal than what he was really entitled to.

That's an example of what you have to do when you're dealing with people who are just totally unreasonable. My view is you try to get along; you try to find ways to accommodate each other because it makes life easier for you, it makes life easier for the other guy. But if you've got somebody who wants to make a fight out of everything—and I've known lawyers, they wouldn't schedule a deposition with you without having a heated argument about it—what I always say to law students, and what I say to lawyers like that, is, "we don't have to have this unpleasant conversation. From this point on we'll just observe the formalities." By that I mean the Civil Practice Act. It is there to guide us both. The rules are there to get us through this even if we don't like each other, and from now on we'll observe the rules.

PROFESSOR LONGAN: You can do it by the book.

JUDGE SIZEMORE: By the book.

PROFESSOR LONGAN: And there is a book.

JUDGE SIZEMORE: There is a book.

PROFESSOR LONGAN: All right. Judge, thank you very much.

(Applause.)

Index